Jewish Identity

The Challenge of Peoplehood Today

JEWISH IDENTITY

The Challenge of Peoplehood Today

Ruth Shamir Popkin

gefen גפן
publishing house בית הוצאה לאור
JERUSALEM ◆ NEW YORK   Est. 1981

Cover Design: Talya Shachar-Albocher
Typesetting: Irit Nachum
ISBN: 978-965-229-671-9

1 3 5 7 9 8 6 4 2

Gefen Publishing House Ltd.
6 Hatzvi Street
Jerusalem 94386, Israel
972-2-538-0247
orders@gefenpublishing.com

Gefen Books
11 Edison Place
Springfield, NJ 07081
516-593-1234
orders@gefenpublishing.com

www.gefenpublishing.com

Printed in Israel

Send for our free catalog

Library of Congress Control Number: 2014957433

To Richard

CONTENTS

INTRODUCTION

The modern era has witnessed dramatic and cataclysmic changes in Jewish life. Beginning with Jewish emancipation in Europe in the mid-seventeenth century and the accompanying urge of the most determined and prominent Jews to escape the constraints of the traditional Jewish world, definitions of Jewish identity have profoundly altered. These definitions underwent an equally dramatic evolution as nationalism burst on the scene and became the driving force in European politics (and subsequently of Jewish politics as well). This development coincided with the spread of racist anti-Semitism which in effect banished the Jews from society at large. The definitions of Jewish identity were subjected to an even more fundamental transformation by the Holocaust and the extermination of a third of world Jewry. This included the near total destruction of the Jews in central-eastern Europe, a community that more than any other had clung to its traditional Jewish identity. With the establishment of the State of Israel in 1948, Jewish identity radically reinvented itself in ways that we are still trying to comprehend.

The flashes of the all-important change in Jewish identity occurring as a result of the establishment of the Jewish state in the Land of Israel were evident long before that event. The early glimmers of this shift were already apparent in the late eighteenth century and over the course of the nineteenth. The *Haskalah* (Jewish Enlightenment) originated in Germany but quickly extended to the Jewish communities of central and eastern Europe, leading to the eruption of a vibrant modern Hebrew culture based on nationalist principles. In parallel there developed a flourishing Yiddish culture in the Pale of Settlement – the only areas of western Russia and eastern Poland in which Jews were permitted to live under the Czarist Empire. These two processes encompassed large numbers of Jews who nurtured a secular Jewish culture that was not merely an alternative to the age-old customs of traditional Jewish religious life but also an open and direct challenge to that tradition.* Israel is but the latest chapter in this cultural clash in which an expanding innovative secular culture consciously confronts a no less determined traditional religious establishment. This confrontation is a basic component of the ongoing struggle for the very identity of the state – a struggle that revolves around a simple but profound question: Does Israel have the ability to strike a balance between cultural pluralism and liberal democracy on the one hand, and giving priority to the preservation of a Jewish identity that, at least in part, is a reflection of the traditional religion, on the other hand?

This question in itself raises existential dilemmas for all Jews who are committed to ensuring Israel's survival. Is Zionism an anachronism or is it still needed and viable? Is the attainment of physical force essential to the survival of a nation? If so, does this apply all the more to a nation with a long history of persecution that reached its peak in the mass extermination of a third of its members? Do the remaining Jewish communities in the Diaspora still need a place of refuge? Are the Jews of the world a nation or merely a religious group? What is the meaning of a "Jewish" state in light of the diverse identities of secular and religious Jews? And how, from a political and cultural perspective, can a state professing to be "Jewish" appropriately accommodate an Arab minority that accounts for 20 percent of the country's population (within the borders of June 4, 1967)?

Among an increasing number of Jews both in Israel and beyond, there is an increasingly noticeable tendency to respond to these questions in the negative. This tendency challenges Zionist mainstream thinking on the evolution of Jewish identity. Broadly speaking, one can attribute much of this trend to "post-Zionism," an incessant debate

---

*   Notes appear at the end of the book.

that encompasses a diverse range of subjects and ideas rooted in the period that preceded the birth of the modern Zionist movement. In part, post-Zionism also includes a number of Zionist philosophies and viewpoints that have developed since Israel's establishment and that are sharply critical of the state. In this context, momentous events like the Six-day War of 1967 and the 1973 Yom Kippur War, as well as political developments such as the Oslo Accords signed in September 1993, intensified the debate both inside Israel and outside it. Indeed, the debate has reached such a level of rancor that there are those who regard the debate itself as a real threat to the very existence of the state.

Over recent years, post-Zionism has spread beyond academic circles and entered the mainstream of Jewish society. It is possible that as a result it has penetrated the Jewish discourse without anyone being able to offer a precise definition of what post-Zionism actually means. For example, temporally speaking, does this term relate to a movement (i.e., Zionism) that has succeeded in achieving its objectives and whose mission has therefore been completed? Or, alternatively, does post-Zionism encompass a complex spectrum of deep-rooted disappointments within Zionism, essentially proving that the realization of a dream necessarily exposes an inability to live up to the ideals of that dream? One way or another, it is clear that post-Zionism is a fundamental evolvement in post-independence Jewish identity.

This book examines the evolution of Jewish identity in the modern era up to and including the surge of Jewish national and post-national sentiments both in Israel and the Diaspora. It will do so by first analyzing the rise of nationalism in modern European society, which in turn led to the emergence in Europe of a Jewish national identity in a form that reached its zenith in the formation of the Zionist movement and the subsequent establishment of the State of Israel. The book then turns to investigating the origins of post-Zionist ideology within the Zionist movement itself and the almost instant development of an Israeli-Hebrew identity separate from Diaspora Jewry. In subsequent chapters the book deals with the thoughts of early critics and pragmatists who appeared on the scene and, in varying degrees, challenged the very legitimacy of a Jewish state. These, in effect, were the precursors of today's post-Zionists, for whom the early critics served as both an inspiration and a role model.

The book surveys changes in Jewish identity in the United States resulting from an increased manifestation of American anti-Semitism during the first half of the twentieth century and the destruction of European Jewry in the Holocaust. There then follows an exploration of the various struggles over identity within Israeli society such as the question "Who is a Jew?"; the rise of diverse and conflicting identities under the banner of "Israeliness"; the influence of postmodernism on Israeli and Jewish identities; and the challenge to Israeli identity posed by the "New Historians" of the late 1980s. Moreover, in this book I attempt to analyze the appearance of post-national, post-Zionist ideologies during the 1990s, including the increasing tendency to question the moral foundation, democratic nature and historical necessity of a Jewish state. This is evidenced in the growing trend to extol the virtues of the Diaspora as a deliberate alternative to the Zionist concept of a national homeland. Lastly, I explore the effects of military power and religious fundamentalism on Jewish identity and the continuing debate as to whether Jewish national life in Israel elevates Jewish identity to a higher plane. Yet this book still cannot be considered a comprehensive exposition on the evolving Jewish identity; it is merely an attempt to represent the most important aspects of this subject at this juncture in time.

CHAPTER 1

THE RISE OF NATIONALISM

J ewish nationalism followed most of the European national movements and its emergence was essentially a response to them.[1] As Hannah Arendt observed, up until very late into the modern era the Jews of Europe were regarded as having "become the "good Europeans" *par excellence*. The Jewish middle classes of Paris and London, Berlin and Vienna, Warsaw and Moscow…were [simply] Europeans, something that could be said of no other group."[2] However, it soon became apparent that this intra-or pan-European identity, specific to modern Jews, couldn't hold out against a tide of nationalisms sweeping the continent – a tide that excluded "foreigners." With the benefit of hindsight it is clear that there was no other possible outcome. This is because nationalism "dominated much of the nineteenth century in Europe and was so pervasive, so familiar, that it is only by a conscious effort of the imagination that one can conceive of a world in which it played no part.…"[3]

The appropriate definition of nationalism has long been a subject of scholarly debate. Yet all historians agree that nationalism is fundamentally a modern phenomenon, even though it is almost certainly deeply anchored in the past and is the consequence of root causes and centuries of earlier developments. Hans Kohn has observed that although nationalism draws on numerous age-old factors, these do not, in and of themselves, constitute nationalism nor are they essential to its emergence. One such factor is the natural tendency of peoples to form an attachment to a "home" and to feel more at ease when surrounded by that which is familiar and that which belongs. This inclination is linked to common descent, language, territory, religion and customs, not to mention a shared political entity. It often leads to feelings of superiority vis-à-vis the "other" and to a distrust of the foreigner. However, even though much importance is attached to a common origin, many modern nation-states, such as Switzerland, are in practice an amalgam of several different peoples. As well, most nations have neither a language nor a religion that is uniquely theirs. And though a common territory or state would appear to be the most important outward manifestation of nationhood, the history of the Czechs in the latter part of the eighteenth century shows that this too is not an essential ingredient, even if a common memory of sovereignty is.

One way or another, Kohn argues, if we are to single out one feature of nationalism that is more important than any other it is the *will* to be a nation. Even if all the other necessary components have been in place for many years, they could not come together and emerge in the image of the newly formulated idea of nationalism without the conscious will to achieve such an outcome. In other words, nationalism is not a natural development that stems from common roots or a people's inborn love of a "homeland." Rather, it is a product of the conscious will of those involved. Thus nationalism is a *state of mind* that must be commonly held by a majority of relevant people; it is not merely the province of isolated, enlightened individuals, as was always the case in premodern times.[4]

Kohn's view clearly reflects the position of Ernest Renan, whose late-nineteenth-century theories on nationalism greatly influenced those scholars who came after him. So far as we know, it was in a lecture given at the Sorbonne in 1882 that Renan for the first time argued that a "nation" is the product of a repeated "daily plebiscite" of its inhabitants. This was because it incorporates the intention of people "to live together" on the basis of their "having done great things together and wishing to do more." Renan saw nationalism as something ethereal, something that defied accurate definition and which was, above all, a spiritual concept. The soul of a nation, according to Renan, is made up of past memories and a present in which people aspire to continue to live together. This desire supersedes the questions of race, language and even of geography.[5]

In a similar vein, Ernest Gellner asserts that nationalism, which constantly sees itself as "re-awakening" a long-dormant nation, essentially "suffers from a pervasive false consciousness. Its myths invert reality…it claims to protect an old folk society while in fact helping build up an anonymous mass society." Gellner admits that there is a basis of truth in the claim that nationalism seeks the revival of a nation's old "folk" society. In particular, this could be so when the rural population or the masses are being governed by a highly developed alien culture and when resistance to that rule involves a cultural renaissance as a first step in the struggle for independence. And yet, when such a national movement is victorious, says Gellner, it doesn't replace the ruling culture with its folk culture of old, but instead "revives, or invents, a local high culture of its own," one that is literate and disseminated by specialists.[6]

Renan's view is also accepted by Eric Hobsbawm, who argues that nationalism requires too much belief in what is patently not so. Approvingly, he quotes Renan as saying that "getting its history wrong is part of being a nation." According to Hobsbawm, this is so because nationalism was an essential fantasy that validated the connection between individuals and large communities, thus fulfilling an important condition for the development of the modern state.[7]

Basing himself on Renan's theory, Benedict Anderson suggests that a nation "is an imagined political community – and imagined as both inherently limited and sovereign." It is *imagined* because those who belong to it believe that they are part of a deeply unified community whereas in reality they are nothing but strangers. "In fact, all communities larger than primordial villages of face-to-face contact (and perhaps even these) are imagined." The nation is imagined as *limited* because no nation, large or messianic as it may be, aspires to include the whole of humanity within its ranks. The nation is imagined as *sovereign* because it appeared on the scene when feudalism and divinely sanctioned monarchial dynasties were being overthrown by the Enlightenment and the French Revolution. And it is imagined as a *community* because it is persistently experienced "as a deep, horizontal comradeship" no matter how unequal or exploitative it may be.[8]

Anthony D. Smith suggests that a nation is "a named population sharing a historic territory, common myths and historical memories, a mass, public culture, and common legal rights and duties for its members." Smith acknowledges that national identity and nationhood are complex concepts. The components that he regards as essential to the nation and nationality "signify bonds of solidarity among members of communities united by shared memories, myths and traditions that may or may not find expression in states of their own but are entirely different from the purely legal bureaucratic ties of the state." In Smith's view, national identity supplies communities and individuals with a range of needs: it has a social purpose and creates a sense of belonging and of standing in the world; it utilizes such instruments as public education, the hope of an inclusive culture and army service; and it creates shared public values with such symbols as flags, national anthems, public ceremonies and national monuments.

Smith's assumption is that the origin of nations is shrouded in mystery. He rejects the theory that nations have always existed but have been holed up in a kind of historical state of dormancy. Nor does he accept the idea that since the existence of nations was always a given the need to explain them never arose. Instead, Smith supports the modernist theory that the nation only emerged at the beginning of the Industrial Age in the eighteenth century. In ancient times, Smith argues, there were neither nations nor nationalisms because they were unable to emerge prior to industrialization and the spread of mass education and culture.[9]

But on the issue of ethnicity Smith equivocates. "An ethnic group," he explains, "is a type of cultural collectivity, one that emphasizes the role of myths and descent and historical memories, and that is recognized by one or more cultural differences like religion, customs, language or institutions."[10] Membership of a particular ethnicity is based on feelings, attitudes and beliefs, all of which may be hard to pin down and subject to change. Thus, for example, Smith reckons Egypt to be an ethnic state but not a nation and speculates that the ethnic entities of old, closest to being nations, were ancient Egypt and the Kingdom of Israel at the time of David and Solomon. As Smith puts it, "Here, if anywhere, we might expect to confront a strong sense of *national* identity and an equally vivid nationalism. Yet even here the evidence is at best ambiguous."[11] The Jews of the period of the Second Temple had what Smith defines as the requisite attributes of a shared mythology of origin as well as similar religious experiences and historical memories. This was so even though the union between north and south at the time of the First Temple did not last for long. After the Assyrians overran the (northern) Kingdom of Israel and exiled its inhabitants in 772 BCE, it was the (southern) Judean priesthood that prevented assimilation. The struggle around this issue continued under the leadership of Ezra and Nehemiah while the Maccabees and later the Zealots followed their example. But since Smith believes that nationalism is a strictly secular phenomenon that only occasionally needs to rely on religious links to mobilize the support of the masses, he questions whether one can indeed see the Maccabees and Zealots as an early example of Jewish nationalism. In Smith's view, "From what we know of the period, it is unlikely that [they] entertained the possibility of a secular concept of the nation separate from Judaism."[12]

Interestingly enough, Smith acknowledges that Judean society in the latter part of the Second Temple possessed those features that he considers essential to nationhood. It had strong links to its territory; it shared a common religion and languages (Hebrew and Aramaic); and all its members had the same religious obligations ("duties and civic rights"). This, he concludes "suggests a closer approximation to the ideal type of the nation…than perhaps anywhere else in the ancient world, and it must make us wary of pronouncing too readily against the possibility of the nation, and even a form of religious nationalism, before the onset of modernity. The profound consequences of the concept of a chosen people, the passionate attachment to sacred lands and centres, and the abiding imprint of sacred languages and scriptures proved to be an enduring legacy for many peoples from late antiquity to modern times, sustaining their sense of uniqueness and nurturing their hopes of regeneration."[13]

Hans Kohn also maintains that the roots of modern nationalism can be traced all the way back to the ancient Hebrews and Greeks. Both peoples, he notes, had the unmistakable sense of being different from other peoples and they both applied their definition of "nation" not only to the ruling classes but to the entire population. Three important characteristics of nationalism originated with the Hebrews: the idea of a chosen people, the emphasis on a shared past and the notion of national messianism. The Hebrews held on to a consistent dichotomy the likes of which can be found in certain modern nationalist movements. Though the concept of a chosen people and messianic fervor often led to chauvinistic and oppressive tendencies, it is nonetheless the case that these concepts were, paradoxically, accompanied by universalist principles and the divine commandment to be a "holy nation" that treats others well. Thus, notions of uniqueness, distinctiveness and a sense of superiority coexisted with feelings of fraternity and universalism.

This was also the way of the Greeks: Their exclusionary form of nationalism was tempered by Alexander's ambition of establishing a global empire and they therefore developed a new universalist approach toward the peoples around them. Hellenic stoic philosophy taught that the Greek fatherland extended across the globe, an idea that greatly influenced the emerging Roman Empire. When the Romans converted to Christianity, the Greek and Hebrew trends merged and their universalist nature became even more pronounced. As a consequence, Kohn writes, under the banner of religion, the Middle Ages in Europe witnessed only universalist trends seeking to expand their influence across borders. Humanity was seen as a single bloc destined to unite under one overarching authority.[14]

According to Arnold Toynbee, it was only in 1775 that "the principle of nationality first asserted itself in the modern world as a dynamic political force."[15] Eric Hobsbawm agrees with this assessment, pointing out that the nation emerged as "an historically novel construct in the eighteenth century, though no doubt anticipations or a few earlier examples may be discovered by those who wish to."[16]

Moreover, Benedict Anderson clearly demonstrates that the modern state could only come about once a number of basic cultural norms – above all the holy scriptures of the dominant religions – had begun to lose their grip on society. Christianity, Islam and other universalist religions were only accessible to the masses through their sacred texts. And yet, people from different parts of the globe who could not speak a word of each other's language were able to communicate via the holy scriptures of their common faith. These languages began to erode once the Europeans discovered other civilizations in the sixteenth century. Additionally, such findings led the philosophers of the Enlightenment and other contemporary scholars to argue ever more firmly that Europe was no more than just one of many great civilizations. The late eighteenth century saw the beginnings of scientific research in comparative linguistics followed by the philology that studied comparative grammar. This development still further reduced the standing of the ancient holy languages.

From this point on, says Anderson, "the old sacred languages – Latin, Greek and Hebrew – were forced to mingle on equal ontological footing with a motley plebeian crowd of vernacular rivals, in a movement which complemented their earlier demotion in the market-place by print-capitalism." Hence the emergence of two additional crucial forces in the development of nationalism: capitalism and print technology. In dealing with the European national movements in the years between 1820 and 1920, Anderson notes that "in almost all of them 'national print languages' were of central ideological and political importance.... The lexicographic revolution in Europe...created, and gradually spread, the conviction that languages (in Europe at least) were, so to speak, the personal property of quite specific groups – their daily speakers and readers – and moreover that these groups, imagined as communities, were entitled to their autonomous place in a fraternity of equals." Anderson adds that among ordinary people, the diminished importance of the religious community and of the old monarchical regimes fostered a new sense of equality and a demand for equal rights.[17]

In their analysis of the rise of nationalism, other historians such as Elie Kedourie and E. H. Carr have stressed the importance of the evolution of certain philosophical ideas.[18] Carr adopts a Marxist perspective and

singles out Rousseau as "the founder of modern nationalism as it began
to take shape in the nineteenth century." Rousseau's most important
contribution, according to Carr, lay in his rejection of the idea held by
most supporters of nationalism prior to the French Revolution that the
nation was to be identified with its leader or its ruling class. Instead,
Rousseau equated the "nation" with the "people" and this definition
became a fundamental principle of both the French as well as the
American revolutions.

Moreover, though the French Revolution's immediate change
of course in relation to the absolutism of the past was inspired by
England's "glorious" revolution of 1688, the move was also influenced
by Rousseau. In the wake of Rousseau's *Social Contract* – which
claims that freedom encompasses obedience to the laws of the state
– the people of France rejected the English emphasis on the freedom
and rights of the individual. Instead, they emphasized the individual's
obligation to participate in the new order. This trend was reinforced by
the massive social upheavals that coincided with the French Revolution
– the dissolution of the feudal order, the growth of urban society and
the mass migration of the French from rural areas to the cities.[19] The
war that soon erupted increased the momentum of such changes still
further both by the imposition of general compulsory conscription and
the demand for absolute loyalty.

The French were victorious in their revolution but then they found
themselves governed by their army. Though not himself a nationalist,
Napoleon came to power on the crest of a new nationalist wave; while
paying lip service to French nationalism, his ambition was to establish
a multinational empire of his own. The French Revolution quickly
evolved into a war between France and the rest of Europe – a Europe that
was increasingly based on national lines. Napoleon's war of liberation,
which was never recognized as a nationalist crusade, finally awakened
nationalism in the countries that suffered its impact – a nationalism that
in the fullness of time was to be the cause of Napoleon's downfall.[20]

The formation of the Holy Alliance between Russia, Austria and
Prussia, created in the wake of Napoleon's defeat, left a whole generation
of young nationalists – whose hopes had rested on the continued spread

of the nationalist spirit represented by the French emperor – dangling in midair. Though the masses had not yet been stirred by the nationalist fervor of those times, youth and intellectual circles were most certainly fired up by the idea. Common and of central importance to all nationalists across the continent was their bitter opposition to the Holy Alliance. This shared hostility, says Jacob Talmon, is what, in practice, finally united all nationalists from every country in Europe. They adopted a form of nationalism that "stressed the collaboration of the peoples against the monarchs and the desire for liberal constitutions to limit the absolutism of the rulers.... The patriots of one people showed their active sympathy whenever and wherever patriots of other countries revolted against the order established by the Holy Alliance at the Congress of Vienna."[21]

In consequence, socioeconomic factors played a significant role in determining the very different path that eastern and central European nationalisms eventually followed. "Nationalism in the West," Kohn reminds us, "arose in an effort to build a nation in the political reality and struggle of the present without too much sentimental regard for the past; nationalists in central and eastern Europe created, often out of myths of the past and the dreams of the future, an ideal fatherland, closely linked with the past, devoid of any immediate connection with the present, and expected it to become a political reality." In agreeing with this analysis, Peter F. Sugar points to the great similarity between the nationalism of eastern-central Europe and that of Germany. This similarity may have stemmed from the fact that most Western ideas, including nationalism, found their way to eastern and central Europe mainly via Germany. Like most of the peoples on the periphery of Europe, the Germans also lacked an independent state of their own at the point in time when their national movement first emerged.[22]

Eric Hobsbawm ascribes the rapid development of ethnic nationalism after 1870 to the political and social changes then occurring in Europe. Modernity shattered the traditional order of life so that large numbers of people migrated to the big cities, thus creating vast urban communities and huge slums. Growing resentment gave birth to new political organizations and proved to be a fertile breeding ground for a novel ethno-romantic form of nationalism.[23]

A number of Marxist theoreticians also tried to analyze the concepts of the nation and nationality. Karl Renner, Otto Bauer, Karl Kautsky and, in days to come also Lenin and Stalin, all made the same discovery – each in his own way. They found that Marxist theory notwithstanding, national movements were continually bursting onto the contemporary scene. Marxism's main contribution to the understanding of nationality was the realization of the linkage between economics and the consolidation of the concept of nationhood. Among Russian Bolsheviks it was Stalin who formulated an accurate definition of the nation as a "historically constituted, stable community of people, formed on the basis of a common language, territory, economic life, and psychological make-up manifested in a common culture."[24] This laid the foundation for the Soviet model that was to remain in place for nearly seventy years: a multiplicity of nations within one large authoritarian framework.

Jewish nationalism was undoubtedly one of the predominant factors that brought home to both Lenin and Stalin Marxism's error in its general analysis of the phenomenon of nationalism. Despite the massive and brutal efforts made by the Soviet regime to suppress this particular nationalism, it persisted with its clandestine presence inside the USSR – surfacing here and there from time to time – and continued to struggle, not always consciously, with its problems of identity. Fundamental strands within the movement included a religious heritage; challenges stemming from an anti-Semitism that reached its barbaric peak during the Holocaust; a fraternity based on a common fate that transcended borders and managed to pierce even the Iron Curtain; and the great achievements in Israel registered by the Zionist movement – the outstanding expression of awakening Jewish nationalism in the modern era.

As said, Jewish nationalism arose after most European national movements and its emergence was a response to them. However, taking its uniqueness into account, it is doubtful that any other timing was possible. Some scholars already referred to – in particular Anthony Smith – have indeed pointed to how close the Jews came in ancient times to the modern national model. But the many upheavals that the Jewish people underwent since then had left it scattered across the globe, living under the shadow of persistent waves of persecution and discrimination. Moreover, the Jews were detached and distanced from the territory in which their historical heritage was rooted – a territory that didn't remain empty of other inhabitants. It would therefore seem that Jewish nationalism's long period of gestation was unavoidable, as were the doubts expressed after its emergence and the early stages of its development.

Zionism did indeed revivify historical memories of Jewish nationality that had been dormant for hundreds of years and did much to adapt these memories to the changes that Jewish identity had undergone as a result of the Jewish people being a persecuted minority – and at times a barely tolerated one. This was so both in the world that preceded the rise of national movements as well as in the period that followed their emergence. To an extent, the doubts that surrounded the birth of Zionism remain to this very day and can even be said to have intensified as a result of it having achieved its major aim. These doubts will be discussed in the following chapters.

CHAPTER 2

THE EMERGENCE OF ZIONISM

T he rise of nationalism required European Jewry to adopt a national identity of its own. It did so in a number of different forms, only one of which – the Zionist movement – was successful. For many Jews, Zionism's appearance on the stage was a shield against the national movements emerging across Europe and represented a fundamental shift in Jewish identity. "At the root of Zionism," argues Shlomo Avineri, "lies a paradox." In the course of nearly two thousand years of exile, the Jewish people didn't even for a moment cease to maintain an emotional link to Eretz Israel (the Land of Israel). This was what, in their own view, singled them out not only as a minority but a minority in exile. Though in prayer they continued to turn three times a day in the direction of Jerusalem, the vast majority never went back there. They mourned the destruction of the Second Temple but didn't set off for the historical homeland to build a new temple. This leads Avineri to conclude that Jewish identity is inherently ambivalent; a constant desire for a "homeland" coupled with a permanent justification for remaining outside its borders.

The shift away from this conception of Jewish identity has long been attributed to the rise, during the last third of the nineteenth century, of a particularly virulent form of racial anti-Semitism that in effect sought to banish Jews from the human community. But it was undoubtedly not the only factor. The Jews had, after all, also faced racial persecution under the Visigoths in the seventh century and in Spain during the fifteenth century, and in the latter part of the Middle Ages they had been expelled from practically everywhere in western Europe. And yet, other than a tiny number that opted to settle in Palestine, the vast majority chose to remain in the Diaspora. This was also the response of the Jews to the pogroms in Russia in 1881. Millions left the country but all of them, save for a handful, turned westward: to America, western Europe, Canada and South America and even to Western outposts in southern Africa and Australia – but not to Palestine.[1]

There clearly was, therefore, another reason driving European Jewry to embrace Zionism. In Avineri's view, the motive was an *unmistakable crisis of identity* among Jews experiencing modernization.

Imagine the dilemma of a modern, emancipated Jew living in Lithuania in the mid-nineteenth century: Having himself escaped the constraints of a traditional Jewish education he wants to send his own son to a school that will provide him with a general education and not to a *cheder*. But to which school should he send him? From a political point of view he is living in territory that is part of the Czarist Empire, so the state school would inevitably be a Russian school; yet there is a sizeable Polish minority in Lithuania which treasures the historical memory of the Polish-Lithuanian Commonwealth and the local Polish school extols the past glory of this union; in Lithuania there is also a significant German minority and its *Gymnasium* offers an excellent German education; and the awakening nationalism of the mostly rural Lithuanian population is also on the ascent, with an emerging school system of its own. The father who doesn't want to give his son a *Jewish* education thus discovers that he is unable to give him a *general* or *universal* education; he is compelled to give him a *particular* education and the only choice he has is whether that education is to be Russian, Polish, German or Lithuanian. Unsurprisingly, the first attempt at a secular, yet historiographically biblical, novel in Hebrew can be traced back to the Lithuania of the mid-nineteenth century – Avraham Mapu's *Ahavat Tziyon* (*The Love of Zion*, 1853), with its dilemmas of identity and crosscurrents of competing nationalisms.

In Avineri's view, this crisis of identity among modern Jews was first addressed by the Haskalah – the Jewish Enlightenment movement in Europe. Long before the rise of Zionism it was this movement that was responsible for the revival of Hebrew as a secular literary language. Avineri notes that when the first political Zionists (Pinsker, Herzl, Nordau and others) appeared on the public scene, "one discerns again and again the same phenomenon: they do not come from the traditional, religious background. They are all products of European education, imbued with the current ideas of the European intelligentsia. Their plight is not economic, nor is it religious: they respond – just like Black leaders in America a century later – to *the challenge of their self-identity*, looking for roots, and acquiring self-respect in a society that has uprooted itself from its traditional, religious background, and has not provided them and their likes with an adequate answer in this quest for self-identity."[2]

It should be noted that apart from its role in the emergence of Zionism, this crisis of identity and the mounting waves of anti-Semitism also played a part in the appearance of a number of other Jewish nationalist movements in eastern and central Europe. The Jewish Peoples Party (*Folkspartei*), headed by the prominent Jewish historian Shimon Dubnov, as well as the Jewish General Labor Union (commonly known as the *Bund*) promoted the idea that Jews were a separate nation worthy of cultural autonomy within a democratic multinational Russian state. The Jewish Socialist Workers Party (SERP) supported "territorialism" and called for the setting up of a separate Jewish territory within the boundaries of such a state. These movements that struggled for a national solution for the Jews *within* Europe and adopted the concept of *doykeyt* – Yiddish for "here and nowhere else" – were all destined to disappear during the Nazi Holocaust of European Jewry.[3] Thus Zionism was to be the only enduring Jewish national movement.

THE INDISPENSABLE PRECURSOR

Baruch Spinoza (1632–1677) was the first philosopher to define Judaism as a modern secular nation rather than a religion. Basing himself on a profound knowledge of Jewish religion and culture, Spinoza was highly critical of "rabbinical theocracy." His views clearly echoed those of the twelfth-century Jewish sage Moses Maimonides, who taught that the Mosaic biblical laws were essentially state laws. According to Spinoza, Moses transformed his people into a nation ruled by law by providing them with a constitution that most resembled a model of democratic rule by its rejection of hereditary governance. Within Mosaic law, Spinoza also discovered the first example of a separation of powers that distinguished between judicial, educational and military spheres of leadership. Spinoza, in fact, regarded Moses as a secular leader who didn't see himself as a messenger of God and refused to name a successor who would rule the people as God's direct emissary. According to Spinoza it was Moses' belief that the original laws written for the people of Israel were laws intended to organize communal life with the ultimate aim of providing a basis for conducting national life.

This philosophy resulted in the rabbinic establishment, which Spinoza had dismissively labelled "dictatorial," branding him a heretic and excommunicating him from the Jewish community. But Spinoza went on to become one of the most influential secular philosophers in the Western world, inspiring such great thinkers as Kant, Hegel and Marx. He was destined to also have an impact on later generations of secular Jews who embraced the concept of a Jewish nation. His conclusion was that Jewish emancipation required the implementation of one of two possible options: the total assimilation of the Jews within the non-Jewish society in which they were living or, alternatively, the removal of Jews to another country, if not to their own land. Indeed, in his *Theological-Political Treatise*, Spinoza daringly prophesied that the Jewish nation would establish a secular state.[4]

THE EARLY "PROTO-ZIONISTS"

Jewish nationalists' focus on Eretz Israel first emerged in the 1850s. Two of them, Rabbi Judah Alkalai and Rabbi Zvi Hirsch Kalischer, were notable exceptions to the rule that Zionists were Jews who had already been assimilated.[5] The most impressive "proto-Zionist" was Moses Hess (1812–1875), a man who "was both a communist and a Zionist. He played a decisive role in the history of the first movement; he virtually invented the second."[6] Alongside Marx, Engels and Ferdinand Lassalle,

Hess was a significant figure in the development of German Social Democracy. Known among his contemporaries as the "Red Rabbi," Hess rapidly despaired of the ability of socialist internationalism to solve the Jewish problem. In 1862 he published his book *Rome and Jerusalem*, in which he called for the revival of a Jewish nation in Eretz Israel and its establishment under a French charter.

Hess tried to disabuse Jews of the idea that it was possible to appease anti-Semitism by their becoming more "Gentile." Hess insisted that "neither reform of the religion, nor baptism, neither education nor emancipation, will completely open...the doors of social life to the Jews of Germany." For it wasn't their religion, their financial dealings or their alleged cultural backwardness that made Gentiles hate the Jews. The source of the hatred was their "Jewish noses."[7]

Hess's fervent and reverberating call fell on deaf ears. This was because he was writing shortly after the Jews of Germany had become emancipated, which made them feel very optimistic about their chances of being fully integrated within German society. In fact, at that time even Russian Jews nurtured a substantial and growing hope for a better future. In the 1860s and 1870s they were allowed to attend Russian state schools for the first time and they therefore assumed that this was the beginning of a "golden age" of one kind or another.

The turning point for Russian Jewry, and a true watershed in modern Jewish history, was the pogroms that erupted in 1881 in southern Russia. In an attempt to bypass the czarist censor these pogroms were dubbed by the Hebrew press in Russia "storms in the Negev" (*Negev* being a Hebrew synonym for *south*).[8] In the wake of the assassination of Czar Alexander II, rumors spread that the Jews had been party to the act. With the blessing of the authorities or by their turning a blind eye, unruly mobs sought revenge among the Jews. The rioters included among their ranks revolutionary factions, who hoped that this would advance the downfall of the czarist regime. In response, the regime launched a discriminatory policy toward the Jews that aimed at suppressing them, damaging them economically and preventing them from gaining either a secondary degree or a higher education. This earthquake, and the refusal of progressive circles in Russia to condemn it wholeheartedly, left the most integrated and most assimilated Jews in Russia feeling shocked and betrayed; some of them became Jewish nationalists, quite literally overnight. Toward the end of 1881, groups of Jewish students were formed in Russia's large cities and debated leaving Russia and "returning to Zion."

The most significant "proto-Zionist" group of this period was Hibbat Zion, inspired and led by Moses (Moshe) Leib Lilienblum (1843–1910) and Judah Leon Pinsker (1821–1891). Lilienblum – an author, publicist and prominent supporter of the Jewish Enlightenment – was already seeking a remedy for the Jewish problem via a change in the community's economic and cultural life. Pinsker, on the other hand, twenty-two years older than Lilienblum, was an entirely assimilated, privileged Russian Jew, who was allowed to study medicine in Moscow and run a medical practice in the city. He also served in the Russian army during the Crimean War as a volunteer doctor. One way or another, in 1881 both found themselves painfully disillusioned and called for a renewal of Jewish nationalism under the banner of political independence. If not, Lilienblum warned, the result would be that the Jews "would forever have…to face the prospect of various pogroms and not be safe even against a major holocaust." Whereas Lilienblum called for a return to Eretz Israel, Pinsker supported "territorialism," which sought any territory in which the Jews would be a majority and govern themselves.

Pinsker outlined his solution in an essay titled *Autoemancipation*, published anonymously in German in the fall of 1882. This treatise was to become the bible of Hibbat Zion (or Hovevei Zion, as they were sometimes known) and a pragmatic prelude to Herzl's political Zionism. Pinsker argued that rather than being disappointed by the outcome of their emancipation, European Jewry had to take practical steps to achieve self-emancipation. He urged them to embark on a collective effort resembling the exodus from Egypt that would lead to the ingathering of the Jews in their own homeland. "If I am not for myself, then who will be for me?" was the motto of *Autoemancipation* and its concluding sentence declared "Help yourselves and God will help you." One way or another, Pinsker claimed that the Jews were a nation but lacked the tangible attributes of a nation.

They lack an independent life – an independence that is inconceivable without a common language, common customs and a common land. The Jewish people don't have a fatherland of their own though they are the sons of many countries, no center of focus or gravity, no government of their own, and no official representation. They have homes everywhere but are nowhere at home. The nations have never to deal with a Jewish nation but always with mere Jews.[9]

Therefore, says Pinsker, "the general question of the Jews has to be resolved by national means." Moreover, he believed that the international circumstances had ripened for this to happen. "For decades we have seen various nations – that in the past wouldn't have dared think about their revival – shaking themselves free and embarking on a fresh start in life. Dawn has already broken and is shedding a new light on conventional political thinking. Governments have already started to listen attentively…to the voice of national recognition that is becoming ever stronger." Pinsker suggested the convening of "a national congress" of all the existing voluntary associations that were engaged in national activities; that congress would be entrusted with selecting a national directorate which would decide where the Jewish national state should be and purchase the territory. The location of such a territory was, in Pinsker's view, a purely pragmatic matter. "It is not toward our Holy Land that we should now be turning our minds," he wrote, "but rather toward a land of our own. Perhaps the Holy Land will again become ours. If so, all the better, but *first of all*, we must determine – and this is the crucial point – what country is accessible to us, and offers us a secure and undisputed refuge."

Pinsker's continued activities within the framework of Hovevei Zion increased his tendency to think that the solution lay in Eretz Israel. However, during the last two years of his life (1890–1891) and against the background of a serious economic crisis in the then existing Jewish settlements in Palestine, Pinsker became pessimistic and supported Baron Hirsch's proposal of the establishment of Jewish settlements in Argentina.

THE REVIVAL OF HEBREW

A common language has long been considered to be one of the central components of a nation, so that a nation without a language is thought to be inconceivable.[10] This characterization did not, of course, apply to world Jewry which conversed in numerous languages, least of all Hebrew. This led some scholars to question the centrality of language to nationalism.[11] Although the Jewish nationalist movements in Europe focused on Yiddish, Hovevei Zion and the Zionists, almost from the beginning, linked their nationalism to the revival of Hebrew. Central to this revival was Eliezer Ben-Yehuda (1858–1922), the father of modern Hebrew.

Even before the founding of political Zionism, Ben-Yehuda insisted that the only way of reviving Hebrew was in the national context of Eretz Israel, to where he himself migrated in 1881. "We will be unable to revive the Hebrew language," Ben-Yehuda wrote, "except in a country in which the number of Hebrew inhabitants exceeds that of the Gentiles. Let us therefore increase the number of Jews in our deserted land and let us return the rest of our people to the land of their forefathers. Let us bring the nation back to life and its language will also be revived."[12] Given the archaic state of the language at that time with less than six thousand Hebrew words to be found in the Old Testament, its revival as a spoken language was clearly an arduous task requiring the assembly of a modern vocabulary to be drawn from every generation of post-biblical Hebrew literature. Ben-Yehuda was able to do a significant part of this himself. He also set up the Hebrew Language Committee, which oversaw rigorous and systematic efforts to adapt the language for everyday usage.

From the outset Ben-Yehuda understood that his initiative would not succeed unless he could mobilize working partners and primarily as many teachers as possible. "If you really want to improve the lot of the inhabitants of this desolate land," he wrote a year before his immigration, "then the language of the past must be used by you as the language of education, the language of teaching." Two years later, when he was already in Palestine, he noted that "we knew that the schools possessed the great strength required to transform the entire people into speakers of one clear language." And indeed a handful of teachers responded to Ben-Yehuda's call and began to teach Hebrew, mostly in the then-existing settlements. Around them groups of Hebrew speakers began to form, including adults. In increasing numbers, such hubs also appeared among Hovevei Zion members in eastern Europe. The process gathered momentum with the accelerated development of Hebrew literature and political journalism.

Three decades after Ben-Yehuda embarked on his stubborn struggle, a "language war" erupted. The initiative of a number of parties, led by the Aid Association of German Jews in Palestine, to set up an advanced school of engineering came up against the demand that the language of instruction at this institution had to be Hebrew and not German. More than ten years later the Haifa Technion was duly opened and at the same time the Hebrew University in Jerusalem began its activities. So far as both institutions were concerned there was no doubt that all the lectures in all fields of study would be in Hebrew. Indeed the number of Hebrew speakers in the twenty-first century is now apparently the largest it has ever been. Moreover, it is now widely acknowledged, even by the detractors of Zionism, that the revival of Hebrew is one of the movement's most impressive success stories.[13]

HERZL

Theodor Herzl (1860–1904), the father of the Zionist movement, and in the view of many also the father of the State of Israel, was born in 1860 to an assimilated Jewish family in the Austro-Hungarian Empire. After completing his studies in the law faculty of the University of Vienna, he chose to become a journalist and playwright. His link to the Holy Land was first revealed in the pen name he chose – Tancred. Tancred was the name of a Norman nobleman who was one of the most prominent participants in the First Crusade aimed at recapturing the Land of Israel from the Muslims. It was also the title of a book by Benjamin Disraeli describing the voyage of an English aristocrat to the Holy Land. As a young man Herzl regularly encountered expressions of anti-Semitism and these in the end led him to the conclusion that the Jewish Question could only be resolved by the establishment of a homeland for the Jewish people. Herzl developed this idea in his book *Der Judenstaat*, which he wrote in German and published in Vienna in 1896. (The English translation, entitled *A Jewish State*, was published that same year in London.)

In 1891, Herzl was appointed as the Paris correspondent of the influential Viennese daily *Neue Frei Presse*, a job he held for a number of years. He arrived in France at a time of great instability. The defeat in the Franco-Prussian war of 1870–1871, the subsequent loss of the territory of Alsace-Lorraine and the obligation of paying substantial reparations to Germany resulted in years of political turmoil which in turn led to increasing levels of anti-Semitism. The overwhelmed French populace was also outraged by a series of crises – including the assassination of the president of the republic, Marie François Sadi Carnot, and the notorious case of corruption known as the "Panama Scandal." The wrath of the French was unleashed against wealthy moguls and well-established businessmen, and focused disproportionately on the Jews within these groups. Herzl reported to his readers on the cases of two of the Jews involved in the scandal, Jacques de Reinach and Cornelius Herz, whose apparent complicity in the crime confirmed the ever-growing accusation of the Jewish hold over the country. This imaginary control was the central theme of the infamous but then highly popular book by Édouard Drumont *Jewish France*, which also got a mention in Herzl's dispatches from Paris.

It was in this volatile atmosphere that Captain Alfred Dreyfus, a Jewish officer in the French army, was arrested and tried. In 1894 Dreyfus was falsely accused of passing on military secrets to the German embassy in Paris. He was court-martialed, dishonorably discharged from the army, and sentenced to life imprisonment on Devil's Island. The resulting scandal, which came to be known in France as "The Affair," increased the polarization between the republican left and the conservative monarchical right – the latter being supported by the armed forces. Even before the Dreyfus affair, Herzl had a hero of his play *The New Ghetto* say these words: "When the ghetto actually existed no one could leave without permission. Anyone doing so could expect to be exposed to serious physical danger. And now the walls and partitions are hidden from sight. However, the moral ghetto is the area we have been allocated." But it was the Dreyfus Affair that ultimately convinced Herzl that emancipation would not end anti-Semitism and that a Jewish homeland was the only viable answer to the problem.[14] As he wrote in *The Jewish State*:

> In those countries in which anti-Semitism was mainly to be found, it itself is a product of Jewish emancipation. When the more culturally civilized nations recognized the heartlessness of the discriminatory laws and liberated us, it was already too late. In our places of residence at the time, we were unable to accept emancipation properly. In the ghetto we had already become, in an odd way, a middle class nation, and we emerged from the ghetto as competitors scaring the middle classes. Thus suddenly after emancipation we belonged to the bourgeoisie where we face pressure both from within and from without.

This leads to the conclusion – which was formulated in a number of different ways – that "in the dark days of their exile, the Jews never ceased to passionately wish for "Next year in Jerusalem!" The time has now come to see that the dream has materialized and will become as bright and illuminating as the light of day."

Herzl's great contribution to Zionism stemmed from his understanding of the need for diplomatic and political activity that would resonate in the international arena. This was in sharp contrast to the likes of Hovevei Zion who preceded him. Their focus was on analyzing the difficult situation in which Diaspora Jews found themselves and giving minimal support to a few settlements in Palestine. Herzl, on the other hand, emphasized the need for a radical solution. In the language of today he was a man of action – the lead actor endowed with first-class diplomatic and organizational skills. As someone who saw himself as being on a spiritual mission to create a Jewish state, he was utterly confident that such a state would bring prosperity and moral renewal to the world. "The world," he wrote, "will be freed by our liberty, enriched by our wealth, become stronger through our greatness." Herzl believed with all his heart that in ridding itself of its Jews Europe would actually guarantee its own citizenry a more liberal order and secure an independent future for the Jews themselves.

In 1902 he outlined his vision of a Jewish utopia in his novel *Altneuland* (*Old New Land*). The book described a Jewish state in which there would be no racial or religious discrimination between its various inhabitants and where religion was to be an entirely private matter. Herzl wrote of a country without soldiers or politicians; instead, the state would be structured along the lines of an aristocratic republic which he saw as more stable than a democracy. It would be ruled by a benevolent council similar to the one that had governed the Venetian republic of old.[15] (This utopia still has not come to pass. However, when the first Jewish city was founded in Palestine in 1909 it was named Tel Aviv, which is a derivation of the phrase "old-new land.")

Possibly the most interesting citizen of the "new society" described in *Altneuland* is the Arab, Raschid Bey. In response to being challenged, Bey insists that Jewish immigration would materially benefit the poor and ignorant Arab population and even questions why any Arab would oppose a Jewish state. In Herzl's utopia there is no mention of either Arab or Palestinian nationalism for the obvious reason that at the time when the novel was being written those concerned were not claiming such nationalism.

Herzl's pamphlet *The Jewish State* turned the establishment of such a state into Herzl's Zionist credo. In Herzl's mind this was the ultimate response to the failure of Jewish assimilation in Europe. No one could have been more assimilated than he was, but this had not proven to be an antidote to anti-Semitism; on the contrary, it had exacerbated it. That being so, Herzl concluded angrily, resurgent anti-Semitism endangered Jews in every European country.

Having so presciently discerned the gravity of the situation, Herzl was ready to consider establishing a Jewish state in a territory other than Palestine. At a certain stage he toyed with the idea of setting up a state in Argentina on the assumption that the inhabitants would willingly part with at least some of their fertile lands. He later changed his mind when he became hopeful that the sultan of Turkey would grant Palestine to the Jews.

Initially, the Jewish leadership in Europe assumed that Herzl would not make any real moves toward establishing a Jewish state because such an approach seemed so quixotic. When it transpired that he was seriously minded to do so, the same leadership defiantly refused to support him – reflecting the views of the vast majority of European Jewry of that period. Undaunted, Herzl quickly embarked on a diplomatic offensive to realize his dream. Shortly after the publication of *The Jewish State* in 1896, he traveled to Istanbul to discuss detailed plans for the establishment of such an entity. This was one of many missions he undertook and which made mainstream Jewish leaders increasingly apprehensive. They feared an anti-Semitic backlash that would accuse Jews of "double loyalty." As the Central Conference of American Rabbis declared in 1897 on the eve of the First Zionist Congress, Zionism will "not only not benefit our still persecuted fellow Jews, it will cause them immeasurable harm by confirming the assertion of enemies of the Jewish people that the Jews are foreigners in the countries in which they are living as loyal and patriotic citizens."[16]

There were doubts expressed also in eastern Europe and even among some of the veteran members of Hovevei Zion who were apprehensive of what some saw as Herzl's daring and others thought was a task far beyond his reach. A blunt expression of this was given by Nahum Sokolow – editor of the Hebrew journal *Hatzfirah* – who mocked Herzl by referring to him as "the Viennese feuilleton playing with diplomacy." But Sokolow quickly recanted and became a devoted supporter of Herzl and rumors about Herzl's *The Jewish State* began to circulate among increasingly wider circles of eastern European Jewry as if to an audience that had been anxiously waiting for just such a message. In time to come Chaim Weizmann described its arrival as "lightning on a clear day," while David Ben-Gurion remembered how he, as a child of ten, had heard that "the Messiah had come – a handsome, dignified, even learned man with blazing eyes, and a black beard – whose name is Theodor Herzl. And he will lead the People of Israel to their ancestral homeland."

In 1897, Herzl convened the First Zionist Congress during which the World Zionist Organization was set up and approval was given to the

"Basel Program." This document opens with the words "Zionism seeks to establish a homeland for the Jewish people in Eretz Israel secured under universal law." The achievement of this goal was to be by way of settlement activity, and organizational and diplomatic steps. But the limited resources of the new organization naturally led to a trimming down of the extent of its activity. In parallel with this, the diplomatic efforts to gain international recognition encountered massive difficulties and Herzl's dream of convincing the Ottoman sultan to agree to a "homeland in Eretz Israel" remained just that – a dream. Though Herzl and the early Zionists did not weaken in their resolve they were soon to be confronted by a dramatic crisis.

In April 1903, in the wake of a blood libel and with the support of elements in the government, a bloody pogrom erupted in the Russian city of Kishinev. Forty Jews were murdered, hundreds were wounded and tortured and thousands of homes and shops were destroyed and looted. The Jewish public was stunned and this sense of shock was accompanied by an international outcry. Among the protestors were Russian intellectuals led by the writers Leo Tolstoy and Maxim Gorky who blamed the Russian government for the pogrom. In response, the authorities issued a hurried invitation to Herzl to visit Russia and gave him permission to undertake Zionist activities in the areas under their jurisdiction. In the course of this visit, Herzl was excitedly received by large crowds of Jews eager to catch a glimpse of the "king" – something that demonstrated to Herzl even more intensely the extent of their distress.

In prior talks held in London, the British government had offered Herzl a sizeable tract of land in eastern Africa for the settlement of a large number of Jews. The territory was in an area that was then part of Uganda and is today within the borders of Kenya. His interlocutor in the British Colonial Office thought that such a settlement would lead to an increase of a white presence in the area and would serve the empire's interests. In the circumstances, Herzl took to the idea that settlement in British East Africa would be the first phase in what he termed "an upside-down miniature England" – the creation of a kind of small Jewish empire based on similar settlements in other places that would be the basis for settling Eretz Israel when the right time came. His rational for this was that if among Jews everything is done in reverse, why establish the homeland prior to setting up the empire and not let the empire whose beginning was within reach set up the homeland? The full plan was not presented at the Sixth Zionist Congress which met in Basel in August 1903. On that occasion Herzl made do with a proposal to immediately evacuate Jewish refugees from Russia to British Uganda as a "night shelter" – a temporary solution to the Jewish problem. "Many of us believed that it was impossible for the situation to worsen," he explained, "but the situation has indeed worsened still further, as proved in Kishinev. Jewry has been overwhelmed by suffering.… Let us save those that can still be saved."

The proposal encountered angry opposition from congress delegates, many of whom thought that it would be interpreted to mean the renunciation of Zion, that is to say of Eretz Israel. Ironically, the Russian Zionists were the bitterest opponents of Herzl's rescue plan. Despite the objections, it was decided at the congress to send a fact-finding mission to East Africa. This decision triggered deep shock among the opponents, to the extent that many feared that the movement would fall apart. So great was the emotional storm that an attempt was made to assassinate Max Nordau, an opponent of the Uganda plan who felt he had to come to Herzl's defense. In the meantime, toward the end of 1903 the British government began to back away from the proposal to settle Jews in East Africa due to pressure from British settlers in the area and because of the significant differences of opinion within the Zionist movement. These dissensions led to a serious deterioration in Herzl's health, and on July 3, 1904, he died. The fact-finding mission that set off for East Africa after his death inspected the "revised" area proposed by the British government in the wake of the pressures it was under, and reached the conclusion that it was not suitable. This conclusion was presented at the Seventh Zionist Congress in July 1905, at which most delegates were in agreement with the opponents of the Uganda Plan. Unsurprisingly, it was decided at this congress to formally reject the British plan and to pledge the total commitment of Zionists to only settle in Eretz Israel.

In response, Israel Zangwill (1864–1926), a supporter of the Uganda plan, broke away from the Zionist movement to form the Jewish Territorialist Organization. This organization sought different territorial solutions to the Jewish problem, given the seeming impossibility of settlement in Eretz Israel. Zangwill considered various settlement projects in north and east Africa, Canada, Mexico and Australia, but none of them appeared to be viable. Finally, in the period between 1907 and 1914, with the help of the American financier Jacob Schiff, he succeeded in settling nine thousand Jews in Galveston, Texas.[17] However, toward the end of World War I, Zangwill returned to the Zionist movement, played a role in the efforts that led to the Balfour Declaration, and in later years was a frequent critic of the Zionist leadership for what he regarded as a shrinkage of the Zionist project. Since it was no longer relevant, the Jewish Territorialist Organization was officially disbanded in 1925, and with this the last threat of a possible split within the Zionist movement over the Uganda plan was finally removed.

A few months prior to his death, Herzl noted in a document that was not published till much later that if it came to a rift in the movement "my heart would remain with the Zionists and my head with the Africanists. I can only resolve such opposition by my resignation." Matters never got to that in his lifetime nor subsequently. His place in the Zionist project remained undisputed. At almost the same time as Herzl died, there was a spontaneous wave of Jewish immigration to Palestine that came to be known as the "Second Aliyah" and which played a key role in fulfilling the vision of the author of *The Jewish State*.

AHAD HA'AM

The Uganda controversy ignited a bitter and prolonged feud between Herzl and the thinker Asher Zvi Ginsberg (1856–1927), known by his pen name Ahad Ha'am (meaning, "one of the people"). This was a conflict between matter and spirit, between political pragmatism and the spiritual-cultural struggle for Jewish identity. Herzl, the pragmatist, believed that a policy of determined diplomacy and negotiations with the great powers was the only way his dream could become a reality. Ahad Ha'am was the most extreme opponent of such an approach. A renowned Jewish writer and Hebrew essayist, Ahad Ha'am was well versed in Jewish affairs from an early age and an outstanding example of the Jewish Enlightenment in Russia.

In 1844 he began to participate in meetings of the Hovevei Zion movement in Odessa. At the movement's Katowice Conference toward the end of that year, he insisted on emphasizing the national character of the movement's activities and its clear affinity to Eretz Israel. Five years later he was to write "my mind has been satiated by all it needed to know about Hibbat Zion, its purpose of reviving our people and the practical ways that are appropriate to achieve this objective." An expression of such thinking is to be found in his article "This Is Not the Way" in which he for the first time signed with the pen name Ahad Ha'am – chosen, he explained, "because I am not an author nor do I intend to join the community of authors in the future." The article itself was written against the backdrop of serious incidents in the few Jewish settlements that had been established in Palestine during the 1880s. Among those events was the uprising of farmers in Rishon LeZion against the representatives of Baron Rothschild, who took over management of the settlements in exchange for financial support. The existence of these settlements was, in the view of the writer, the result of serious shortsightedness. "What ought we to have done?" he asks rhetorically and answers:

> We should have devoted our initial efforts to a revival of people's hearts to inspire men with a deeper attachment to the national life and a more ardent desire for its success, until the will would be aroused and workers would act faithfully.... Though such an effort is difficult and takes a long time, not one year nor one decade... hence it is probable, in fact almost certain, that if we had chosen this method we should not yet have had time to produce concrete results in Eretz Israel itself: lacking the resources necessary to do things well, we should have been too prudent to do things badly.... But this is not what the standard-bearers of our idea did. Not satisfied with working among the people to train up those who would ultimately work the land, they wanted to see the latter and its results with their own eyes.

As a result, Ahad Ha'am argued, the bearers of the flag began to disseminate fictitious reports about the strong economic foundations that settlers could expect to find in Palestine and the possibility of immigrating "to the good country, to eat and be satiated and to live a happy and comfortable life." And there were those who responded to the temptation – most of whom had no intention of submitting with love to suffering for the sake of a common ideal. Though trapped, they did not refrain then and until this very day from creating a hue and cry and sowing confusion." This, therefore, is not the way, concluded Ahad Ha'am: "not by force of arms or might but by our spirit, and then the day will come when our efforts too will yield results."

The article produced a wide array of reactions and was also thought of as a landmark in the development of essay writing in Hebrew. Among other things it served as an ideological platform for the society known as Bnei Moshe. This body, set up through the initiative of the journalist and author Yehoshua Eisenstadt Barzilai and led by Ahad Ha'am, was intended to be a secret organization, a kind of parallel to the Freemasons. Its declared objective as explained by Shulamit Laskov was "to cleanse Jewish nationalism from all the material dross that had stuck to it, and inspire trust in the purity of its intentions."[18] Members of the society, Ahad Ha'am decided, "would work slowly, would remember that there is a form of inaction that produces far more good than the deed itself," and their beliefs would be gradually absorbed through education. Naturally it didn't occur to Ahad Ha'am or his followers to engage in high diplomacy of the kind that Herzl would in eight years' time place at the top of the Zionist movement's agenda.

The clandestine nature and elitist pretensions of Bnei Moshe troubled many of Hovevei Zion's members, and minimized the membership of the society. Throughout its existence over a period of about eight years, the society didn't even manage to attract as many as two hundred members. Some also didn't agree to their leader's edict to refrain from "doing." At least three of them – Yehoshua Eisenstadt Barzilai, Vladimir Temkin and Menachem Ussishkin – became involved in practical efforts to advance immediate settlement in Eretz Israel without waiting to cultivate Zionist consciousness. A year after the society's establishment, members of

its Warsaw branch formed the Menuchah v'Nachalah (Repose and
Homestead) Company, which almost immediately joined in the work
of establishing a new settlement – Rehovot. But Ahad Ha'am himself
continued to stick to the principles of his essay "This Is Not the Way."
It can be safely said that his oppositional stance became still firmer in
the years that followed.

In 1891, Ahad Ha'am set off for a three-month visit to Palestine.
On the ship returning him to Odessa he summed up his impressions of
this visit in an article entitled "The Truth from Eretz Israel." In it he
wrote: "I have now departed from the land that is my heart's desire.
I left broken hearted and saddened…, all I wish for…is to waken my
brothers in the love of Zion from their sweet sleep and advise them, as
an eyewitness, of the negative aspects of the movement, so that they too
will know how to judge it."

He concluded that "Eretz Israel cannot now absorb the mass of our
people migrating from their homelands.… The Arabs, in particular
those who inhabit the cities, realize what it is that we seek in this
land.… The *baksheesh* [bribe] is powerful in Turkey and leaders are
also susceptible to the temptation but…the important ministers are at
the same time patriotic and zealous devotees of their religion and their
government." And so "if, in all sincerity, we wish to achieve our aims in
the land of our ancestors, we cannot any longer ignore the fact that we
are embarking on a major war."

In time to come Ahad Ha'am noted that in the summer of 1897 "the
society [Bnei Moshe] was nullified by the hubbub at Basel," thereby
expressing his clear disapproval of the convening of the First Zionist
Congress in Basel. In the Hebrew monthly *Hashiloach* which began
publication under his editorship in 1896, Ahad Ha'am had nothing to
say ahead of the congress's opening. He did attend the congress itself –
the only one at which he was present – thinking that "perhaps I can be
of some use because it saddens me to see that everything there is in the
hands of youngsters whose enthusiasm exceeds their understanding."
This hope was frustrated. "The great majority of those who attended," he
wrote to his friend, "were senseless youths." Herzl, he wrote, is "by my
intuition an actor." Elsewhere he called him the "new Shabtai Zvi." To

comprehend the severity and bitterness of equating Herzl with the man who went down in Jewish history as the "false Messiah," it is necessary to digress from the subject of this book with a short biography: Shabtai Zvi (1626–1676) was a Sephardic rabbi and kabbalist who claimed to be the long-awaited Jewish Messiah. He was the founder of the Jewish Sabbatean movement. In 1666, at the age of forty, Shabtai Zvi was forced by the Ottoman sultan Mehmed IV to convert to Islam.

The only thing that enabled Ahad Ha'am to calmly sit through the congress in Basel – "this comedy," as he called it – was Max Nordau's lecture on the plight of the Jews all over the world. Immediately after the congress he explained that, initially, "the Basel assembly surpassed itself in letting the whole world know that the people of Israel are still alive and want to live." This he followed by declaring, "For having done so the assembly deserves to be engraved in letters of gold for the generations to come, were it not…that it wanted to do much more." He predicted that Herzl's diplomatic efforts would antagonize the Ottoman government to such an extent that it would lead to the destruction of the Zionist movement. Additionally he opined that only "a fantasy bordering on madness" could lead to a vision of mass Jewish migration to and the establishment of a Jewish state in Palestine. "We have seen what diplomacy can do in matters of this kind if a large fully armed military force doesn't stand at its side." Moreover, he vehemently disagreed with Herzl's prediction that a Jewish state would put an end to anti-Semitism in the Diaspora and insisted that such a state based only on materialistic success would ultimately endanger the very existence of Judaism. This led to his scathing conclusion that the "salvation of Israel will be achieved by prophets, not by diplomats."

Soon afterwards, Ahad Ha'am sharply ridiculed Herzl's utopian novel *Altneuland*. He had a range of queries about the feasibility of the "new society" described by Herzl in his book, its nature, and the absence of national Hebrew or Jewish symbols. However he did point out that "we don't find fault with *Altneuland* for being full of miracles." In another article Ahad Ha'am explained that "the secret of our nation's existence lies in what the prophets taught in ancient time: to honor only spiritual power and not to revere brute force…. But a political idea that doesn't rely on a national culture [i.e., a Jewish state such as Herzl visualized] is apt to seduce us from our loyalty to spiritual greatness and to beget in us a tendency to find a path of glory in the attainment of material power and a political state that will undermine the nation's historical foundation."[19]

Ahad Ha'am did not participate in the Sixth Zionist Congress at which Herzl brought up the Uganda Plan, but the plan itself aroused both his anger and his despair. He wrote to one of his close friends that "what you did in Basel is considered by me to be a public act of religious conversion." And in an article titled "The Weepers," which he published a short time later, he wrote against any attempt at compromise between supporters and opponents. "The Zionism of Basel," he ruled, has died, whereas "historical Zionism" can wait and needs to be driven slowly along what is "a long path."

Ahad Ha'am's prognosis in relation to the Zionist movement did not come to pass. The crisis over the Uganda scheme was not an act of "religious conversion" and Ahad Ha'am himself was not only to participate in various efforts to strengthen the Yishuv in Palestine (including the establishment of the Haifa Technion) but was also involved in the political activity that preceded the Balfour Declaration. In 1922 he immigrated to Palestine and lived the remaining years of his life there. One way or another, he remained firmly committed to his view that Jewry was aspiring to "return to its historical center, in order to live a life of natural evolution, to develop and perfect its national assets…and thereby in the future introduce to humanity's treasure chest a great national culture…. In the achievement of this goal it can make do for now with little, and does not need a political government but requires only to create for itself in its homeland…a decent group of Hebrew people who can work without interference in all branches of the culture ranging from agriculture and art to intellectual and literary endeavors. This group, which will gradually come together, will in the fullness of time become the core of the nation…. And once the national culture in Eretz Israel reaches such a level we will be able to rely on it, for it will itself produce people from its offspring that will, when the moment is right, be capable of establishing there a state – not merely a state of the Jews, but an authentic Jewish state."

Thus Ahad Ha'am correctly spotted the cultural-spiritual vacuum in political Zionism. Yet his opposition to a state or to mass migration to Eretz Israel would in time come to be seen – in circumstances that he himself would not live to witness – as a tragic mistake. Undoubtedly his clash with Herzl ran along the same fault lines and addressed the same issues as those that would decades later typify the clash between Zionism and post-Zionism. And Ahad Ha'am's preference for spiritual growth and cultural development over political power represents a clash of views that continues to echo in the contemporary debate and attempts to conceptualize Jewish identity today. It would seem that in the final analysis Herzl and Ahad Ha'am were both right. Cultural and political power are both essential and ultimately complementary elements. In other words, in optimal conditions they are two sides of the same coin.

THE POST-HERZL ERA

Following Herzl's premature death in 1904, there were fears among the Zionists that the movement was in danger of fragmenting due to a lack of leadership. Yet, despite the enormous difficulties in finding someone to step into Herzl's very large shoes, the Zionists regrouped and continued to vigorously debate the movement's past policies as well as what its line of action should be in the future. The most passionate debate was the one that erupted between Russian and western Zionists. The Russians objected to political Zionism's attempts to reach an agreement with a major world power as a means of securing the immigration of large numbers of Jews to Palestine. The Russian preference was for a slow, systematic settlement of Palestine that would create "facts on the ground" and ultimately lead to a diplomatic breakthrough. This approach came to be known as "practical Zionism." Herzl's elected successor, the uncharismatic banker David Wolfsohn, attempted in 1907 to get the Ottomans to agree to the settlement of five thousand Jews in Palestine – in areas that excluded Jerusalem – in exchange for which the Zionists would organize a "loan" on easy terms for the sultan's depleted treasury. In the early stages of negotiation over the loan, the Young Turk Revolution erupted in Istanbul. In the ensuing unstable political climate all additional Zionist settlement in Palestine was forbidden by the Ottoman Empire until the end of the First World War.

And yet, the same political instability offered new opportunities for circumventing the Ottoman prohibition on entry into the country. More than thirty thousand Jewish immigrants were able to reach the shores of Palestine between 1905 and 1914. The new settlers managed to create a more autonomous, Hebrew-speaking community and demonstrated a capacity to conduct their affairs without overly fearing the Ottoman authorities. In this way the Zionist movement began to lay the foundations for self-rule. Among other things it set up the Palestine Land Development Company (PLDC) which engaged in the purchase of land from Arabs and prepared that land, as well as land owned by the Jewish National Fund, for modern agricultural cultivation. In doing this, the PLDC was helped by funds donated by Zionists throughout the Jewish world. Despite all the upheavals and difficulties no less than 127,000 Jews in the Diaspora were members of the Zionist Organization during WW1; they joined by purchasing the "Zionist shekel."[20]

THE BALFOUR DECLARATION

The event that unified the political and practical wings of the Zionist movement was the publication by the British government on November 2, 1917, of the document that came to be known as the Balfour Declaration. In this document the then British Foreign Secretary, Arthur James Balfour, confirmed his government's support for the creation of a Jewish national home in Palestine. Many commentators attribute this astonishing development to the diplomatic skills of Chaim Weizmann. At the time Weizmann worked as a chemist in the British navy's ordnance program, in which capacity he developed an efficient method for the production of acetone; Dr. Weizmann went on to become the State of Israel's first president in 1948.[21] But the precise reasons for the British government's actions have long been regarded as an elusive question. In the classic book on the Balfour Declaration, Leonard Stein thoroughly examined all the factors leading up to the publication of the declaration but didn't reach any definitive conclusions.[22] Nor is there any authoritative proof that either the foreign minister, Balfour, or the prime minister, David Lloyd George, understood this declaration to mean support for the establishment of a Jewish state in Palestine.

Either way, by 1918, only months after the publication of the declaration, many British politicians had begun to distance themselves from it – claiming that it was not a legally binding document but rather a political statement that could be altered at any time. But even though Great Britain began almost immediately to scale down its commitment to Zionism, it left the movement with enough maneuvering room to attain its main objectives.[23] As the war ended, Britain was handed the mandate to govern Palestine and prepare it for sovereign rule by its inhabitants. The British gained this authority from the Allies and subsequently by a resolution of the League of Nations. In this latter resolution the Zionist movement succeeded in getting the Balfour Declaration included in the text of the mandate. From the Zionist point of view, there were two articles of great importance in this document, articles 2 and 4. In article 2 it was stated inter alia that "the Mandatory shall be responsible for placing the country under such political, administrative and economic conditions as will secure the establishment of the Jewish national home...." Article 4 stated that "an appropriate Jewish agency shall be recognised as a public body for the purpose of advising and co-operating with the Administration of Palestine in such economic, social and other matters as may affect the establishment of the Jewish national home and the interests of the Jewish population in Palestine.... The Zionist organization...shall be recognized as such agency. It shall take steps...to secure the cooperation of all Jews who are willing to assist in the establishment of the Jewish national home."

Like the Balfour Declaration itself, these articles included the following proviso: "it being clearly understood that nothing shall be done which may prejudice the civil and religious" rights of existing non-Jewish communities in Palestine. And the recognition of the Zionist Organization would remain unaltered "so long as its organization and constitution are in the opinion of the Mandatory power appropriate." There can be no doubt that after the publication of Herzl's *The Jewish State* and the convening of the First Zionist Congress, the Balfour Declaration was the most significant step in the realization of the Zionist dream.

SOCIALIST ZIONISM

In the mid-1930s, Socialist Zionism, or the Zionist Labor movement, became the dominant force in the Zionist Organization and continued to hold the reins of power in Israel until 1977. But the process that brought that about had already begun in the early 1920s.[24] The preeminence of this movement within Zionism is, among other things, indicative of the overwhelming prominence of socialist ideas in eastern and central European Jewish communities at the turn of the century. It is also an indication of the way in which cosmopolitan socialists and internationalists were woken from their illusions in much the same way as happened to Moses Hess nearly fifty years earlier.

Socialist Zionism initially had two primary theoreticians. Nahman Syrkin (1868–1924) participated in the First Zionist Congress and about a year later published the pamphlet entitled *The Jewish Problem and the Socialist State of the Jews*. In Syrkin's view "waiting for the revolution" – socialism's general prescription for ending anti-Semitism – was not a viable option. The socialists were utterly convinced that the increasingly intense class struggle against the advance of capitalism would ultimately lead to a socialist revolution – a regime of equality. But to Syrkin it was clear that this struggle would also inevitably serve to increase anti-Semitism. On one side of the barricade were the new "native" urban classes whose aim was to replace Jewish artisans and commercial traders; on the other side were the "casualties" of advancing capitalism – the petite bourgeoisie made up of small shopkeepers, impoverished landowners, large numbers of farmers, the middle classes and civil servants. None of these lost any time in blaming the Jews for their dire straits. "As life becomes more difficult and less secure," Syrkin wrote, "and as the danger of an assault on the middle classes and the fear of a proletarian revolution aimed at Jewry, capital, the monarchy and the state grows, so the waves of anti-Semitism will gather momentum. The warring factions will be drawn closer to one another in their common war against the Jews."

Syrkin was, in fact, the first to identify the roots of Fascistic anti-Semitism – a widespread amalgam of anticapitalist sentiments. He identified it firstly among the victims of the new order, for whom capitalism and Jews were one and the same. Secondly he saw it emerging among non-Jewish capitalists who redirected the popular anticapitalist feeling toward Jewish capitalists by advancing the idea of a "safe" revolution – not of class but of blood. On the other hand, Syrkin argued that the state of the Jews could only be established on the basis of the Jewish proletariat in the Diaspora. Therefore "under the guise of socialism, Zionism can become the property of the whole Jewish nation…. All Jews will have an interest in its success; no Jew will keep his distance. The messianic hope that was always foremost in the thoughts of Diaspora Jews will come into being through a political act…. Something that is usually the province of the imagination of the few will, among Jews, become a massive, great national movement; what is elsewhere regarded as utopian will among Jews be seen as inevitable."

Dov Ber Borokhov (1881–1917) went even further. In his view it wasn't just that the socioeconomic tilt toward socialism would lead to greater anti-Semitism, socialism itself would produce that outcome. As a result of it becoming a mass movement, Borokhov argued, the socialist parties would adopt the kind of anti-Semitism widespread among the public at large and this would happen for two reasons. Firstly, socialism does not preclude ethnic-nationalist competition with the Jews; Jewish "overrepresentation" in the economy would continue to be an issue in socialist and communist societies. Secondly, anti-Semitism contains an irrational hatred that cannot simply be reduced to economics – meaning that anti-Semitism actually refutes the basic tenet of Marxism. The problem of class was *not* the most important issue, certainly not the sole issue of significance in the growth of anti-Semitism. Yet at the same time Borokhov tried to position Jewish nationalism within the framework of socialist-Marxist assumptions, which brought him to the following conclusion: "The contradiction between the need to move over to the primary manufacturing sectors and the impossibility of getting there by focusing on the developed capitalist countries where the means of production…are already in the hands of the country's population and non-Jewish immigrants – this contradiction makes it necessary to focus the migration to a country in which the Jewish immigrants can immediately take control of the primary phases of production.... In conclusion, there is a need for a territorial solution to the Jewish question." After considerable vacillation, Borokhov concluded that such a solution was possible only in Palestine.

Both Borokhov and Syrkin saw national liberation as an important precondition to internationalism. All peoples, both argued, must first enjoy national sovereignty and only then would there be a basis for the expectation that they would waive their right to such sovereignty.[25]

One way or another, the Zionist Labor movement did not overly preoccupy itself with the writings of Syrkin or Borokhov but focused instead on the creation of facts on the ground in Palestine. It did so encouraged by the acute political consciousness of its leadership – first and foremost that of David Ben-Gurion, who was to coin the slogan "From Class to Nation." The tough core of the Second Aliyah laid down the foundations for a system of trade unions, welfare services – especially health insurance – and educational, journalistic and cultural projects. These were joined by new forms of settlement – the kibbutz and the moshav – that were structured to take root in the border areas controlled by the Zionist movement. There was, in addition, the body known as Chevrat Ha'ovdim (Society of Workers) which developed a wide range of economic projects based on socialist values. The movement also established a countrywide Jewish militia – the Haganah – subordinate to the civilian echelon.

Within this structure there were plenty of ideological disputes that morphed quite often into bitter conflicts both from within and from without. However, throughout it all the mainstream espoused the cause of a Jewish state in Palestine without explicitly determining its borders. Though the socialist strand was never a majority either in the Zionist movement or the Jewish Yishuv in Palestine, from the mid-1930s and on it succeeded in forming coalitions under its direction. This required a great deal of pragmatism. The backdrop to this throughout was what Shlomo Avineri has described as the view that it was not enough to extract Jews from the Diaspora, one had to also extract the Diaspora from the Jew.[26]

However divided these early Zionists were in their views, they were nonetheless united in that they all saw the need to deal with an evident crisis of Jewish identity in the modern world, resulting from the rise of nationalism across the European continent.

CHAPTER 3

REINVENTING JEWISH IDENTITY:
DIASPORA NEGATION

N egation of the Diaspora was the central premise of Zionist ideology. It entailed the delegitimization of Jewish life beyond the borders of a Jewish state once it had been established. As a concept in the evolution of Jewish identity, the negation of the Diaspora had its origins in debates within the Jewish nationalist movement in eastern and central Europe. The two sides to the debate were the political Zionists and the "autonomists," led by the historian Shimon Dubnov (1860–1941).

Though Dubnov himself was sceptical about the possibility of ensuring Jewish survival in the Diaspora, he didn't believe that a Jewish state would resolve the problem. According to Dubnov, every period since the destruction of the Second Temple had seen a community of Jews surpass the others in their capacity for self-rule and Jewish creativity. In their time, each of these communities became the center of the Jewish people. It was Dubnov's hope that such a center would come into being in Russia-Poland after the establishment of "states of nationalities," which would maintain the imperial integrity of czarist Russia and Austro-Hungary while bestowing autonomy on the many nations within the empires. It was Dubnov's further hope that within this center Jewish creativity would be freed from the envelope of the religiosity of the Talmudic and medieval periods and would develop mostly in Yiddish.

The political Zionists, like the autonomists, did not mandate that all Jews migrate from the Diaspora to a Jewish state. Even Herzl noted that the Jewish state would be established only for the sake of those Jews unable to assimilate in their places of abode. The Jewish state would then serve as a catalyst for the full assimilation of those Jews who wanted to integrate within the surrounding societies.

And yet, Zionists strongly believed that Jewish survival could only be assured through the creation of a political Jewish entity in Eretz Israel. The debate on this issue intensified when Ahad Ha'am began to distinguish between objective and subjective negation of the Diaspora. He argued that a realization of the dangers confronting a minority and the fear of extinction did not amount to an objective negation. That would necessitate an absolute recognition of the impossibility of a continuation of Jewish life in the Diaspora. In his words, "Exile is indeed a very bad and bitter experience. Yet we must live, and we can live in the Diaspora despite all its awfulness and bitterness. The exodus from the Diaspora has been and will continue to be a national hope for the end of days. But the time of that end is a divine secret, concealed and unknowable, and our national existence does not depend on it." Loyal as ever to his unique Zionist vision, Ahad Ha'am thus inferred that "the new bulwark for Jewish national life in exile has to be built outside the Diaspora – in the land of our forefathers.... We must improve and broaden our national lives in the Diaspora to the utmost extent possible while at the same time seeking the perfect solution beyond the limits of the Diaspora."[1]

Though no one could possibly have foreseen the enormity of the Holocaust, the objective negation of the Diaspora ultimately developed in line with the Zionist prediction of a major tragedy that was liable to engulf the Jewish people. The negation of the Diaspora, which began to appear on the movement's agenda in the early days of Zionism, dictated a radical change in national identity. It renounced the lack of worldliness, modernity and European culture in the life of Diaspora Jews. Even before then, writers such as Avraham Mapu and David Frishman lamented the backwardness of Jewish shtetl life, its impoverishment and its obliviousness to the world around. These sentiments clearly expressed a yearning for a modern, entirely new Jewish identity. Similarly, the poet Y. L. Gordon called for the opening up of the shtetl to European culture, for its inhabitants to begin engaging in "real" agricultural work and for a return to nature and a departure from the constricted horizons of traditional Jewish life. In their negation of the Diaspora, the Zionists sought to mobilize Jewish resources in the noble cause of creating a Jewish homeland. The Jewish community in Palestine, on the other hand, in its effort to strengthen the national spirit and reinforce the commitment to the building of a new state, called for the negation of the Diaspora long before statehood.

Negating the Diaspora meant the creation of a new kind of national identity that would be manifestly different from that of the typical shtetl Jew. The new Jew, freed from the handicaps and complexes of the Diaspora, was to be proud and strong, tilling the soil, affirming his Hebrew culture and embracing the Land of Israel. Thus, when in the first quarter of the twentieth century a kibbutz member compared himself to the father he had left behind in Russia, it was easy for him to reach the conclusion that he, the new man in the old land (and since 1948 the new Israeli), was very different from the previous generation shackled by the Diaspora. He was enthralled by his ability to operate, manage, be decisive, demonstrate courage and independence – in stark contrast to the cowardly Diaspora Jew living in constant fear of anti-Semitism.

An intergenerational clash was now clearly evident. The new, even prestate Israelis became the epitome of the negation of the Diaspora to a degree that seemed flawed to their parents, who were committed to such human virtues as compassion, consideration of others and spiritual involvement. The antagonism reached its peak after 1945 when many of the younger generation in Palestine expressed contempt for the Diaspora and the victims of the Holocaust. They believed that such a fate could never have happened to them because they – the new Jews – would have never gone to their deaths without fighting. Moreover, many thought that the tragedy would not have occurred at all if, at the time, a Jewish state in the Land of Israel had already been established. The encounter between the new Israeli and the Jewish Diaspora was painful and reproachful, lacking empathy or compassion and marked by an overt sense of superiority and overbearing.

Upon their arrival in Eretz Israel in the course of the First Aliyah (1882–1903), these European Jews encountered a hedge plant belonging to the cactus family which in Arabic is called *tzabar*. This plant – sweet on the inside and prickly on the outside – led the newly arrived Jews to dub the children born to them in the country *Sabra*s. The prickly shell covering a hidden sweetness symbolized to them the new Israeli settling the homeland and also the hard work demanded of him if he was to survive the arid and unforgiving soil of this homeland. Most of the native born, the Sabras themselves, were keen to adopt the metaphor. Their Jewish identity bore no resemblance to that of Diaspora Jewry, unaffected as it was by fear, doubt or submissiveness.[2] For the Sabras, the right to live in the ancient homeland was unquestionable and they were prepared to sacrifice their lives to sustain and defend it. The idea that Zionism was the only legitimate Jewish ideology was accepted by them as a given.

The drawbacks of such personality traits quickly became apparent. Many Sabras were abrasive and arrogant and lacked compassion for the "other" – be they Arabs or the Jews of the Diaspora. These Sabras had a pronounced air of elitism about them and saw themselves as part of an inner circle which was naturally superior to everyone outside it. It appeared that the mission of the Sabras was to survive in the Jewish homeland and defend Zionist ideology. One of the most famous personifications was Moshe Dayan – the son of settlers, courageous, shrewd, ingenious, at times rude and irreverent, unconventional, protective of his people and with an apparent understanding of how to deal with Arabs. A consequence of these characteristics was a weakening of the solidarity and camaraderie that the embryonic Israeli society so needed. Those Israelis not born in the country felt inferior to their Sabra contemporaries and to a certain extent sensed that they were not part of Israeli society.

In his quest for a new Jewish identity, David Ben-Gurion drew a straight line connecting the biblical era and the nascent state. He attempted to erase the intervening two thousand years of Jewish exile from the collective memory of the Jewish community by simply not referring to it. In his view, Jewish history was a matter of archaeology: the uncovering of an ancient Jewish civilization in Eretz Israel rather than the study of the vicissitudes of Diaspora history. Indeed, Ben-Gurion considered the Bible, not the plight of persecuted Jewry in the Diaspora, to be the basic and inherent moral justification for the establishment of a Jewish state in Eretz Israel.

Jewish identity in the Yishuv (the prestate Jewish community in Palestine) became intimately linked to biblical Israel. The first Zionist settlers embraced the Old Testament not as a religious text but rather as a national-cultural saga documenting the history of their motherland. The pioneers of the Second Aliyah (arriving in the years 1903–1914) were mostly Russian Jews enamoured with socialism. Ironically, they turned to the Old Testament to justify their immigration to Palestine. When asked why they had come to this country, they said nothing about pogroms in Russia or the persecution of Jews in the Diaspora. Instead they cited God's commandment to Abraham in the book of Genesis to go to a new land and create a people. This sentiment, echoes of which can be heard in the works of writers and poets such as Shaul Tchernichovsky, reflected the intrinsic attachment of Zionists to the Land of Israel and their increasing detachment from the Diaspora.[3]

An extreme negation of the Diaspora in an attempt to mold a new national identity in Eretz Israel was the Canaanite movement. This was a radical cultural movement founded by the Hebrew poet Jonathan Ratosh (1908–1981). Originally named Uriel Halperin, Ratosh was born in Warsaw and emigrated to Palestine as an eleven-year-old child.[4] The Canaanites believed that all efforts should be dedicated to securing the survival of temporal Israel. In Ratosh's view, the Jews in Israel had to be distinguished from the Jews of the Diaspora who, he insisted, were not a nation but merely a religious group. Therefore, Ratosh argued, Israeli Jews should go their own way and create a new Hebrew identity that would not be limited to the followers of the Jewish religion. Israel had to become not a Jewish state but a Hebrew state in which only Hebrew would be spoken. Muslims and Christians would be entitled to adopt the Hebrew language and culture and whoever did so would be welcomed as part of the new Hebrew society.[5]

Ratosh was influenced by the historian Adolf Gurevitz (Adia Horon) who participated in deciphering ceramic clay tablets discovered by a French archaeological expedition that began its excavations in 1929 on a site in the northern Syrian town of Ugarit. The expedition unearthed early writings describing the lives of Canaanite gods in a language that resembled Hebrew. Based on these tablets Gurevitz-Horon developed a theory of there having been a "Land of the Hebrews." During the second and first millennia BCE, according to this theory, the inhabitants of the Middle East from Mesopotamia to the Mediterranean and south to the Red Sea had one culture and were all Hebrew speakers. In biblical times the entire area was known as Eretz Hakedem (the Land of Kedem) meaning the "ancient land" or the "land of the east." The Hebrew inhabitants of the region worshiped the Canaanite gods, as did other tribes in the same area. Gurevitz-Horon posited that the Jewish religion did not appear on the historical stage as a universal monotheistic religion until after the Jewish nation was exiled to Babylon (in the fourth or maybe fifth century BCE), where the Jewish religion originated. All of this became the basis of Ratosh's Canaanite ideology. Ratosh claimed that historical proof had been found showing that the Hebrews and the Jews belonged to two different civilizations. The first had developed in the Middle East and was authentic to the region. The Jewish civilization, on the other hand, argued Ratosh, had developed after the dispersal of the Jews to various countries. The greater Hebrew nation visualized by Ratosh would integrate within its borders all the non-Jewish minorities into one Hebrew-speaking nation.[6]

The Canaanites embraced the Zionist concept of the "new Jew" untainted by the Diaspora, and took it to an extreme level. One of the writers who joined the movement was Benjamin Kamerstein (1919–1989), who changed his family name to Tammuz (the name of the god of spring, growth and fertility in Sumerian mythology). In his novella, *Jacob*, Tammuz's hero casually dismisses the fate of European Jewry. "We cannot be responsible for them. If, for example, I was told that famine in China had led to the death of a million people it would of course be distressing. But what could I possibly do about it?" When asked how one could possibly equate the fate of his own people, the

Jews, with that of the Chinese, he snapped. "Of course you can't.... There are six hundred million Chinese and only sixteen million Jews."[7]

This response mirrors Ratosh's attitude toward the Eichmann trial (April 1961). When asked whether the Holocaust shocked him he answered: "If tomorrow you are killed does that make you my cousin?" The Turks, he added, had killed two million Armenians, but this fact didn't make him an Armenian. In fact, the Eichmann trial was to be the final parting of the ways for the Canaanite movement. The Canaanites contradicted their ideology of denigrating the Diaspora by blaming the leaders of the Jewish community in Palestine for not having taken action to rescue European Jewry. At the same time they opposed the Eichmann trial itself, claiming that its sole purpose was to instruct young Israelis about the persecution of Jews in the Diaspora.

Following the trial, the influence of the Canaanites rapidly declined. Even before then, their impact had not been significant. New immigrants arriving in the country after the establishment of the state didn't want to sever themselves from the Diaspora, and the Zionist principle of Israel becoming the "guardian of the entire Jewish nation" reigned supreme.[8] The writer A. B. Yehoshua has since claimed that the waves of Jewish immigration at the beginning of the 1950s convinced all Israelis that "neither we nor our forefathers were born of the sea or in the fields of the Philistines." He concluded that Canaanite ideology "is an excellent ingredient for spicing up the flavor of Zionism but only if used sparingly." The departure of the Canaanites from the scene enabled the Israelis to appreciate the movement more seriously as an episode in the process of an evolving Jewish identity in a sovereign state.[9]

The concept of "negating the Diaspora" that had been taken to an extreme by the Canaanites became an element in the criticism of Zionists in general. Writers such as Tom Segev, Idith Zertal and Moshe Zuckerman claimed that Zionism's negation of the Diaspora had led to a confrontation between Israel and Diaspora Jewry and hence to the lack of any real effort by the Zionists to save European Jewry during the Holocaust. The Zionist leadership, according to these writers, at all times gave priority to building up the Jewish community in Palestine instead of aiding the threatened Jews in Europe.[10]

Long before that, there were those who were enraged by the Jewish leaders who, in 1935, reached a "transfer" deal with the Nazi government of Germany. The agreement allowed approximately fifty thousand Jews to emigrate from Germany to Palestine after having exchanged their property and assets for German products to be exported to Palestine. (This was done in a way that undermined the Jewish boycott of German goods but profited the local Jewish economy in Palestine).[11] Others blamed the Zionists for putting Yitzhak Grunbaum, a second-rank member of the leadership, in charge of rescue operations during the war.[12] Others accused the leadership of having missed opportunities to ransom thousands of Jews at a later stage of the war, citing such examples as the Transnistria episode, the Europe Plan and the deal proposed by Adolph Eichmann to exchange one million Jews for ten thousand trucks and other goods,[13] a deal the Nazis called *Blut gegen Waren*, "blood for goods." Zionist leaders were also denounced for having blocked a proposed transfer of Jews to the Dominican Republic and other countries and for opposing every rescue plan not linked to bringing Jews to Eretz Israel for permanent settlement.[14]

The highly regarded historian of Zionism, David Vital, alludes to a particularly distressing example of this stance. On September 13, 1944, a senior and authorized representative of the Zionist movement visited the US State Department to meet with members of the team handling Middle Eastern affairs. The heading of the "Memorandum of Conversation" as recorded by the State Department was "Zionist Position towards Eretz Israel." Among other topics the memorandum gave an account of two references to the rescue of Jews in occupied Europe. The first was to a proposal tabled in Congress to provide temporary emergency shelter in Palestine for Hungarian Jews. The Zionist representative made it clear that he didn't attach any special importance to this proposal, partly because of a lack of trust in the motives of those who lobbied members of Congress to raise it and partly because he didn't think there was any way for Hungarian Jews to successfully flee the country. He went on to say that "in any case, Zionists are opposed to every plan whose purpose is to settle Jews in Eretz Israel only on a temporary basis and on the understanding that they would be sent elsewhere after the war."

The second reference in the memorandum was to an ongoing debate at the time between the British Colonial Office and the Jewish Agency about the final allocation of fifteen thousand certificates that still remained to be allocated in accordance with the White Paper of 1939: "The Colonial Office chose to give preference in the issuing of certificates to those Jews in occupied Europe who were in danger of being killed. Though the Jewish Agency was unable to object to the priority that these people were entitled to…it argued that a certain minimum number of certificates had to be also promised to potential immigrants from 'safe' areas such as Italy, North Africa and Yemen." In a handwritten comment in the margins of the document it was noted that the US officials listening to our representative found it hard to believe what they were hearing.[15]

Segev traces the origins of this policy to a number of comments made by Ben-Gurion during the 1930s. "If I knew that it was possible to save all the children of Germany by transporting them to England, and only half by transferring them to the Land of Israel, I would choose the latter, for before us lies not only the numbers of these children but the historical reckoning of the people of Israel."[16] Admittedly, Ben-Gurion said this before the war and before the Nazis began their "Final Solution." At the time he, of course, had no idea of the magnitude of the danger those children faced. From the moment when the plan for the Final Solution was exposed neither Ben-Gurion nor any of his colleagues had any real influence over the Allies, to say nothing of their ability to save the Jews of Europe. By the time of the Bermuda Conference at the end of April 1943, the Nazi plan for the "Final Solution" was already known to the participants. In the wake of this conference it became apparent that apart from intensifying the war effort in general, the Allies would be doing nothing to prevent the implementation of the Final Solution. In light of this Ben-Gurion reached the conclusion that the Jewish people had no ability to rescue the Jews of Europe "and saw with almost brutal clarity, as was his way, the limited options the Yishuv had for saving the Jews." From then on, in Dina Porat's estimation, Ben-Gurion "no longer saw the matter as central and continued to be entirely immersed in questions related to the political future in Eretz Israel."[17] Perhaps because of that, and in order not to increase pointless public pressure to do something, he tried for a time to prevent publication of reports of the murder of the Jews of Europe.[18] In Palestine, according to Anita Shapira's analysis, a sense of helplessness was the main reason for the unsatisfactory responses of the Zionist leaders. Shapira attributes their opposition to efforts to rescue Jews by moving them to other countries to occasional mistaken interpretations of the priority that Ben-Gurion attached to the creation of a Jewish state.[19]

Be that as it may, many post-Zionists insisted, and continue to insist, on emphasizing the fact that the Zionists didn't even try to save European Jews because their agenda was limited to the establishment of a Jewish state in Eretz Israel – a consequence of their doctrine of negating the Diaspora. "Never since the beginning of the emancipation," writes Boaz Evron, "were the Jews weaker or more helpless than during the Nazi period. Possibly this also explains the Zionist inertia. And yet a reading of the material [from the debates in Zionist institutions on the matter of a rescue plan] makes it difficult to overcome the suspicion that in addition to these reasons there was the Zionist loathing of Diasporic Jewry, from which they were attempting to detach themselves, to the point that they now found it difficult to identify with its catastrophe."

In Evron's view this was a natural development in light of the Zionist movement's evolution "from a rescue movement to a movement intent on building a motherland and a nation – a change that in fact was responsible for its success. The creation and development of the Yishuv in Palestine necessitated great zeal, incredible commitment to the goal, and even a degree of brutal resoluteness that disregarded any other considerations, including even Jewish interests, all in the name of success."[20] In other words, the venture of creating a state in Eretz Israel itself necessitated the disengagement from Diaspora Jewry.

In any case, the Holocaust has since become the cornerstone of Zionist ideology and has served as the ultimate cautionary tale of the supreme importance for Jewish survival of possessing territorially based political power. This turned out to be so despite the fact that Ben-Gurion himself rarely talked about the Holocaust and even created the impression that his attitude toward the survivors was coldhearted and unsympathetic. Instead of dwelling on the tragedies of the past, he clearly preferred to identify with assertive and successful Jewish leaders such as the biblical Joshua and Judah the Maccabee. The creation of a self-reliant Jewish state required, in his view, a culture that extolled proud and self-confident heroes as an antithesis to the victimhood of the Holocaust.

The Eichmann trial marked a turning point at which Zionism renounced its negation of the Diaspora and merged Israeli identity with Europe's exterminated Jewry. In a painful way this trial recreated the collective memory of Israelis who till then had refused to identify with the Jews of the Diaspora. Whereas in the 1950s, the memory of the Holocaust was sadly absent from the state's symbols and national ceremonial events,[21] Israel now began to embrace the Holocaust as its own tragedy. In truth, it was possible to discern signs of this change even before the trial. A law establishing "Holocaust Day" as a national day of mourning was passed in 1959 and the very acts of Eichmann's capture and trial in Israel proved Ben-Gurion's desire that Israelis become more aware of the Holocaust and identify with its victims.[22] In retrospect, the trial was the decisive point when Israel began to demonstrably put into effect political Zionism's vision of being the "guardian of the Jews."

Yoram Hazony has traced the origins of this concept to Montesquieu's theory that the founding of a political state is based on a unique mission that varies from state to state. According to Hazony the mission of the Jewish state is to be found in the hope expressed by Herzl that this state would become the "guardian of the Jews."[23] The need for such a guardian was underscored in 1781 by Edmund Burke, who attributed the persecution of Jews during the nineteenth century to their total lack of military power and representation.

> Having no fixed settlement in any part of the world, no kingdom nor country in which they have a government, a community and a system of laws, they are thrown on the benevolence of nations.... If Dutchmen are injured and attacked, the Dutch have a nation, a government and armies to redress or revenge their cause. If Britons are injured, Britons have armies and laws...to fly to for

protection and justice. But the Jews have no such power and no such friend to depend upon. Humanity then must become their protector and ally.[24]

Events after that speech proved that Burke's expectation that the Jews would be protected by the world's nations was more than just naïve. Anyone who had read Montesquieu would have been able to anticipate the failure of all nations, particularly the United States and Britain, to come to the aid of the Jews during the Holocaust. The goal of states, Montesquieu contended, was the "the creation of conditions for political liberty" within their own countries, which left little room for attending to the needs of a persecuted foreign people.

A mission such as this on behalf of Jews was a matter exclusively for a Jewish state – a fact that Herzl clearly understood nearly a hundred years after Burke. The mission of the Jewish state was not only to protect the Jews within its borders but to come to the assistance of Jews wherever they were persecuted. In other words, the state is to serve as the guardian of the Jews wherever they live and wherever they are threatened, be that in Yemen, Ethiopia or Entebbe – as well as by the capture of enemies such a Adolph Eichmann. The need for such a mission has become less and less apparent to younger Jews in the post-Holocaust world who have come to see themselves as neither persecuted nor exiled. Nevertheless, this mission has become a central component of Israeli Jewish identity.[25]

CHAPTER 4

HARBINGERS OF POST-ZIONIST IDENTITY BEFORE AND AFTER STATEHOOD

The questions that continue to be raised to this day about Jewish identity all lead back to the issue of Jewish nationality. Is such a concept too narrow and limiting? Is it possible to reconcile the Jewish links to Eretz Israel with the rights of the indigenous Palestinian population? These questions have become central not only to post-Zionists in Israel and elsewhere, but also to the thinking of liberal-progressive Jews in the Diaspora. Troubled by the increasing delegitimization of Israel in academic circles and among progressive groups of people throughout the world, many liberal Jews yearn for a more humane, moderate, "politically correct" version of Zionism that they can embrace without reservations. This has led to the re-emergence of known critics of Zionism from within the movement itself, now hailed as exemplary role models inspiring a return to a Jewish national identity with progressive ideals.

MINIMALIST ZIONISM

When the British government published the Balfour Declaration in November 1917, the mainstream of the Zionist movement also included the "synthetic Zionists" – previously known as "practical Zionists," they had meanwhile recognized the need to combine practical activity in Palestine with political and diplomatic action. The mainstream included such figures as Chaim Weizmann and Ze'ev Jabotinsky, as well as the Zionist Labor movement. In the political sense all of these were at the time "maximalists," seeking mass Jewish migration to Palestine, the creation of a Jewish majority throughout the country and the establishment there of Jewish sovereignty. Notably, Weizmann himself was inclined to formulate his position more moderately. He never referred to a "Jewish state" and supported a relatively modest increase in the rate of immigration. In any event, given that the British government was providing the support Zionism required to turn the dream of a Jewish homeland into a reality, the Balfour Declaration and British rule over Palestine were enthusiastically welcomed by these various factions within the movement.

A small minimalist opposition disagreed with the mainstream view. In Palestine this opposition was led by Chaim Margalit-Kalvarisky (1868–1947), an agronomist and a senior intelligence officer within the Yishuv. Kalvarisky purchased tracts of land for Jewish settlement and dreamed of mixed Jewish-Arab clubs and schools throughout the country. He "bribed" newspaper editors, writers and other prominent members of the Arab community in an attempt to prevent them from openly opposing the Zionist enterprise, and called for the establishment of a binational state that would be integrated within the Semitic region. In Germany, Martin Buber and his disciples – adherents of Ahad Ha'am's spiritual brand of Zionism – were key figures in this faction. The minimalist opposition did not welcome the Balfour Declaration, arguing that it would merely antagonize the Arab community and increase its hostility to Zionism. Thus the minimalists argued that instead of relying on British support it would be better to seek an understanding with the Arabs. In the 1920s this opposition was joined by Hashomer Hatzair (the Youth Guard), a new Marxist faction influenced by Buber that supported the establishment of a binational state almost until the outbreak of the War of Independence toward the end of 1947.[1]

In 1925, a small group of Jewish intellectuals in Palestine formed Brit Shalom (Covenant of Peace), which became the most prominent proponent of the minimalist opposition. This group's manifesto called for a binational state in Palestine, espoused the necessity of an Arab-Jewish agreement as a condition for the realization of Zionism and proposed that immigration and economic expansion should be slow and incremental. The group's members were, in the main, Jewish academics who had left Germany and found a home in the recently established Hebrew University in Jerusalem.[2] Among these were the group's founder, Arthur Rupin, who left the faction in 1929; the historian Hans Kohn who, in that same year, decided to immigrate to the United States; and professors Gershom Scholem and Samuel Hugo Bergman. The university's chancellor (and later its first president), the American Reform rabbi Judah Leon Magnes, didn't officially belong to Brit Shalom but was nonetheless a major influence. This was also true of the well-known philosopher Martin Buber who immigrated to Palestine and joined the university's faculty only in 1938. Buber, like Ahad Ha'am before him, always considered himself a Zionist but at the same time made sure to distance himself from the Herzlian school of Zionist thought and opposed the establishment of an independent Jewish state. Instead, he called for the creation of a spiritual-cultural entity where neither Jews nor Arabs would enjoy supremacy, a state that would be run in accordance with the consensus of all its citizens.[3]

Judah Magnes was one of the first to warn of the potential Arab threat to the Jewish community in Eretz Israel. Fearing that the Balfour Declaration would forever stigmatize the Zionists as "invaders," he insisted on viewing it as an immoral act that had no juridical basis since the British were not entitled to offer Palestine to anyone.[4] His call for a binational state appeared to be more realistically based after the Arab riots of 1929, reflecting a general feeling of alarm within the entire leadership of the Jewish community in the country.

The frightening and bloody attacks against Jews in the course of that year bewildered the Zionist leaders and led to a crisis of credibility among them. The mainstream's hope that modernization and economic expansion would lead to a rapprochement with the Arabs was now completely shattered and skepticism about Zionism's future greatly increased. Moshe Beilinson, one of the leading publicists and spokesmen for the Zionist Labor movement, noted at the time that "the mouth of a volcano is not the place to build a durable structure intended as a refuge for an entire nation."[5] Their sense of alarm increased when the British responded to the riots by significantly retreating from the positions expressed in the Balfour Declaration. In the White Paper published in 1930 by the colonial secretary Lord Passfield, it was announced that the continuation of Jewish immigration to Palestine would be dependent from now on "on the economic capacity of the country to absorb new arrivals." The White Paper promised the immediate establishment of a legislative council based on proportional representation. That, in effect, meant that the council would have an Arab majority that could easily block the Zionist enterprise. Although within a few months Britain's prime minister, Ramsey MacDonald, rescinded the limitations on immigration (though not the initiative to set up a legislative council), the Zionist leadership saw the writing on the wall: David Ben-Gurion noted in his diary that the British were attempting to appease both sides by continuing to permit unrestricted Jewish immigration but only until the Jews reached 40 percent of the population; when that occurred they would implement their plan to convene a legislative council based on majority Arab rule.[6]

For the Zionist leadership, the lessons to be drawn from these developments were unmistakable. Firstly, they could no longer rely on the British – neither for their continued support of the Balfour Declaration nor for their readiness to provide physical protection to the Jewish population of Eretz Israel; secondly, they must now prepare to establish a real military force that could defend the Yishuv; thirdly, they had to reach an agreement with the Palestinians. "We have erred for ten years," Ben-Gurion declared to his colleagues. The crux of the matter, he explained, was not cooperation with the English but with the Arabs.[7] Under his leadership Mapai, the recently formed political party, adopted the motto of "nondomination": no single community would impose majority rule over the other. In fact, at the Seventeenth Zionist Congress in March 1931 the Zionist leadership went even further. There it was decided to strive for the most important characteristic of a binational state, equality or political parity between the two national

entities in the country. "Basically," writes Israel Kolatt, "the period
after 1929 was the time when the Zionist movement was most willing to
open a dialogue with the Arabs at the cost of far-reaching concessions,
such as the relinquishment of the idea of Jewish majority rule. Many
Brit Shalom members even believed that their ideas had captured the
heart of the Zionist movement."[8]

However, the Palestinian leadership was not impressed by any of this.
They continued to consistently demand the imposition of majority Arab
rule that would put an immediate end to Jewish immigration. Such an
approach was, of course, utterly unacceptable to the Zionist movement
including even many members of Brit Shalom who had hoped that their
suggestion of political parity, without reference to the numerical size of
either community, would lessen Arab fears about Jewish immigration.
As Arthur Rupin wrote in 1931: "What we are able to get from the
Arabs we don't need and what we need we won't be able to get." In the
wake of Hitler's rise to power in 1933, and the Palestinian request for
help from the Nazis, Ben-Gurion and the Zionist leadership reached the
conclusion that there was no longer a possibility of coexistence within
the framework of one state. In its acceptance of a British proposal in 1937
(subsequently shelved) to partition Palestine and establish a truncated
Jewish state, the Zionist mainstream irrevocably broke its links with the
opposition. Magnes isolated himself still further by offering to concede
on the issue of immigration by agreeing not only to binationalism
but also to a ceiling on Jewish immigration. Magnes's proposal was
that in the course of the following ten years the Jewish population of
the country would not exceed 40 percent and that emergency Jewish
immigration be diverted to neighboring countries.[9]

Buber, Kalvarisky and members of Hashomer Hatzair refused to
give up on the issue of immigration. However, up until the establishment
of Israel in 1948, they did maintain their support for a binational state
and their opposition to a sovereign Jewish entity. Toward the end of
that year, Buber admitted that history had rejected binationalism and he
began to encourage friendly cooperation between the Jewish and Arab
nations.[10] He viewed the formation of a Jewish army as an anathema,
and Israeli militarism as an exercise in state power akin to that of the

Nazis. By following the dictates of force rather than of spirit, Ben-Gurion, according to Buber, was modeling himself on Hitler. Buber found the essence of Jewish force objectionable, arguing that force corrupts irrespective of who possesses it. However, after the Holocaust it seemed that only a handful of Israelis were prepared to accept Buber's views on this subject.

The same was true of the positions espoused by Judah Magnes and the remnants of Brit Shalom. The Arabs' absolute rejection of their proposals also consigned their approach to the dustbin of history. In fact, Magnes, Buber and Brit Shalom were ahead of everyone else in anticipating the Arab-Jewish conflict and in warning that such a conflict would inevitably destroy the Zionist dream. At a certain stage it appeared that the Zionist mainstream was prepared to accept their thinking; however, the two sides went their separate ways following Hitler's assault on Europe and the advent of the Holocaust.

It is easy to recognize in the ideas of these minimalist Zionists the harbingers of the post-Zionist ideas that were to emerge after the establishment of the State of Israel. The Zionist/post-Zionist schism was to become in essence a repeat of the heated debates between Theodor Herzl and Ahad Ha'am at the turn of the century.

THE HEBREW UNIVERSITY OF JERUSALEM

The idea of setting up a Hebrew university in Jerusalem was initially raised at the First Zionist Congress in 1897. The initiator then was Zvi Herman Shapira, a yeshiva student who was to become a professor of mathematics at the University of Heidelberg; he was also responsible for the idea of establishing the Jewish National Fund, dedicated to acquiring land in Palestine. But it was not until 1913 that Chaim Weizmann persuaded the Eleventh Zionist Congress to decide on immediate action to establish the university. And it was only in the spring of 1918, shortly before the end of the First World War, that Weizmann was finally able to lay the foundation stone on Jerusalem's Mount Scopus. Weizmann even succeeded in mobilizing Albert Einstein to join the effort of setting up the university; Einstein accompanied the Zionist leader to the United States to raise funds for the new institution and for a number of years was chairman of the Academic Committee of the university's Board of Governors. In 1923 Einstein delivered a lecture in Jerusalem on the Theory of Relativity, considered to have been the first lecture given within the framework of the university even though the institution's official opening ceremony was to take place two years later.

Weizmann himself remained the university's president until 1935, but in name only. Despite all his efforts he had no real standing on Mount Scopus; even his desire to engage in research work there, after his resignation as president of the Zionist Organization in 1931, was foiled. In the first twenty-three years of its existence, the intellectual reins of the university were in the hands of a group of German-Jewish scholars who were contemptuous of the Herzlian model of political Zionism and opposed Weizmann's leadership of the Zionist movement. Judah Magnes, the confidant of most of the American donors funding the university, ran it from 1925 to 1935 as chancellor, and was its president from 1936 until his death in 1948. During his incumbency some of the leading scholars of the day in the humanities joined the faculty: Martin Buber in sociology, Hugo Bergman and Leon Roth in philosophy, Shlomo Goitein and L. A. Mayer in Islamic studies and Norman Bentwich in international relations. Magnes gained satisfaction from the fact that the university had become the country's intellectual focal point and rejected criticisms of there being antagonism between the academy on the mount (Scopus) and the tillers of the valley (Jezreel), as well as any attempt to depict the university as a bastion of the opposition to the Zionist leadership. "The charge is made against the university," he declared, "that it is the stronghold of those who are against chauvinism and terror and who are for peace.... I think that this is so, and it is this which gives me more genuine cause for thankfulness than anything in life."[11] It was also in this spirit that he used to open the academic year. Only years later was it revealed that directly beneath the rostrum from which he spoke, the Haganah had concealed one of its arms caches.

The events that preceded the War of Independence, and the war itself, shattered the composure and complacency of the university – making it painfully clear that it could no longer remain a cloistered and aloof ivory tower. It found itself on the verge of closure both because it was forced to abandon its campus on Mount Scopus (which, until 1967, became a demilitarized Israeli enclave in the Jordanian part of Jerusalem) and because of its financial difficulties, caused in part by Magnes's death. The Israeli government headed by Mapai – the largest party within the Zionist Labor movement – responded quickly to this situation, taking advantage of the university's predicament to alter the ideological leanings of its leadership. In January 1949, Selig Brodetsky, a member of the Zionist Organization in London and professor of mathematics at the University of Leeds, was appointed as president. He resigned two years later because of disagreements with the senate and was replaced in 1953 by the archaeologist, Professor Benjamin Mazar. The university was now headed by a man who clearly identified himself with the Zionist Labor movement (and who also happened to be the brother-in-law of Israel's second president Yitzhak Ben-Zvi).

In light of the needs of the new state – or, as some would have it, the needs of pragmatic Zionism – the period following the War of Independence saw the university opening schools of medicine, dentistry, social work and business administration, as well as a faculty of law. To these was added an agricultural faculty, a successor to the Institute for Agricultural Studies that had already been set up within the framework of the university as early as 1942. After a number of ups and downs the university's new departments became established in a new central campus in Givat Ram in Western Jerusalem, as well as in a medical campus in Ein Karem and an agricultural campus in Rehovot. Naturally, a significant part of the activities of these departments focused on the training of professionals that were so needed by Israel's burgeoning society. However, any dream of the university's ideological disposition taking on a new direction quickly faded away. The humanities remained the province of the antinationalists. Its illustrious faculty, according to Yoram Hazony, was not openly hostile to the state yet it continued to teach its students in a way that entirely ignored the founding of the state. As was the case prior to 1948, the pedagogic line in the humanities clearly leaned toward universalism and antinationalism, so that tenets of post-Zionism and the delegitimization of the Jewish state remained at the core of its curriculum.[12]

An instructive example of this was Professor Richard Koebner, who headed the university's history department until 1955. As one of his students, the historian Joshua Prawer, said of him, Koebner established a department with a far more universalist outlook than any university that Prawer himself experienced anywhere else in the world.[13] Koebner was an ardent binationalist and joined Buber and Magnes in opposing the establishment of a Jewish state. He insisted that national sovereignty was not an urgent need for the Jews of Eretz Israel "as it is neither directly nor indirectly the most important means of creating sound economic and cultural conditions." He pointed to Ireland as a cautionary example. De Valera's success in setting up an independent state in 1920, he argued, had brought only disaster to the Irish people.[14]

Hugo Bergman, the head of the philosophy department and the university's first rector, held similar views which he based on the universality of Kantian philosophy. As late as the 1960s Bergman still maintained that the assumption that Jewish sovereignty would fundamentally improve the situation of the Jews had been "entirely false." In a similar vein, Ernst Akiva Simon, teaching Jewish values in the philosophy department, expounded that the Pharisees in the period of the Second Temple had had the good sense to doubt the necessity of a Jewish state.

The same was true of the highly revered biochemist, Yeshayahu Leibowitz, whose substantial influence also impacted the Faculty of Humanities. With an intellectual ambivalence that is to this day difficult to understand, Leibowitz would occasionally defend the Jewish state while at other times he would angrily criticize it, saying that it was no more than a mechanism of coercion and the expression of violence for violence's own sake. Arguing that courage on the battlefield was not a praiseworthy virtue, Leibowitz attributed Israeli military might to Judeo-Nazi influences and categorically opposed Israel's occupation of the West Bank and the Gaza strip during the Six-day War of 1967.[15]

It is important to note that the university's various faculties also included enthusiastic supporters of Ben-Gurion and even a number of right-wing Zionists.[16] And yet, the views of the Revisionist Zionist Dr. Joseph Klausner, the author of a four-volume history of the period of the Second Temple, were sufficient to throw the university into a spin. Although Dr. Klausner was a member of the committee that oversaw the establishment of the Hebrew University in 1925, he was refused a professorship in the History of the Jewish People despite the fact that he was the only candidate for the position. Many have suggested that this was because of the sympathetic two-volume work he wrote on Jesus. Yet it is difficult to believe that Klausner's candid support for Ze'ev Jabotinsky was not also a contributory factor in his being rejected. Eventually, Magnes appointed Klausner as head of the Department of Hebrew Literature, apparently in an attempt to prevent him from unduly influencing the student population. This banishment remained in place until 1943. Only then, when Klausner was already sixty-nine and a few years before mandatory retirement, was he allowed to teach the history of the Second Temple at the university.[17]

The second generation of academics came to the university from east-central Europe in the course of the 1930s. Among the most prominent of these were the philosopher Nathan Rotenstreich and the historians Joshua Prawer and Jacob Talmon. The three were born and raised in Poland, where they were influenced by German culture. Rotenstreich was one of a number of key activists in the Gordonia youth movement named after A. D. Gordon – a major spiritual force behind practical Zionism. The Gordonia movement was inspired by Hapoel Hatzair (the Young Worker), an antimilitarist pro-labor group that Gordon had founded in Palestine. Its leader Pinhas Lavon embraced binationalism and in fact continued to support it up until 1948. For obvious reasons Rotenstreich, Prawer and Talmon were more comfortable, both culturally and ideologically, with the university's first generation of German-Jewish scholars. And yet the Holocaust convinced them of the imperative of a Jewish state. Indeed, "some of them…were ardent patriots whose devotion to the Jewish state cannot seriously be questioned,"[18] even though they remained under the lasting influence of the university's first generation.

It was this influence that led Rotenstreich – who had translated Kant into Hebrew together with Hugo Bergman – to adopt Bergman's highly critical view of Ben-Gurion's "messianic" policies. And it was due to this influence that Joshua Prawer, when writing a history of the Crusades, took an entirely new approach to early Palestinian history that emphasized the Arab point of view.[19] This was to have a significant impact on the way in which some of his students viewed Zionism. In time to come, Prawer's student, Meron Benvenisti, was to emphasize the similarity between the Arab response to the loss of Jerusalem and the response of Muslims to the conquests of the Crusaders.[20] Benvenisti himself would emerge in due course as one of Israel's leading advocates of a binational, post-Zionist State of Israel.

As was the case with the minimalist Zionists of the first generation, the second generation of Hebrew University academics, while supporting Zionism and the necessity of Israel, simultaneously planted the seeds of the post-Zionist movement.

CHAPTER 5

HANNAH ARENDT: ON THE FAULT LINE OF CLASHING IDENTITIES

H annah Arendt is one of the most influential thinkers of the twentieth century. It could also be said of her that she never ceased to baffle and exasperate her disciples and admirers as well as her many opponents. She appears to have avoided being labeled politically and to have, instead, been adopted both by progressives and conservatives, historical sociologists and philosophers, as well as by anarchists and conventional political theoreticians alike. Her influence on thinkers and researchers in the field of Jewish scholarship was profound, complex and contradictory in equal measure. In her life and in her work she embodied the dilemmas and ambiguities of Jewish identity both before and after the Holocaust. Her audacious readiness to take on sacred shibboleths and fearlessly question the majority view on core Jewish issues makes Arendt the preeminent role model for contemporary post-Zionists both in Israel and abroad.

History placed Hannah Arendt at the crossroads of the pivotal events of the twentieth century. With the Holocaust and the establishment of the State of Israel, Arendt's Jewish identity was challenged by momentous tests. Arendt's attempt to interpret these historical events while living them undermined her ability to judge them. She didn't analyze the Holocaust from a broad Jewish perspective, but rather from an individual, albeit penetrating and profound, examination of totalitarianism. Yet the catastrophe that befell the Jewish people was too monumental an event to be simply reduced to an acute phenomenon of totalitarianism. In an attempt to be objective and analytical, Arendt chose to provide her own interpretation, one which was out of step with the prevailing Jewish understanding of what had happened. At the end of the day her analysis became irrelevant, unrealistic, infuriating and profoundly flawed. Though here and there she demonstrated a brilliant understanding of exceptional situations, she failed in her overall assessment of events; she was unable to differentiate between the trees and the forest.

Arendt, the authentic German who continued to be devoted throughout her life to German culture, was bitterly disappointed by Germany's betrayal in turning to Nazism and was unable to come to terms with the disintegration of everything she believed in. She could not adjust to the loss of her beloved "Germanness," which she held to be more humane and more aesthetic than every other civilization but that in the end became more cruel than any of them. She felt an estrangement and repulsion toward the Jewish cultures of eastern Europe and the Middle East which, in her view, were crude and unsophisticated. But her alienation from them was mainly grounded in the fact that Germany insisted on regarding and defining her as someone who was no different and no better that the *Ostjuden* (east European Jews), toward whom she was condescending and disparaging.

The roots of Hannah Arendt's abandonment of her illusions can be traced back to the Enlightenment and the promise of emancipation and integration which that period inspired within the Jewish community of Germany. The main exponent of a resolution of the Jewish Question through culture and enlightenment was Moses Mendelssohn, a prominent philosopher of the late eighteenth century known throughout Europe as the "German Socrates." His exceptional example of a Jew transcending traditional Jewish norms and reaching the heights of European culture became the paradigm for the nineteenth century's movement of Jewish emancipation. Mendelssohn had demonstrated that the path to acceptance was through acculturation and education. Mendelssohn's achievement was popularized in Gotthold Ephraim

Lessing's play *Nathan the Wise*, which was premiered in Berlin in 1783. The play's sympathetically portrayed hero was clearly intended to personify Mendelssohn and was, just as obviously, the antithesis of Shakespeare's Shylock as he emphatically declares *"ich bin ein mensch"* (I am a human being).[1]

However, as Hannah Arendt was to note, if *Nathan the Wise* was indeed a carbon copy of Mendelssohn, then this copy was "nothing but a grotesque and dangerous evasion of reality."[2] Indeed, Mendelssohn's exalted example did not lead to an acceptance of Germany's Jew's by the country's cultural elite. Instead, it served only to intensify that elite's animosity toward Mendelssohn for having actually chosen to remain a Jew. Rising above the crowd, as was prescribed by the Enlightenment, did not lead to greater acceptance by that crowd, but quite the opposite. Proving one's humanity or cultural excellence was not sufficient to guarantee the civil rights of a persecuted minority.

Hannah Arendt was born into an assimilated, prosperous German-Jewish family. Her grandfather served as the chairman of Königsberg's city parliament in the early years of the twentieth century. In that capacity he was responsible for the passage of legislation that denied Zionist organizations access to municipal facilities for their activities. In a television interview in 1964 Arendt told her interviewer that as a child her Jewish identity was vicarious and defensive.

> The word "Jew" was never mentioned at home. I first encountered it…in the anti-Semitic remarks of children as we played in the streets. Then I became, so to speak, enlightened…. As a child – now a somewhat older child – I knew, for example, that I looked Jewish…that is that I looked a bit different from the rest. But not in a way that made me feel inferior. I was simply aware of it, that is all…. For my mother the "Jewish Question" was irrelevant. Of course she was a Jewess! She would never have had me baptized and turned into a Christian. And she would have given me a real thrashing if she ever had had reason to think that I denied being Jewish. The matter was never a topic of discussion. It was out of the question for it to be.…

You see, all Jewish children encountered anti-Semitism. It
poisoned the souls of many children. The difference with me was
that my mother always insisted that I not denigrate myself. A
person has to stand up for himself! When my teachers made anti-
Semitic remarks they were usually directed not at me but at my
Eastern European classmates. In such situations I had my mother's
orders to get up immediately, leave the classroom, come home
and leave the rest to the school's procedures. My mother would
write one of her many letters and with that she would put an end
to my involvement in the matter. I got a day off from school and
that, of course, was very nice. But if other children made remarks
about me I wasn't allowed to leave the school and go home. That
was unacceptable. I had to defend myself against the comments
of those children. There were rules of conduct, house rules, if they
can be so called, that completely protected my self-respect.[3]

The "house rules" that forbade ever kowtowing to anti-Semites paved
the way for Hannah Arendt's short-lived romance with Zionism. The
romance began in 1929 when she met Kurt Blumenfeld, one of the
leaders of the Zionist movement in Germany with whom she was to
maintain a close friendship – particularly after his immigration to
Palestine – until his death.[4] In Blumenfeld's view, Zionism was the sole
legitimate response to the "objective Jewish question." His reasoning
was that all Jews, irrespective of their political views, their cultural
sophistication or their reservations about Judaism, will, in the eyes of
non-Jews, always be considered first and foremost as Jews. Therefore,
Blumenfeld argued, Jews had no choice but to accept this reality and
"look the German gentile straight in the eye unashamedly."[5]

   Arendt wholeheartedly adopted Blumenfeld's psycho-sociological
argument that sounded like an echo of her mother's demand to stand
tall in the face of anti-Semitic comments. In the years 1933–1942, she
joined in the activities of various Zionist organizations in Germany,
France (to where she fled in 1933) and the United States (following her
second flight after France fell to the Nazis in 1940). As she was to write
later, Zionism was the "only political response to anti-Semitism ever

found by the Jews and the only ideology that enabled them for the first time to relate seriously to the hatred that was destined to place them at the center of world events."[6] But Arendt didn't accept Blumenfeld's second assumption that all Zionists had to emigrate to Eretz Israel. This option was certainly not part of her agenda[7] – especially after her visit to Palestine in 1935, a visit that left her with very unpleasant memories.[8]

Arendt distrusted Herzlian Zionism and preferred the approach to Zionism of Bernard Lazare, the somewhat obscure French Zionist-anarchist. In her view, Herzlian Zionism was by its very nature "escapist." It was an attempt to flee from anti-Semitism, which it considered a permanent and universal phenomenon in non-Jewish society. Its means of doing so was the establishment of a Jewish homeland in Eretz Israel, even if that required an agreement with the European anti-Semites. Lazare, on the other hand, downplayed the importance of territory and argued, instead, that the creation of a Jewish homeland had to be combined with a struggle for Jewish civil rights in Europe and combating anti-Semitism within the continent. This had to be done by building coalitions with non-Jewish allies who were not anti-Semitic. Secondly, Lazare contended that Herzlian Zionism conducted its politics from above and sought the agreement of the great powers. In contrast, his aim was the creation of a mass movement that would join forces with other oppressed peoples in Europe.[9]

In the spring of 1942, more than a year after her immigration to the United States, Arendt's dissident version of Zionism found expression in her establishment of the Jungjüdische Gruppe (the Young Jewish Group). Arendt detailed the group's principles in a manifesto she titled "The Revolutionary/National Principles of the Jewish National Freedom Movement": Jews were an oppressed people with non-Jewish allies who were also fighting for freedom; all oppressed peoples had to struggle against oppression by their own privileged classes; Eretz Israel alone could not save the Jews – it could only serve as a nucleus for a new, populist Jewish politics throughout the Diaspora.[10]

On the other hand, Arendt supported the conventional Zionist view of the right of Jews to settle in Eretz Israel. In the mid-1930s her husband, Hans Blucher, a German communist who wielded considerable influence over her, wrote to her lamenting the fact that the

> Jewish people…wants to be handed a whole country (in Eretz Israel). But you can't just be given a country, any more than you can be given a woman; both must be earned…. To want a country, a whole country, from a gangster who first of all has to steal it? Instead we should join forces with Arab workers and laborers to liberate the land from the British robbers and the Jewish bourgeoisie allied with them.

Arendt's response to this was:

> Palestine. Good God, sadly you are right. But if we are pitching conquest against gift, then it seems to me that a military campaign against swamps, malaria, desert and rocks – for that is what our Promised Land looks like – is also worthy of praise. If we want to become one people, no ancient territory that world revolution might someday want to offer us would be of any real use to us. For whichever way you look at it, that land is inevitably bound up with our past. Palestine is not at the center of our national aspirations just because two thousand years ago some people lived there from whom in some sense or other we are supposed to have descended, but because for two thousand years the craziest of peoples was pleased to preserve that past in the present.

In the end, however, Arendt broke with the Zionist movement. The break came because in 1942 the movement adopted the Biltmore Program, which called for the establishment of a "Jewish commonwealth" in Eretz Israel. She continued to strongly support the minority, minimalist position within the movement, championed by Brit Shalom and Hashomer Hatzair and their call for the establishment of a binational state in Eretz Israel. In an incisive essay entitled "Zionism Reconsidered" which she published in 1944, Arendt argued that by calling for a Jewish state "the Zionists have now indeed done their best to create that insoluble 'tragic conflict' which can only be ended through cutting the Gordian knot. But only the most naïve of people can believe that this breach would necessarily benefit the Jewish people or result in a lasting solution."

> Nationalism is bad enough when it trusts in nothing other than the sheer might of the nation. A nationalism that necessarily and openly depends on the force of a foreign power is certainly worse.... The Zionists, if they continue to ignore the Mediterranean peoples and watch out only for the big faraway powers will be painted as nothing more than tools of these powers, the agents of foreign and hostile interests. Jews who know their own history should be aware that such a state of affairs will inevitably lead to a new wave of hatred against the Jews; the anti-Semites of tomorrow will say that not only did the Jews profit from the presence of the big foreign powers in the area, but that they themselves had actually conspired to ensure that presence and are therefore responsible for its consequences.[11]

In his judgment of Hannah Arendt's position the Israeli philosopher Elhanan Yakira concludes that Arendt's "pact with Zionism appears to have been conditional – when the Zionist movement turned a deaf ear to her, she turned her back on it." Arendt's approach, Yakira adds, was loaded with contradictions. On the one hand she called for a Jewish army to fight the Nazis in Europe, not because such an army could hurt the Nazis – a possibility she knew was nonexistent – but simply in order to redeem Jewish honor. On the other hand, she was unable to see the link between such a redemption of honor and the achievement of Jewish sovereignty. She failed to understand the value of a sovereignty that could mobilize Jews to an army, enable Jews to fight in a meaningful way as Jews, pass judgment according to laws legislated by Jewish institutions – the kind of sovereignty whose highest expression is an independent Jewish statehood.[12] In Arendt's opinion, Jewish sovereignty in Eretz Israel would only doom the Zionist project. "What's the point in establishing sovereignty," she demanded to know, "whose only sovereign right would be to commit collective suicide?"[13]

Arendt's insistence on being judgmental inflamed her reporting of the Eichmann trial in Jerusalem in 1961. Journalists from across the globe arrived to cover the trial's opening but quickly abandoned the legal proceedings and their coverage to Holocaust survivors, jurists and the local Israeli press. The two writers who remained until the end of the trial were Hannah Arendt and the Israeli poet Chaim Guri.[14] Whereas Guri was present at every session of the court, Arendt only came to very few and instead preferred to rely for her reports on court transcripts and other sources. What she missed, and what she ignored in her reportage, was the large number of testimonies from Holocaust survivors that accounted for about half of the trial's sessions (62 out of 121). Later she would write that she thought that these witness accounts were superfluous and had no bearing on the question of Eichmann's personal guilt. The same could, of course, have been said about the activities of Jewish leaders at the time of the Holocaust. But this didn't prevent Arendt from delving deeply into those very activities in a highly provocative way.[15]

Perhaps Arendt chose to absent herself from the sessions at which survivors gave their testimony because the witnesses spoke in Hebrew and she had to rely on an inept German interpreter.[16] Another possible reason for her behavior may have been her inability to tolerate the atmosphere in the Jerusalem courtroom. "The trial and everything around it," wrote Arendt to her friend Mary McCarthy, "is banal, inferior and repulsive in an indescribable way."[17] In a letter to the psychiatrist and philosopher Karl Theodor Jaspers, she went beyond mere snobbery and adopted a markedly racial tone. "On top are the judges, the elite of German Jewry. Below them are the prosecutors, Galitzianers [a disparaging reference to Jews from the area of west Ukraine and southeastern Poland] but nonetheless Europeans. Everything is organized by the police who give me the shivers, speaking Hebrew only and looking like Arabs. Among them are some types who look particularly brutish. They will obey every order. And outside are the oriental masses as if we were in Istanbul or any other semi-Asian country."[18]

Whatever Arendt's reasons may have been, her decision to absent herself from the testimonies of the survivors, concludes Yakira, is of considerable importance because it was precisely these reports, the fact that the "extermination of the Jews...was presented for the first time by eye witnesses in such a complete way, detailed and in public," that "gave this trial its historical value and significance."[19] It was the poet Chaim Guri, born and raised in Eretz Israel, who made this point most emphatically and clearly. Guri admitted that the witness reports at the trial had made him comprehend the Holocaust for the first time. "Not one of us will emerge from this trial the same as we were," he declared, thus personifying an evolutionary development in Israeli identity in relation to the Holocaust.[20]

The questions relating to Israel's legal right to put Eichmann on trial have been raised continually since he was kidnapped in Argentina. Though there were countries that fell to the Nazis during the war and in due course held anti-Nazi trials without it causing a stir, only Israel's right to do so was questioned.[21] Arendt recognized Israel's right to try Eichmann, but thought that Israel should not do so on its own and solely with its own judges. While agreeing that the Holocaust was a unique crime against the Jewish people, Arendt ultimately judged it to have been directed against humanity as a whole. The enormity of the Holocaust, she argued, transcended its purely Jewish dimension. Therefore, Arendt argued, the case against Eichmann was not one solely for Israel to prosecute. The judgment should have been placed in the hands of the international community as a whole. As Yakira notes disparagingly, Arendt "did want young Jews to fight as Jews against Germany…but she refused, a decade and a half later, to allow the Jews to judge – as Jews – those who had murdered them."[22]

Arendt's report of the trial was published first in the *New Yorker* and later in book form under the title *Eichmann in Jerusalem: A Report on the Banality of Evil*. For the Jewish world these publications were nothing short of a bombshell. "Despite all the efforts of the prosecution," she wrote, "everybody could see that that this man is not a 'monster.' But it was really difficult not to suspect him of being a clown."[23] She reported that Eichmann "had never harbored any enmity towards his victims,"[24] was not animated by "fanatical anti-Semitism" and was "neither a pervert nor a sadist"; instead she described him as very banal and "terrifyingly normal."[25] In Arendt's view, Eichmann's problem was clear and simple: he suffered from "an inability to think."[26] In a postscript that was added to later editions of the book Arendt phrased this idea to read that Eichmann "simply had no concept of what he was doing."[27]

But Arendt's most controversial accusation focuses on the role of the Jewish leaders in Nazi-occupied Europe. Arendt's charge was that having been nominated to positions in the *Judenrate* (Jewish councils) and given "enormous powers," these leaders not only complied with Nazi orders but cooperated with them – a cooperation without which "there can be no doubt…it would hardly have been possible for a few thousand people, most of whom, moreover, worked in their offices, to liquidate hundreds of thousands of other people."[28] The leaders cooperated, Arendt noted, by volunteering to hide the truth of the Final Solution from the Jewish people. Apart from that

> Jewish public figures could be relied on to compile lists of persons and their property to obtain the funds to cover the costs of the deportation and ultimately the annihilation of these very same people. The Jewish leaders kept track of vacated apartments, assisted in policing by helping in the seizure of Jews and getting them onto the trains until, as a final gesture, they handed over the assets of the Jewish community in an orderly way for it to be finally confiscated.

Arendt placed this cooperation in a context which, she concluded furiously, was "for a Jew…undoubtedly the darkest chapter in the whole dark story."

> True that the Jewish people as a whole had not been organized, that they had no territory, no government, and no army; that, in the hour of their greatest need they had no government in exile to represent them among the Allies (the Jewish Agency for Palestine… was, at best, a miserable substitute), no caches of weaponry, no youth with military training. But if one is to be entirely truthful, there were community organizations as well as Jewish party and welfare organizations at both the local and the international level. Wherever Jews lived there were recognized Jewish leaders and this leadership, almost without exception, cooperated in one way

or another, for one reason or another, with the Nazis. The whole truth was that if the Jewish people had really been unorganized and leaderless, there would have been chaos and plenty of misery but the total number of victims would hardly have been between four and a half and six million people."[29]

As Sharon Muller insightfully observed, Hannah Arendt's "scathing indictment" of the *Judenrate* "reflected a vision of the development and significance of modern Jewish history to which she had been committed for three decades."[30] This vision drew a critically sharp distinction between parvenus and those who consciously chose to be "outcasts." In Arendt's view, the Jewish people were essentially condemned to be outcasts from European society and had two options as to how to react to this difficult situation. They could continue to live under the illusion that the Jewish Question was simply a matter of not fitting in and assimilating socially and that the solution was to be found in the formula recommended by Mendelssohn and the Enlightenment. That solution required rising above the despised Jewish mass by excelling in non-Jewish culture while at the same time silently maintaining a Jewish identity at home (or not maintaining it, as more and more Jews tended to do). In doing so the parvenus showed themselves to be ready to willingly abandon their solidarity with the Jewish people merely in order to excel as exceptions, uncharacteristic of their kind and thus worthy of praise.[31]

In contrast to that position, Arendt suggests, those Jews who consciously chose to be "outcasts" determinedly refused to bend to petty social pressures, and accepted their pariah status in the clear realization that the Jewish Question was not simply, or even primarily, a matter of social assimilation. Rather, they understood it to be essentially a political problem that had to be resolved publicly and by political means. "Conscious pariahs" rejected the idea of seeking personal fame and fortune or acquiring cultural excellence so as to stand above the fray, and entirely understood that the only way of putting an end to "the 'disgrace' of being a Jew…was to fight for the honor of the Jewish people as a whole."[32]

Arendt identified the classic parvenus in modern Jewish history to be the court Jews of the seventeenth and eighteenth centuries. From time to time these Jews possessed significant power because of the dependence of various absolute monarchs and a long line of other rulers on their financial resources. However, not one of them considered, even for a moment, using their power as a bargaining chip to advance the political rights of their fellow Jews.[33] On the contrary, the court Jews had a personal stake in ensuring that the political standing of the mass of Jews was not improved so that they and they alone would stand out as the "exceptions" while the mass of Jews remained isolated, discriminated against and trampled upon.

"Against this background," noted Arendt, "their glory as exceptions shone more brilliantly." The successors of the court Jews, the notables and well-known bankers of the nineteenth century, "made great efforts to ensure that the bleak circumstances of poverty, wretchedness and absence of rights of the Jewish masses be maintained.... So it was that in the 1820s the Rothschilds withdrew their pledge to donate a large sum to their native community of Frankfurt. They did this in order to curb the influence of reformers who wanted Jewish children to have a general education and thereby create new options for the poorer classes.... The poorer the masses became, the more secure the rich Jews felt and the brighter their glory shone."[34]

According to the logic on which Arendt's argument is founded, it is the tendency of high-ranking Jews in the modern period to betray the masses that ultimately led to the catastrophic circumstances of the *Judenrate*. Similarly, she argued, the mind-set of parvenu assimilated Jews led to their being "unable to distinguish between friend and foe, between compliment and insult," and being naively inclined "to feel flattered when an anti-Semite gives his assurance that he doesn't mean them, that they are exceptions, exceptional Jews."[35] And so, when the Nazis launched their attacks against German Jewry, this community "split into many splinters each of which believed and hoped that its basic civil rights would be protected by special privileges: the privilege due to having been a veteran of the First World War, or for being the descendant of those involved in that war or of someone killed in action in the course of it." It was this approach of special-case pleading that Arendt believes "explains the nonviolent destruction and disintegration of the Jewish people and that it was this that ultimately led the Jews to unintentionally collaborating in crime with the Nazis."[36]

As Arendt herself noted, the one group that could be said to have been the perfect model of "conscious pariahs" and and to have rejected the approach of the parvenus were the Zionists. As she was to recall in one of her interviews: "In 1933 I reached the conclusion which at that time I always put into one sentence, a sentence that for me clarified my position: When one is attacked because he is a Jew he must defend himself as a Jew.... Once I understood this it became my clear intent to link up...with the Zionists. They were the only ones prepared for action."[37] Following the publication of *Eichmann in Jerusalem*, Arendt came under severe attack by a wide range of critics while anti-Zionists attempted to recruit her to their cause – most notably the anti-Zionist American Council for Judaism, which offered to come out in her defense and provide her with a platform from which she could respond to her critics. But Arendt turned them down flat. In a letter to the council she wrote:

> You know that I was a Zionist and my reasons for cutting off my relations with the Zionist Organization are very different from the anti-Zionist position of the council. I don't oppose Israel as a matter of principle, I object to specific aspects of Israeli policy. I know, or believe that I know, that if this Jewish state is hit by a catastrophe for whatever reason (even if it is as a result of its own foolishness) this will perhaps be the final catastrophe for the entire Jewish people whatever views we may hold at this moment.[38]

As her biographer Elisabeth Young-Bruehl describes her, Arendt always saw herself as part of the Zionist "loyal opposition." She therefore welcomed Marie Syrkin's fiercely critical review of her book published in the Zionist Labor movement's journal *Jewish Frontier*. Arendt even went so far as to declare that Marie Syrkin "is the only person with whom I would want to discuss this whole subject" – precisely because Syrkin wrote her scolding rebuke as a Zionist.[39]

And yet, Arendt singled out the Zionists for a particularly vehement attack when criticizing the Jewish leaders in her book *Eichmann in Jerusalem*. As she described it, Zionist ideology had laid the groundwork for the "universal collaboration" of wartime Jewish leaders with the Nazis. It was her view that the "belief on the part of Herzlian Zionists in the eternal and ubiquitous nature of anti-Semitism...was responsible for the dangerous inability of the Jews to distinguish between friend and foe." She strongly condemned the "Transfer Agreement" between the Zionist establishment and the Nazi regime, and scorned the Zionists' motives for saving German Jewry through immigration to Palestine. She insisted that the Zionists had little interest in rescuing the community as a whole and were only concerned with securing a selection of "suitable human material." She made a number of hurtful and sarcastic innuendos that implicitly linked Zionist aspirations with Nazi plans – going as far as to describe the prewar years as a "pro-Zionist" period of Nazi Germany, depicting Eichmann as a "convert to Zionism" and portraying the enormous ghetto that Eichmann had at one time envisioned setting up in Madagascar for all of Europe's Jews as being no different than a "Jewish state."[40] These altercations became increasingly acrimonious and Arendt's attack on Zionism smacks of the fury of a disillusioned insider who has bowed out.

It would appear that in the same way as she welcomed Syrkin's criticism Arendt was glad to be in a correspondence with Gershom Scholem over the controversy she had aroused. Scholem, after all, had been a Zionist member of Brit Shalom – in other words a Zionist after her own heart and her close friend for nearly forty years. But his outrage at *Eichmann in Jerusalem* was so great that it put an end to their friendship.[41] As Scholem was to say in later years, their conflict over the book was "one of the most bitter controversies of my life."[42] In his letter to Arendt, he angrily accused her of being "heartless, often adopting an almost sneeringly malicious tone....Your account ceases to be objective and it exudes a whiff of malevolence." At best she was guilty of "speaking out without thinking...which was wholly inappropriate given the gravity of the issues you are discussing." Moreover, wrote Scholem, "a discussion such as the one that is attempted in your book demands the utmost seriousness and caution precisely because of the feelings aroused in people by this issue – the destruction of one-third of our people. I regard you as being entirely the daughter of the Jewish people and nothing else." But according to Scholem, none of this seemed to concern her. "In Jewish tradition there is a concept that is difficult to define but is nonetheless very real, *ahavat Yisrael*, loving your people. I find nothing of that feeling in you, my dear Hannah, as is the case among so many whose origin was the German left."

In the matter of the *Judenrate*, Scholem was highly critical of what he regarded as Arendt's "demagogic zeal to exaggerate."

> Who among us can today say how the "elders of the Jews" should have acted in the circumstance in which they found themselves? ... Some of them behaved as villains, and some behaved righteously. I have read a great deal about both of these types and there were many who were no different than us and who were forced to make horrendous decisions in circumstances that we cannot even imagine. I don't know if they were right or wrong, and I don't see myself as being qualified to judge since I wasn't there.

At the end of the letter, Scholem explained to Arendt that "your comments about Eichmann as a 'convert to Zionism' could only have been uttered by someone filled with animosity toward anything linked to Zionism, and from this I have to conclude that your intention was to ridicule and discredit Zionism."[43]

In her reply Arendt wrote to Scholem: "I was puzzled when reading your comment that you regarded me 'as a daughter of our people, and nothing else.' The truth is I never pretended to be anything else, to be in any way other than what I am; I never felt tempted in that direction." As to her supposed lack of "love of our people," she retorted:

> You are quite right – I am not moved by any "love" of this sort, and for two reasons: I have never in my life "loved" any people or community – not the German people, nor the French, nor the American, nor the working class or anything of that sort. I really only love my friends and the only kind of love I know of and

> believe in is the love of specific persons. Secondly, this "love
> of the Jews" seems to me, Jewish myself, as something quite
> suspect.... I don't "love" the Jews, nor do I "believe" in them; I
> merely belong to them as a matter of course, beyond dispute or
> argument.

Instead, Arendt insisted, her patriotism as a Jew was first and foremost
expressed by her duty to criticize her people and to demand that it
adheres to standards higher than those of others. "There can be no
patriotism," she wrote, "without constant opposition and criticism....
Wrong perpetrated by my own people naturally grieves me more than
wrong done by other peoples." She also elaborated on her thesis with
regard to the actions of the *Judenrate*: "I said that there was no possibility
of resistance, but there was the option of doing nothing. And in order
to do nothing a person didn't have to be a saint. All they had to do was
to say: I am just a simple Jew, and I have no desire to play any other
role.... These people still had a certain, limited freedom of decision
and of action. Just as the SS murderers also had, as we now know, a
limited range of choices. They could have said "I wish to be relieved
of my murderous duties," and nothing would have happened to them.
Since we are dealing with the politics of mere mortals and not with
heroes or saints, it is precisely this policy of 'non-collaboration'...that
is decisive from the moment that we begin to judge, not the system and
the method, but the individual, his choices and his argumentation."[44]

Finally Arendt adamantly rejected what she saw as Scholem's and
other critics' fear of judging. As she would later write:

> There exists in our society a widespread fear of judging.... For
> behind the unwillingness to judge lurks the suspicion that no one
> is a free agent, and hence the doubt that anyone is responsible
> or could be expected to answer for what he has done.... "Who
> am I to judge?" actually means We're all alike, equally bad, and
> those who try, or pretend that they try, to remain halfway decent
> are either saints or hypocrites, and in either case should leave us
> alone. Hence the huge outcry the moment anyone fixes specific
> blame on some particular person.[45]

It is worthwhile to note that Arendt's thesis on Eichmann's banality has recently been challenged by the historian David Cesarani, who has unearthed evidence that shows Eichmann to have been an extreme anti-Semite and that his hatred of the Jews had indeed motivated his wartime activities.[46]

As for Arendt's critique of the *Judenrate*, this was essentially based on her reading of Raul Hilberg's monumental work *The Destruction of the European Jews*, the first extensive history of the Holocaust published just before Eichmann's trial. Hilberg too criticizes the *Judenrate*'s collaboration, though he does so far less sweepingly and provocatively than did Arendt. The Holocaust historian Yehuda Bauer, however, regards both Hilberg's and Arendt's analysis as too generalized and inadequate since "no *Judenrate* behaved in quite the same way as any other *Judenrate*." This was clearly established in the research carried out by the historian Aharon Weiss, who questioned survivors of Polish ghettos as to their opinions of the various *Judenrate* in their areas.

The answers reflected their perceptions of the morality and decency of their official leaders – whether their intentions were good or bad – and not their success in preventing disaster. Weiss examined "first," "second" and "third" *Judenrate*. By first *Judenrate*, Weiss meant those appointed at the beginning of the German occupation; in most cases they were replaced frequently precisely because they did not fulfill the aims set by the Germans. Then a second *Judenrate* was appointed and often, later, a third.

Of the 146 first *Judenrate* in Poland with a sufficient number of responses, 30.9 percent of the heads of *Judenrate* were judged by survivors to have been "good" leaders – they assisted the community, refused to carry out German financial directives, warned of imminent Aktions. An additional 37.7 percent resigned because they were unwilling to carry out German orders, were removed by the Germans because of such disobedience, or were murdered because they refused to hand over Jews to the Germans. Another 9.1 percent committed suicide, or had connections with the underground, or died after taking office. The evaluation of another 9 percent was ambiguous, and 14.3 percent were judged negatively. At least 86.6 percent of these heads, according to Weiss, did not go beyond a limited, forced cooperation with the authorities and were thought by the survivors to have been devoted public servants. Second *Judenrate* were judged negatively by an overwhelming majority.[47]

Moreover, Bauer points out that the Nazis established the *Judenrate* between 1939 and 1941, that is to say before their decision to implement the Final Solution. Thus the *Judenrate* were no different from other councils or administrations of occupied peoples under the Nazis. In that period the Nazi aim in all cases was "subjugation, enslavement, exploitation, control, accompanied by brutal repressive measures escalating to mass murder." But Hilberg and Arendt didn't at all look at the non-Jewish administrations and thus were unable to provide an important non-Jewish context to the actions of the *Judenrate*.

> How many French, Belgian, Dutch, Polish, Czech and other mayors, local bureaucrats, police chiefs and others, even if they were personally against Germany, rebelled against the Germans or openly disobeyed their orders even though such disobedience did not always put their lives directly at risk? Why do Hilberg and Arendt have to impose criteria that differ to such an extreme from the criteria by which they would judge non-Jewish administrators? And when one takes into account the degrees of coercion to which Jewish and non-Jewish administrators were subjected, were not the *Judenrate* in a much worse situation so that every overt act of resistance became an act of suicide? Nonetheless, in many places there clearly was resistance. Thus for example the *Judenrat* of Minsk, headed by Eliahu Mishkin, joined the underground resistance group led by Hersh Smolar immediately after it was set up. The Minsk ghetto was the fourth largest in Eastern Europe and at the beginning more than eighty thousand people were held there. I know of no comparable non-Jewish municipal authority or local government that was involved in similar activities while under Nazi occupation.[48]

Arendt's almost complete ostracism from the Jewish community following the publication of *Eichmann in Jerusalem* led to her not writing anymore about Jewish affairs. "Dissident" Jews enthusiastically approved of her definition of Jewish patriotism as a mandate to criticize their people. They adopted her as a heroic role model. More recently anti-Zionists and post-Zionists started to use her writings, especially *Eichmann in Jerusalem,* as supporting authorities in their campaign to delegitimize the State of Israel and Zionism.[49] Moshe Zimmerman sees in some of what Arendt wrote to Kurt Blumenfeld in 1957 confirmation that she presciently recognized the post-Zionist belief that there is no longer any point to Zionism and that the movement has no constituency among Diaspora Jewry. "At this moment," Arendt wrote, "the Zionist movement is dead. It has withered away because of its victory [the establishment of the state, which was its objective] and because of the fundamental change in the essence of the Jewish Question in the post-Hitler period. European Jewry is no more...perhaps for ever.... To me it seems that at this time there is no chance of a Zionist renaissance."[50]

However, after *Eichmann in Jerusalem* Arendt displayed an increasing link to Israel, both publicly and privately. She admired the Israeli military victory of 1967,[51] proudly telling Jaspers that the Israelis had done a "marvelous job" and "I very much like Moshe Dayan,"[52] and that she was so "amazed by Israeli heroism that a friend had told her that she was behaving as if she were a 'war bride.'"[53] In the autumn of 1973 when it seemed for a time that the surprise Egyptian and Syrian attacks on Yom Kippur threatened the very existence of Israel, Arendt was unable to work and was afraid that Israel might be destroyed. In an interview to French television on October 9, 1973, her mind was entirely on the war and she declared that "the Jewish people is at one with Israel," along with an explanation absent of all criticism that Judaism is a national religion.[54] She also participated in a solidarity rally at Columbia University's school of law, donated money to the Jewish National Fund (as she had done in 1967) and sent money to relatives in Tel Aviv. As she told Mary McCarthy, "A real catastrophe in Israel will have a profounder impact on me than nearly any other event."[55]

Therefore Elhanan Yakira is undoubtedly right when he says that despite all of her post-Zionist acolytes, "Hannah Arendt was not an anti-Zionist or even a post-Zionist.... She had no doubt that Israel is a

Jewish state and must remain so." Nonetheless she is considered to be one of the most celebrated role models of post-Zionist identity.[56]

This contradiction is but an example of the manner in which Hannah Arendt epitomizes the perpetually ambivalent modern Jew, the "conscious pariah" constantly on the fault line of clashing identities.

CHAPTER 6

JEWS ASSIMILATED
AND POST-ASSIMILATED

J ewish identity prior to the modern era was unquestionably an
amalgam of religion and ethnicity. Jews saw themselves – and
were seen by others – as a separate, unique people. Apart from a few
noteworthy exceptions (primarily the Jews of Spain and Italy toward the
end of the Middle Ages), the Jews of Europe maintained social contact
with the Christians around them solely for utilitarian purposes. Their
lives were characterized by internal cohesion and cultural autonomy.
"The boundary between Christian and Jew," Todd Endelman reminds
us, "was clear and stable...for over a thousand years."[1]

The rise of modernism brought about a dramatic change in
this situation. One of the salient features of modernism was the
universalization of human society. The clear and distinct "estates" that
typified the society of the Middle Ages were no longer tolerable (nor
was the institutionalized discrimination against these separate groups).
Also doomed was the cultural uniqueness within these various societies.
But cultural universalism did not imply multiculturalism: minorities
were forcefully and rudely required to adopt the culture of the majority.[2]

This axiom was at one with the formula favored by the Jewish
Enlightenment's quest for Jewish emancipation. It was the movement's
assumption that the Jews would attain civil rights through education

and adoption of the majority's culture. Moses Mendelssohn, the pioneer among those who launched the Jewish Enlightenment, wholeheartedly believed that the Jews would be accepted by the surrounding society only if they acquired a general education. Therefore he called on them to substitute Yiddish, which he saw as "the root cause of the cultural decline," with pure German or Hebrew. The *maskilim* (proponents of the Enlightenment), who followed his lead, established new Jewish schools, wrote textbooks in Hebrew for Jewish students and attempted to fundamentally alter the structure of the Jewish economy. All of these concepts, of course, stemmed from the classical tenets of the Haskalah – the product of the belief that enlightenment of the people and their "acculturation" would be only to the good.

It should be noted that both Mendelssohn and the Haskalah movement as a whole sought to have Jews become part of the general culture, but not to assimilate. By no means did they want the Jews to disappear into European society. Their argument was that the Jews had to undergo modernization but must remain Jews; they must adopt the majority culture, but they mustn't abandon the Jewish faith. In other words, the Haskalah called on Jews to renounce the national or ethnic components of Judaism and retain only its religious aspects.[3]

Making the Jews' emancipation contingent on their becoming part of the majority culture and undergoing modernization, as the Haskalah movement proposed, was an idea that gained a great deal of traction during that period. The advocates of Jewish emancipation claimed that inequality and oppression were the factors corrupting the Jewish character, making them backward, strange and immoral. Logically this meant that Jewish liberation was dependent in equal measure on their own self-improvement and on the Gentiles ending their intolerance.[4] In this spirit, modern society implicitly offered the Jews of Europe an "assimilation pact": Become enlightened, modern, and part of the majority culture and you'll be accepted.[5]

Many Jews (particularly in western Europe and in the center of the continent) rejoiced at this offer. They enthusiastically adopted universalism by eagerly embracing the majority culture.[6] In the German principalities, this phenomenon mainly manifested itself by a combination of *bildung* (self-improvement by becoming part of the majority culture) and *sittlichkeit* (adoption of proper behavior). The Society for Jewish Culture and Science (*Verein für Kultur und Wissenschaft der Juden*), which was established in order to advance the cultural integration of German Jews and improve their image among non-Jewish Germans, prepared a list of "matters that require improvement among the Jews for their *bildung* and *sittlichkeit*."[7] The list included "religious concepts, especially the love of God and his exclusive preference for Jews; prayers in the synagogue...; superstitions...; peddling; greed; the pervasive illusion that it is permissible to deceive non-Jews in contravention of the law; harmful customs that have become obsolete...; tyrannical rabbis – forceful, fanatical and useless...; charity that is wasted on the indolent; bad schools or the lack of schools; effeminate boys, and therefore cowardice...; neglect of women (and discrimination against them)...; avoidance of physical labor, the lack of agriculture; self-neglect...; the lack of physical activity; bad language, behavior, social relations, manners."[8]

"Self-improvement" was interpreted as ridding oneself of typically Jewish speech and mannerisms (*mauscheln*), which many non-Jews regarded as repulsive and effeminate. Included in this was the renunciation of Jewish physical traits: the Jews' reputed stench (*foetor Judaicus*), their supposed physical ugliness, and what was considered to be their "blackness" (in European science, Jews were literally seen as black, and nineteenth-century Europeans regarded black as the epitome of ugliness). According to the list Jews possessed a disease-stricken nature, their blackness being one of the manifestations of this sickly nature. "By the mid-century," reports Sander L. Gilman, "being black, being Jewish, being diseased, and being 'ugly' came to be inexorably linked."[9]

The "Jewish nose" supposedly signified Jewish ugliness and Jewish bad health, and was also considered as being direct evidence of the Jews' unnaturally big penises. These "Jewish penises," according to the widespread belief, were themselves regarded as being a pathological consequence of syphilis, the origin of which was also attributed to the Jews.[10] No wonder then that many Jews wanted to change their physique. Cosmetic surgery first became available to the general public toward the end of the 1890s – simultaneously with psychoanalysis – and Gilman believes this was no coincidence. At that time, there was a widespread belief that one could "heal" the mind by "healing" the body.[11]

All this was an integral part of the mass-assimilation project undertaken by modern European Jewry. Jews who assimilated and became embedded within the culture of the majority in their countries of residence didn't make do with merely adopting those cultures – they embraced them with a passion and zeal that were not seen in any other group, least of all among the majority nationalities. "The Jews who related to enlightenment with the utmost seriousness and equated emancipation with a refinement of manners and, in a more general way, with self-improvement," claims Zygmunt Bauman, "became cultural fanatics. In every Western nation, they were the ones who treated national cultural heritage most seriously."[12] Moreover, as has been pointed out by Michael Stanislawski, by adopting a dual or hybrid identity, so common in today's postmodern world, they were actually preserving an ancient Jewish tradition.

Decades ago Gershon D. Cohen, the great Jewish historian and former chancellor of the Jewish Theological Seminary of America, wrote a deliberately provocative article published under the title "The Blessing of Assimilation in Jewish History." He claimed that assimilation in its commonest form – the way in which Jews embraced non-Jewish cultures, languages and lifestyles – has been a central, essentially beneficial motif in Jewish history since ancient times and to the present day. In many senses, Cohen argued, it was the main factor that made it possible for the Jews to adapt and survive through the ages; whoever thinks of an eternal essence unaffected by foreign influences, Cohen argued, exhibits a lack of understanding of Jewish culture and Jewish life, be it in ancient Eretz Israel or in the Diaspora, and paints the Jews as caricatures of themselves.[13]

Be that as it may, the problem lay in the "threatening and dangerous dialectic" that characterized this process of assimilation in the modern era. The very fact that the Jews were willing to give up their Jewish identity in order to gain equal rights merely led to a sevenfold increase in the Gentiles' hatred of them.[14] We can attribute "this classic situation of a conflict of relations" to what Gilman describes as the "conservative curse": "The more you are like me, the more I know the true value of my power which you want to share, and the more I am aware that you are but a shoddy counterfeit, an outsider."[15] In any case, the Jews eventually had to face up to the fact that the "assimilation pact" was nothing but a con.[16] Assimilated Jews submissively obeyed the conditions that had been laid down for them to become integrated but the "rules kept changing, so that every gain the hapless players made promptly became a loss.... The closer the success came, the more elusive it became." Whenever the Jews got close to the desired final destination, that destination became ever more unattainable. When the Jews overcame the cultural differences, they were presented with new conditions – ultimately racial conditions which, of course, they would never be able to meet.[17] The thing they were required to change, first and foremost, was the fact that they were "the other," which, like race, was immutable.[18]

This agonizing dilemma in its entirety was personified by the nineteenth-century German-Jewish poet Heinrich Heine. In the gloomy, detailed account by Bauman, quoting from the historian S. S. Prawer, Heine did

> everything he had been advised and goaded to do to "rid himself" of his Jewishness. Heine tried to acquit himself of the task "by ostensibly showing himself being unfit for the kind of mercantile or banking career in which so many Jews...had been signally successful; "by seeking predominantly non-Jewish company at the universities of Bonn and Göttingen and subscribing to the dueling ethos of student fraternities"; by openly and publicly disavowing the Judaist lore as a fossil of bygone and shameful times, devoid of use or value for the modern man; by angrily objecting to being defined as a Jew by either enemies or friends; even by accepting that Jewishness was a "disease" in need of a cure, and excelling in the derision and ridicule of all aspects of conduct or physique

which had been stereotyped as specifically Jewish, like "physical clumsiness and gracelessness, the 'Jewish' nose, the insanitary appearance of Jews from Eastern Europe, Jewish pawnbroking and trade in cast-off clothing, the mercantile 'genius' of the Jews, the *parvenu* behaviour of Jewish *nouveaux riches*, the *Fresser* or guzzlers who 'despised the higher flights of the mind,'" or the traces of Yiddish in speech.[19]

Yet Bauman goes on to demonstrate the failure of Heine's enterprise:

Indeed, Heine drew liberally from the catalogue of Jewish sins and faults which, by the resolution of the dominant cultural elite, had to be repented of or repaired as a condition of the "all is forgiven" verdict. He used them with a passion which often dwarfed the fervour of the outsiders, thanks to his own supreme gift of wit and irony as much as to his singeing feeling of shame; having once accepted the superiority of the ideals which had not been his by birth, Heine must have been overwhelmed by the desire to cleanse himself of the birthmarks which the accepted ideals condemned. And yet Heine's efforts remained inconclusive and in the end unrewarded. The louder he protested his emancipation from Jewishness, the more his Jewishness seemed to be evident and protruding.... The display of assimilatory passion was perceived as the most convincing proof of his Jewish identity.... Nothing Heine did and could do helped him.[20]

In the second decade of the twentieth century, the German-Jewish author Jakob Wassermann (who never renounced his roots, but fervently aspired to be German) realized that his writing, no matter how German it was, would leave a Jewish mark on every matter. "Everything his German readers – admirers and detractors alike – found impeccably, unchallengeably 'German' in his work, free of a single hue or shade setting it apart from the accepted standards of the German novel, they ascribed to Jewish zeal, shrewdness or uncanny gift of imitation, rather than to Wassermann's Germanhood."[21]

Ultimately Wassermann had no choice but to conclude that it is

Vain to present the right cheek when the left has been smitten. This does not move them to thought; it neither touches nor disarms them: They strike the right cheek also.

Vain to interject words of reason into their crazy shrieking. They say: "He dares to open his mouth? Gag him."

Vain to set an example in your life and behavior. They say "We know nothing, we have seen nothing, we have heard nothing."

Vain to seek obscurity. They say: "The coward! He is creeping into hiding, driven by evil conscience!"

Vain to go among them and offer one's hand. They say: "Why does he take such liberties with his Jewish obtrusiveness?"

Vain to keep faith with them, as a comrade-in-arms or a fellow citizen. They say: "He is Proteus, he can assume any shape or form."

Vain to help them strip off the chains of slavery. They say: "No doubt he found it profitable."

Vain to counteract the poison. They brew fresh venom.

Vain to live for them and die for them. They say: "He is a Jew. A Jew he was, a Jew he will remain."[22]

The incessant rejection and humiliation left many assimilated Jews deeply depressed and insecure, a condition that turned into one of neurosis. They willingly and easily relinquished social cohesion and the security that comes from a united community, but got nothing in exchange. The result was a doubled alienation, emotional confusion, craven conformism and self-hatred.[23] "Self-hatred," argues Paul Mendes-Flohr, a preeminent scholar of modern Jewish thought, "is a product of assimilation.... There can be no doubt that this complex emotion had its impact on the Jew as he was wrenched from his ancient community in the course of the accelerated assimilation that characterized his entry into the modern era. There is no way of understanding the phenomenon of self-hatred other than in the context of assimilation."[24]

Kurt Lewin notes that when a minority is denied entry into society by the majority, the feelings of frustration lead to belligerency. However, aiming the aggression at the real culprit, the envied majority, is an impossibility since it is all-powerful and symbolizes the unattained ideal. Consequently, the aggression is turned inward, toward the minority from which the individual is unable to escape and finally toward the individual himself.[25] Moreover, many tended to vent their frustration on the "Jews who were too Jewish," the Jews who they considered to be responsible for their being rejected by the majority. According to the rationale of the frustrated assimilating Jews, if it were not for the fact that the Orthodox Jews and *Ostjuden* had polluted their countries and re-ignited the old hatred, they would have been able to attain the desired social integration.[26]

But internalized aggression was not the only response. There were those among the frustrated assimilating Jews who took a step back into a renewed Jewish identity – one that had nearly always been either secular or nationalistic. And again it would seem that Heinrich Heine's persona epitomizes this paradigm. Because his path to assimilation was so strewn with endless obstacles, Heine rejected both traditional Judaism as well as the culture of the Enlightenment. Instead, he opted for a third way: an instinctual secular Judaism that derived its vitality from a collective memory and national solidarity and was the precursor of Zionism.[27]

Heine was perhaps the first pioneer of Hibbat Zion and Zionism: Hess, Pinsker, Herzl, Nordau, Jabotinsky and a whole generation of others were all, like Heine, assimilating Jews whose expectations were disappointed.[28] They were joined by intellectual and international socialist Jews, countless cosmopolitans whose disillusionment in the face of deep-rooted anti-Semitism (especially among colleagues and those who shared their views) led them to return and adopt a Jewish identity.[29] It is even tempting to consider the cosmopolitan ideals and the striving for assimilation as essential stepping-stones on the path to a secular or national Jewish identity: for the assimilators and the cosmopolitans who preferred the universalist path but were blocked by hostility and incessant rejection, there remained no alternative other than to return in one way or another to the Jewish preserve.

But this process was in no way a mere reaction to nor was it just a step compelled by the bitter reality. In what came to be termed "dissimilation" and "post-assimilation," assimilating Jews began to renew their Jewish identity not only because of the frustration and continuing rejection but also because they developed a growing feeling of "affirmative solidarity" with other assimilating Jews. "They heaped praise...on national art and literature and suddenly noticed that their audience was mostly made up of people like them. They were avid readers and it became clear to them that they could only discuss what they had read with people who, like them, aspired to be Germans or Frenchmen."[30] They longed to be integrated into the non-Jewish society only to find that they in fact preferred the comradeship of urban intellectual Jews, who were as cultured as they were. From the 1890s, says Shulamit Volkov, German Jews found themselves "pulled in a positive way toward their own unique *milieu* by the force of a mass of common experiences, life strategies, hopes and aspirations."[31] Inadvertently, concludes David Sorkin, they created a Jewish-German subculture which they themselves were not conscious of but believed that the path they had chosen for themselves was merely a way to leave the Jewish preserve.[32]

This subculture was from the very outset flawed by a deep ambivalence.[33] Assimilating German Jews who had apparently galloped at record-breaking speed toward the gates that would allow them to leave the Jewish community were also holding on to a vague form of Jewishness "as a sort of heritage, a principled belief, an incomprehensible and undefined foundation that was nevertheless clearly present in their consciousness."[34] While in the process of making significant inroads into German society (particularly at the beginning of the twentieth century) these Jews remained in a separate social group; their spouses, their friends and their social circle were mostly other Jews.[35]

As Todd Endelman has explained, in central Europe from the 1870s and onward, "even Jews who had been baptized remained entangled in a Jewish network of family and friends, a mingling of Jews, Jews converted to Christianity, and mixed couples whose Jewish partners were considered to be of no faith (since they formally resigned from the *Gemeinde* – the community – without having changed their faith). As the extent of social discrimination increased, so did the number of converts and Jews of no faith who were compelled (or preferred) to choose friends and spouses among former Jews such as them."[36] This was also the lot of the richest German Jews who, for many years, were thought to have been the ones who nurtured the aspiration to meld into Prussian aristocracy by marriage. Research has shown that even they preferred to continue associating with other Jews.[37] "Their starting point was a deep primal loyalty to their families and the steadfast maintenance of their allegiance" to the Jewish community[38] – a collective identity that German Jewry increasingly defined by their social behavior and not via the religion itself.[39]

A major part of this secular-Jewish identity in Germany revolved around an expansive array of Jewish secular clubs and organizations that flourished at the turn of the twentieth century. The biggest countrywide Jewish organization of this kind, the Central Association of German Citizens of Jewish Faith (founded in 1893), was involved in political and ideological disputes with the Zionist movement, which had begun to rise in popularity. But in one respect there was a great similarity between them: these two organizations were robust carriers of a secular-Jewish identity and of Jewish communal solidarity.

And so the dissimilation of Jews during the period of the Weimar Republic took a further step forward. Influenced by the trauma of the First World War and the contacts with eastern European Jews, more and more secular Jews in Weimar Germany began to search for a lost spirituality and a "Jewish renaissance." This was the background to the increasing popularity of Martin Buber who, in 1901, wrote an article titled "Jewish Renaissance" and whose monthly journal, *Der Jude*, represented a plain-speaking minority who, in time to come, was to determine the tone of a significant part of Jewish life in the Weimar Republic. One of the most outstanding figures of this period was the Jewish philosopher and theologian Franz Rosenzweig, who became an advocate of a renewed commitment to Jewish spirituality and Jewish scholarship. The period witnessed the rise and continued growth of a Jewish youth movement, advancing a renewed Jewish consciousness that frequently expressed itself by rebelling against the assimilation of its parents' generation. It was also during this period that there was an eruption of Jewish scholarship and Jewish cultural activity across the whole country – a mirror image of a similar phenomenon taking place at the same time in eastern Europe.[40]

The tragic fate of this community and of the Jews of Europe as a whole was not, concludes Zygmunt Bauman, a portent of things to come despite its profound historical significance. "In contemporary history, the agonies and splendor of assimilation," wrote Bauman, "were a relatively short, and relatively local, episode." Today, Western multiculturalism enables Jews to enjoy ethnic uniqueness as well as religious and cultural diversity. "The sting of assimilation has worn off…because the pressure has gone – in this late-modern or post-modern world, a world of universal particularism; a world integrated by the power of its diversity, a world that has become used to obfuscation and is not bothered by differences."

According to Bauman, the migration of the *Ostjuden* to the west drove western Jews into even more rapid assimilation because they were afraid of being identified with their brethren from the east. However, Bauman adds, the sad truth is that the *Ostjuden* are no more and no longer exert an internal pressure to assimilate. "All around there is no reminder of the 'shameful past,' there is no reason for embarrassment…. All in all, much of the internal flame of the dream of assimilation and its practice has been extinguished."[41] Today, the Jews of the Diaspora are free to choose not to assimilate and free to adopt a durable Jewish identity (even though it is undoubtedly dual or hybrid). The question is whether they will choose to do this or whether Jewish identity is, in fact, at all durable in an open society that integrates all who enter it.

The data on the Jewish community in America is no grounds for optimism. The Jewish identity of very many Jews who migrated from eastern Europe and Russia to the United States toward the end of the nineteenth century and the beginning of the twentieth revolved around a secular Yiddish culture that developed in areas of dense Jewish population (be it the czarist Pale of Settlement or in segregated Jewish neighborhoods).[42] After World War II, the majority of Jews who had become culturally assimilated in the United States continued to emphasize their Jewish secular and cultural identity[43] that was primarily based on the Holocaust and the support for Israel.[44] This identity – a form of what has been termed ethnic "familism" – was in any case a current and ongoing phenomenon, irrespective of what the Jews themselves chose to do.[45]

In the wake of a number of developments religion returned to the forefront of American Jewish identity. These developments include the replacement in the United States of Yiddish by English, the departure of the Jews from their urban ghettos and their integration into American society, the lessening of American Jewish identification with Israel and the fading of the personal impact of the Holocaust.[46] According to Stephen Whitfield, in the United States "only religion can provide the inspirational core for a meaningful and durable Jewish culture."[47]

The return to a primarily religious Jewish identity coincides with an increasing demographic decline – mainly due to an enormous increase in the number of mixed marriages. For most of the twentieth century the rate of such marriages was stable and stood at approximately 7 percent. But in the final third of the last century it grew substantially as part of a general trend among all ethnic, religious and racial groups in the United States. According to one study, in the 1990s the rate of Jewish mixed marriages in the United States reached 52 percent; another study put the rate at a lower figure of 41 percent. But even if the more conservative estimate is correct, it nonetheless suggests a fivefold increase in mixed marriages and a situation in which a third of American Jews live in mixed Jewish-Gentile households. Moreover, 70–82 percent of all mixed-marriage couples either bring up their children under an umbrella of religious duality, or detached from religion altogether, or as Christians; only 25 percent of the children of such couples declare their Jewish identity when they reach college age. Perhaps, as could be expected, these rising rates of mixed marriages coincide with the decline in the identification of American Jews as being part of the Jewish people. In a research undertaken in 1998, it was found that only some 52 percent of American Jews agree with the statement "I regard the whole Jewish community as my extended family."[48]

We therefore return to the fateful question. We have established that the post-modern Jewish identity assimilates within its surroundings, becoming a dual, or hybrid, identity. That being the case, can such an identity be transmitted from one generation to another in a pluralist, multicultural society? If the fate of secular cultural Jewish identity in the West is anything to go by, the chances are not high. Such an identity does not appear to be durable in any Western society – with the notable exception of Israel.[49]

CHAPTER 7

AMERICAN JEWISH IDENTITY IN THE NAZI ERA AND AT THE TIME OF ISRAELI STATEHOOD

The Nazi period led to changes in Jewish identity not only in Palestine but also in the United States. American Jewry was involved in a continual struggle between the desire to adopt an "American" identity and their wish to hold on to a "Jewish" identity. Jewish immigrants who came to the United States from Germany in the first part of the nineteenth century were proud to be both Jews and Germans. They tried to discard a strictly Jewish identity and make the most of the emancipated status they had attained in Europe. This was in sharp contrast to their east European brethren who kept their deep-rooted religious and communal ties. The behavior of the German Jews was in line with American norms: to be an American in those days meant shedding one's past personal identity and melding within the melting pot.[1]

The first crisis to test American Jewish identity was the Damascus Affair of 1840, when Ottoman officials accused the town's Jewish community of the ritual killing of a Capuchin monk and his assistant. The subsequent witch hunt resulted in the detention, torture and deaths of seventy-two Jews. The international outcry that followed prompted many American Jews to rekindle the flame of their Jewish identity and demonstrate their support for Damascene Jewry, a development that dismayed not a few Americans.[2]

There was a similar reaction by American Jews to the Kishinev pogrom of 1903. But their call for intervention by the American administration fell on deaf ears in Washington. Theodore Roosevelt's government consistently refused to respond to any ethnic minority's request to change the foreign policy of the United States. It would appear that the establishment in 1906 of the American Jewish Committee (AJC) was a reaction to this official American position. The AJC was the first ethno-religious organization to be established in the US – its objective being to defend and promote Jewish interests in the United States.[3]

American Jewish identity was tested on a number of occasions in the course of the twentieth century. During World War I, German Jews in America were openly accused of disloyalty, as was anybody else who had links to Germany. In particular there were mounting suspicions about Jacob Schiff, one of the wealthiest members of the American Jewish community, who was barely able to contain himself from publicly expressing pro-German views. Schiff had himself questioned the loyalty of American Zionists, saying that it was impossible for someone to be both an American and a Zionist.[4] This was also the stated position of Rabbi Louis Grossman, the head of the Central Conference of American Rabbis; in his view, Eretz Israel could not really be considered the homeland of American Jews since they were, after all, an integral part of American society. On the other hand, another prominent American Jew, Louis D. Brandeis, adopted a very different position. Brandeis, a close confidant of President Wilson and the first Jew to be appointed to the US Supreme Court, was an ardent Zionist and regarded the movement as exemplifying the American ideals of justice and political democracy. National identities, Brandeis argued, are only damaging if they operate on opposing sides, which was not the case with American Jewish aid to Eretz Israel.[5]

As the Israeli historian Gulie Ne'eman Arad has pointed out, more than one and a half million Jews emigrated from eastern Europe to the United States between 1890 and 1920, a period during which American xenophobic and isolationist nationalism was at its height. "The old motto proclaiming America a haven for the oppressed," Arad notes, had changed. "Now it was said that 'hyphenated' Americans were not wanted."[6] During the 1920s, the situation only got worse. Three forces combined to frustrate the integration of Jews within American society: an aggressive form of nationalism that was exacerbated by World War I, a growing opposition to foreigners and to immigration, and American anti-Semitism. In 1921, Congress passed the Emergency Immigration Restriction Act which set the immigration quota for national groups at 3 percent of the number of people of that nationality who were then living in the United States; in 1924 it passed the National Origins Immigration Act, which reduced the quota from 3 percent to 2 percent and changed the year on which the quota was based from 1910 to 1890 when considerably fewer Jews, Slavs and Italians lived in the United States. The same period witnessed a growth in anti-Semitism. However, the "red scare" of the early 1920s changed the grounds of anti-Semitism from prewar anticapitalism to the new anticommunism. This was augmented by the very popular accusations voiced by Henry Ford against international Jewish power.[7]

The rise of the Nazi regime in Germany and the Second World War posed grave tests for the identity of American Jews. The activities of Stephen S. Wise (1874–1949), president of the American Jewish Congress, epitomized the struggle between Jewish and American identities. Wise tried to navigate his work for the American Jewish community in conjunction with his efforts to help European Jewry. Though he always endeavored to maintain open access to the White House by repeatedly demonstrating his loyalty to America, he never allowed American politics to thwart his vigorous pursuit of his European-Jewish agenda.[8]

Compared to the open fury among American Jews in response to the Kishinev pogrom of 1903, the reaction three decades later to the Nazis was very different. This change was apparently due to the increasing restraint of American Jews about raising specifically Jewish issues on the public agenda of their "new Zion" in the western hemisphere.[9] Judge Joseph Proskauer, a leading member of the American Jewish Committee, insisted in 1935 that the Jews of America had "no moral right to coalesce as a separate group inside the United States, to disturb the economic and diplomatic relations between America and a country with which America is at peace."American Jews must never forget, Proskauer added on the same occasion, that they were expected to "fulfill their basic obligations as American citizens dutifully and loyally."[10]

Rabbi Stephen S. Wise's approach reflected no such reticence. The duty of American Jews, Wise insisted, was to publicly protest against the Nazi regime. Upon his return from Germany, where he was profoundly shocked by the persecution of Jews, Wise accepted Judge Brandeis's pessimistic view that the only solution was a Jewish exodus from Germany.[11] Ironically, it took the Jews of Germany until 1935 and the passing of the Nuremberg Laws to take this view on board. It was only then that they began to urgently request the help of the Jewish communities in Eretz Israel and in the United States. But American Jewry was slow to internalize the Nazi threat, many fearing accusations such as those that appeared in the Protestant weekly *The Christian Century* to the effect that Jews were an ethnic community incapable of integration into Christian society.[12]

At that time, American Jewry consisted of two identity groups: those who considered themselves to be first and foremost Americans and denied that their Jewishness entailed any ethnic or national component, and those who considered themselves as being part of a particular ethnicity and wanted to be accepted as such. The former encompassed most of the German-Jewish elite including such figures as Rabbi Bernard Felsenthal who, in 1924, declared that "racially I am a Jew because I was born a Jew…but from a spiritual point of view, I'm German since my inner life has been influenced by Schiller, Goethe, Kant and other great German intellectuals."[13] Many Jews were very sensitive to the perception by Gentiles that they were "clannish" and so did their best to display a lack of solidarity with other Jews; others shuddered at the prospect of being identified with the less-sophisticated *Ostjuden* and spoke of shedding "many of our most primitive impulses."[14]

In contrast, the second group consisted of Jews who had failed in their attempts to integrate into the society or embrace the idea of cultural pluralism and American nationality that incorporated self-validating minority cultures and ethnic identities. They adopted a resurgent and energized Jewish identity by establishing synagogues as community centers, Jewish employment agencies, professional clubs, fraternities and educational facilities. All these were designed to strengthen the Jewish community and not necessarily serve as instruments of assimilation into the society, as had been the case with such institutions in the past.[15]

Both groups were fearful of the backlash that could result from an overly public debate focused on issues of Jewish concern only. Those who felt this way included prominent Americans who served President Franklin D. Roosevelt as advisors and confidants, among them Felix Frankfurter, Isador Lubin and Nathan Straus. American Jewish leaders hoped that these very same people would mobilize American support for German Jewry, but were quickly disappointed. At this moment of unprecedented crisis, Jews holding positions at the highest level of government were gripped with intense fear of being accused of double loyalty and refused to use their influence with Roosevelt to advance the cause of specifically Jewish issues. Fear and intimidation turned out to be the determining features of American Jewish identity.

One of the first to defy such self-negation was Rabbi Abba Hillel Silver (1893–1963). A Zionist leader who enthusiastically supported cultural pluralism in America, Silver insisted that Jewish solidarity was not harmful to the United States and demanded a Jewish-American response to Hitler. The Jewish leadership followed Silver's lead only after the annexation of Austria by the Third Reich in March 1938 which put an additional two hundred thousand Jews in harm's way, and after the Nazi pogrom known as *Kristallnacht* in November of that same year.[16] From then on, the Jewish leadership openly lobbied for steps to be taken to help German Jews despite the accusation hurled at them that they were "running their affairs as a state within a state." They called for the removal of immigration restrictions for Jewish refugees but their pleas fell on deaf ears. The Great Depression had led to a wave of opposition to immigration throughout the United States that Roosevelt was unwilling to challenge. The Jewish community became increasingly disillusioned with Roosevelt and the Jews close to him.

The draconian immigration restrictions enforced by the United States were dramatically expressed in May 1939 by the refusal of the American authorities to allow desperate Jewish passengers on board the *St. Louis* ocean liner to disembark, a decision that in effect doomed them to death. At the very same time, Britain imposed severe restriction on the number of Jews allowed to enter Palestine. The White Paper, published in May 1939, allowed for only seventy-five thousand Jewish immigrants during the following five years; after that, the White Paper decreed, further Jewish immigration would be subject to Arab consent.[17] The British move prompted American Jewish leaders to renew their demands to issue additional entry permits for Jews to come to the United States, but to no avail. An attempt in 1939 to get Congress to pass a law enabling two hundred thousand Jewish children to immigrate was unceremoniously rejected, thus escalating the painful conflicts of identity within American Jewry.

ECHOES OF THE HOLOCAUST IN THE UNITED STATES

The ensuing catastrophe and the evident helplessness of American Jewry to either halt or somehow alleviate its severity deeply scarred the American Jewish consciousness. The historian Peter Novick claims that evidence of this can be found in the fact that more than sixty years after the event America is still very "Holocaust conscious." This is unquestionably an unusual phenomenon given that most historical events cease being of interest to the public within just a few years. In this instance it's not only that consciousness of the Holocaust in the United States hasn't declined, it's actually growing and doing so in tandem with the growth in awareness of Jewish identity in America. One can find reasons for this in Maurice Halbwachs' writings on collective memory. According to Halbwachs, "it is in society that people normally acquire their memories. It is also within society that they recall, recognize, and localize their memories."[18]

Therefore, he argues, it is impossible for individuals to remember the past in any coherent or permanent way outside their groups' context. Being part of a society provides individuals with the necessary material for memory, and group membership prompts individuals to remember certain events and forget others. As a matter of fact, membership of a group may even create in individuals memories of events that they had never directly experienced.[19]

Current public interest, Halbwachs concedes, influences our remembrance of past events. Conversely, past experiences influence present collective memory. Collective memory is not historical and does not depend on the passage of time, but is linked to the critical truth that lives on as part of an "eternal collective memory"; this memory is viewed from the perspective of one major hallowed event, usually a tragedy, and it casts a shadow over all subsequent interpretations of that event.

Halbwachs also differentiates between historical memory and autobiographical memory. The former is maintained only through written and pictorial records and is kept alive through collective rituals and festivals. The second type of memory consists of personally experienced recollections of the past that "tends to fade with the passage of time unless it is periodically reinforced by contact with people with whom those past experiences were shared." Thus autobiographical memory is rooted in contact with others, and will fade and disappear if it is not bolstered by such contact.[20]

Moreover, Halbwachs argues, memory fixates the experiences and ensures the continuity of collective groups. Historical events have always been pivotal to the collective memories of groups and nations. For example, the Serbian collective memory is anchored in the continual struggle to be rid of Muslim dominance. The massacre in 1871 at the Communards' wall, in which one hundred forty-seven combatants of the Paris Commune were killed, will forever symbolize the clash between the proletariat and the bourgeoisie in France. Disagreeing with Freud, Halbwachs argues that such memories are selected consciously – and the choice is made under the influence of present experiences and the cultural development of a given nation. As the interest of American Jews went from delving into America's melting pot to safeguarding particular group identity, so their collective memories have also evolved. In the current environment, while the leadership is trying to cope with assimilation and increasing levels of intermarriage and with the growing fears that Jews may have lost the ability to survive as a distinct group in America, the collective memory of the Holocaust serves as the objective purpose of unity and self-preservation.[21]

In a negative way, the unity and identity of American Jews has been strengthened by acknowledging that their very existence is an accident of history. Had their parents and grandparents decided to stay in Europe rather than immigrate to the United States, they too would have perished in the Holocaust.

At the beginning, according to Novick, Jewish reaction to the Holocaust was polarized, ranging from feelings of guilt and despair to outright indifference. Those whose Americanization had significantly weakened their Jewish identity felt more distanced from the tragedy than those who had maintained a strong Jewish identity. But in the late 1960s and early 1970s, the significance of the Holocaust shifted from being a marginal issue in the lives of American Jews to become the focus of their attention. This shift coincided with new fears of a growing anti-Semitism in the United States which was at odds with the objective reality of greater security and integration. The true causes, Novick thinks, were the perceived existential threat to Israel in 1967, and the perilous plight of Soviet Jewry. The feeling grew that another Holocaust was a possibility. "American Jewry," Jonathan Sarna has suggested, "was obsessed with the question of whether a Holocaust is possible in America."[22]

This increased sensitivity to Jewish vulnerability reinforced long-simmering feelings of guilt stemming from the feeble response of American Jews to the Holocaust. The slogan "never again" acquired an almost holy meaning in a community whose dedication to Soviet Jewry in the 1970s appeared to be inflamed by a need to make amends for the past. Many lamented the fact that saving the Jews of Europe during the Holocaust had not been at the top of the agenda of Jewish organizations in the United States. "While Mordecai Anielewicz and his comrades fought their lonely battle in the blazing ghetto under seige," said Elie Wiesel in anger, "…a large New York synagogue invited its members to a banquet featuring a well-known comedian."[23]

Jews were forced to deal with the fact that many Jewish-owned newspapers had paid little attention to German atrocities during the war. According to the historian Laurel Leff, this was especially true of the *New York Times*:

> From the start of the war in Europe to its end nearly six years later, the story of the Holocaust made the *Times* front page only 26 times out of 24,000 front-page stories, and most of those stories referred to the victims as "refugees" or "persecuted minorities." In only six of those stories were Jews identified on page one as the primary victims.
>
> Nor did the story lead the paper, appearing in the right-hand column reserved for the day's most important news – not even when the concentration camps were liberated at the end of the war. In addition, the *Times* intermittently and timidly editorialized about the extermination of the Jews, and the paper rarely highlighted it in either the *Week in Review* or the magazine section.[24]

Some attributed this angrily to a craven fear of mounting anti-Semitism that had prevented Jews from acting during their people's greatest crisis. Others, however, point to the fact that similar lapses also occurred among the Jews in Eretz Israel, implying that the situation was too complex for it to be simply described as American Jewish cowardice. In any case, the sorrowful conclusion of many was that nothing American Jewry could have done would in the end have changed the situation. "Even if we had done everything that was suggested... – and within twenty-four hours – it still would not have saved any Jewish lives," was to be Nahum Goldmann's gloomy verdict. "We are helpless."[25]

And yet, in the final analysis, it was not the fear of resurgent anti-Semitism in America nor the threats against Israel and Soviet Jewry that raised the consciousness of the Holocaust in American Jewish life.[26] Toward the end of the 1960s and the beginning of the 1970s, Novick concludes, American Jewish leaders were increasingly alarmed by the escalation in the rate of assimilation and intermarriage. The Holocaust became the primary weapon in the struggle to contain this phenomenon and ensure the continuity of Jewish solidarity. Novick goes so far as to claim that the Holocaust in effect became the sole unifying force behind American Jewish identity.

Novick views the Holocaust as the all-powerful argument, and considers Jewish survival to be the ultimate imperative in the wake of the loss of the six million.[27] As Rabbi Irving Greenberg rightly put it, "Holocaust consciousness became a channel for the resurgence of the rest of Jewry." The idea of "never again" represented not only the refusal of Jews to once more becoming helpless victims but also their determination to ensure that assimilation did not hand Hitler a posthumous victory. At least in part, Jewish identity in America began to revolve around the determination to survive.

THE ESTABLISHMENT OF THE STATE OF ISRAEL

American Jews did not reach a consensus on the idea of a Jewish state until 1940. Prior to that, members of Jewish organizations in America (about a quarter of all American Jews) were divided into three groups: Zionists (the majority), non-Zionists (B'nai B'rith, the American Jewish Committee [AJC] and most Reform synagogues) and anti-Zionists. Since its establishment in 1906, the AJC had sought to become the recognized representative of American Jewry. It focused specifically on the issues of civil rights and the persecution of Jews within the United States and beyond. From the time of the publication of the Balfour Declaration at the end of 1917, the AJC adopted a position of neutrality toward Zionism, a position that was labeled "non-Zionist": the committee supported philanthropic projects intended to benefit the Jewish community in Eretz Israel but totally opposed the idea of that community becoming a Jewish state. In the view of Judge Joseph M. Proskauer, who was elected president of the AJC in 1943, the Zionist position expressed in the Biltmore Program of May 1942 calling for a Jewish commonwealth in Eretz Israel was nothing less than a "Jewish catastrophe." The prospect of such a state panicked the AJC's leaders who feared its potential negative impact on American Jewry – particularly, they feared the accusation that the Jewish community was guilty of dual or divided loyalty.[28]

News about the Holocaust published in the middle of World War

II led to a radical change within the American Jewish establishment: it was enough to turn both anti-Zionism and non-Zionism into untenable positions. In November 1947, the AJC supported the United Nations' partition resolution that mandated the creation of a Jewish state in parts of Palestine. Proskauer's support for partition faltered in March 1948 when the US State Department backed away from its commitment to this plan and attempted instead to set up an international trusteeship. The background to this was a series of Jewish military setbacks at that stage of the War of Independence. But Israel's Declaration of Independence in May of that year, and the success of the young state in repelling the Arab onslaught, essentially put an end to any debate about whether or not a Jewish state should exist.[29]

However, the AJC's recognition of Jewish statehood was accompanied by a new list of controversial issues between the committee and Israel and the Zionist movement. Though the AJC's new president, Jacob Blaustein – elected in 1949 – rejected the continuing anti-Zionist stance of the American Jewish Committee, he didn't shrink from trying to apply pressure on David Ben-Gurion on a series of substantive issues. Blaustein opposed unrestricted Jewish immigration to Israel; was critical of the socialist policies of the Israeli government led by Mapai (Labor Party), which he felt would stifle private investment; and pushed for a settlement with the surrounding Arab states.[30]

But it was the potential minefield of dual loyalty that concerned American Jewish leaders most of all. The extent of their unease in this matter was clearly evident in the position adopted by Dr. Emanuel Neumann, president of the Zionist Organization of America. Dr. Neumann demanded that the Zionist movement be active only in the Diaspora, entirely divorced from any link to the Israeli government so as to avoid the suspicion of dual loyalty. Blaustein himself categorically rejected the term "Jewish nation," fearful that it would arouse precisely such suspicions.

The issue was headlined in 1949 when Ben-Gurion called on America's Jewish parents to send their children to Israel. While threatening to reassess the AJC's stance toward Israel, Blaustein entered into serious negotiations with Israel's government that ultimately led in

1950 to the famous understanding between him and Ben-Gurion. In the document between the two, Ben-Gurion clarified his position both on the matter of relations between Israel and the Diaspora and on the issue of dual loyalty. He pointed out that world Jewry consisted of three categories: citizens of Israel; Jews in nondemocratic countries who were not free and must therefore emigrate to Israel; and Jews who lived freely in democratic countries. Ben-Gurion agreed not to engage in any propaganda suggesting that Jews in the third category were in danger and must emigrate to Israel. He also renounced any Israeli interference in the internal affairs of Diaspora Jews. "The Jews of the United States," he stated, "as a community and as individuals, have only one political attachment and that is to the United States of America. They owe no political allegiance to Israel."[31]

Thus from the very beginning of Israel's existence, and throughout the first few stormy years of the Cold War, American Jewish leaders were embroiled in a struggle with Israel's government over the core issue of Jewish identity. It was to be some time before American Jews came to the realization that they could openly show their support for Israel, even engaging in intensive lobbying on its behalf, without risking the accusation of dual loyalty.

CHAPTER 8

IDENTITY STRUGGLES WITHIN
ISRAEL

I n the afternoon of May 14, 1948, David Ben-Gurion declared the
establishment of the State of Israel, thus fulfilling Theodor Herzl's
prescription of a "Jewish state" a mere fifty years after the Zionist
leader had first clearly voiced the idea. The ceremony was attended by
representatives of the various Jewish political parties: from the socialist/
labor parties (Mapai, Achdut Ha'Avodah, Mapam) to the Orthodox
(Agudat Israel and its associate party Poalei Agudat Israel), as well as
the more moderate religious parties (Mizrachi and Hapoel Hamizrachi).
It also included the right-wing revisionist movement – as distinct from
Etzel, which later on reconstituted itself as the Herut Party – and on
the far left the Communist Party. The Declaration of Independence
came in the wake of the United Nations' General Assembly resolution
of November 29, 1947, to partition Palestine into two states – one
Jewish, one Arab – a decision that was met by violent Arab opposition.
In the course of the declaration, Ben-Gurion spoke of the need to settle
homeless Holocaust survivors in their ancestral homeland but didn't
specify what the geographical borders of the new state would be. He
did call on Arab nationals who were now residing in the State of Israel
"to keep the peace and to play an active role in the building of the state,
based on full and equal citizenship and an appropriate representation
in all of the country's temporary and permanent institutions." But the
language of the declaration made it perfectly clear that the new state in

Eretz Israel was to be a "Jewish" state, not a "state of all its citizens."

A few hours after Ben-Gurion's historic declaration, Egyptian war planes began bombing the newly born state and the armies of a number of Arab countries crossed into the borders of what was British mandatory Palestine. These actions turned what had been a six-month civil war between Jews and Arabs in Palestine into a full-blown multifront conventional war. Herzl's Jewish state was ultimately ratified on the battlefield at a very high cost in blood. The number of Jews killed was no less than 1 percent of the entire Jewish population of Palestine on the day the state was proclaimed.

Naturally, the struggle over the future identity of the State of Israel began even prior to May 14, 1948, and reflected the various ideological strands within the Yishuv. Was it to be an unambiguously Jewish state? And if so, would it be a secular or a religious state? How liberal would its policies be toward non-Jews living within its borders? Would the rights and obligations of the non-Jews in fact be equal?

Anita Shapira has delved deeply into the topic of Israel's various evolving identities. Identity, we learn from Shapira, is an elusive term that is subject to different interpretations. This is because we live in a constantly changing world that creates corresponding changes in the meanings, definitions and understandings of the term. There is the identity of the individual, the collective identity, and the interrelationship between them. In fact, every individual has a number of identities: as a family's son or daughter; as part of a tribe or specific ethnic group; as belonging to a certain generation with whom one shares common experiences that are defined by one's mutual identities. The "group identity" of the individual is the sum total of individual and group identities, even if it does not accurately or even approximately represent the individualistic identities of the group's members.[1]

Mordechai Bar-On applies Erik Erikson's definition of individual identity as a conditioned sensibility of increasing sameness and continuity also to "communal" or "collective" identity. The terms "sameness" and "continuity," he explains, can also apply to the aggregate perceptions of individuals that define a group. As Erikson wrote, "We are dealing with "a process 'located' in the core of the individual and yet also in the core of his communal culture, a process which establishes, in fact, the identity of these two identities." Erikson describes this process of crystallizing identities as "cultural consolidation."[2]

Bar-On points out that social psychologists, particularly those committed to theories of "role" and "reference groups," focused on the process of what Gordon Allport has described as "the sense of emotional merging of oneself with others." This shaping of collective or group identity, Bar-On adds, is also determined by how others view and distinguish the group, as well as how the group perceives itself and its situation in relation to others. As Erikson described it, the "affiliative" bonds of individuals to collectives include "a passion of excluding others, that is, of knowing against what and whom one will stand and fall together.[3]

In the final analysis, Shapira suggests, the ideal collective identity is imaginary. It can be best defined as a model of the ideal society in the eyes of a particular community. Thus, the collective identity of a nation represents the ethos and the acceptable norms of a specific society at a given time. These norms constantly evolve, leading at times to a cultural clash of identities within a particular community.

In Shapira's view, prior to the Holocaust and the establishment of the Jewish state, there were two absolutely distinct Jewish identities: that of the traditional or Orthodox Jew and that of the modern Jew. The Zionist movement created a third ethos, that of the "new Jew": secular, revolutionary and with allegiances that were inseparably linked to historical Eretz Israel. "Negation of the Diaspora" was one of the fundamental beliefs of the new Jew. It was a conviction that made the new Jew an equal among his non-Jewish peers and ultimately led to a new collective Jewish identity. The model for the new Jew was a person who had left his home and culture of the old Diaspora behind him, and made a home for himself in his "newly restored" homeland. He dressed simply, content with the little he had, and was dedicated to the collective goal of building a new Jewish nation. The new Jew tilled the soil, built roads and drained swamps – in sharp contrast to the image of the merchant or moneylender that typified the "old" European Jew. Jews born in Eretz Israel were automatically classified as new

Jews; they were part of a radical new beginning and proud of it. They wore their dissimilarities with Diaspora Jews as if they were badges of honor: they were courageous, fearless, simple and hardworking – not bookworms or money-grubbing misers – and they were committed to an independent Jewish state, without self-abnegation.

It is not surprising, therefore, that native-born Israelis (Sabras) didn't eagerly embrace Jewish immigrants who arrived after the state's creation. In their minds, these immigrants personified all the negative aspects of the life led by Diaspora Jewry. In fact, many of the immigrants had at first tried to emulate the collective Sabra identity. As Shapira reminds us, given that collective identity is not a reality but an ideal, such attempts quickly crumbled and gave way to various evolving Jewish identities.

Even the new immigrant who took on the Israeli way of life out of a sense of veneration was far from resembling the native-born Sabras. He loved the land, but was no fanatic. He found himself alienated from the kibbutz's collective way of life and from the mythology that elevated agricultural work to be society's highest ideal. Moreover, for many immigrants, the Sabra's "negation of the Diaspora" seemed heartless and unjustifiable in light of the Holocaust.

Thus, Israel's "society of immigrants" shaped its own identity. Ever since then, and in fact from an even earlier period, Israel has experienced a continuous evolution of identity. The collective, according to Shapira, seeks increasingly to represent the parts rather than the whole. Similarly, post-modernism favors minorities over the privileged. As Israel developed, the stark differences between its many component parts became increasingly evident. Holocaust survivors contrasted sharply with the Sabras' new Jew; the *Mizrachim* – Middle Eastern Jews mostly from North Africa and Iraq – differed from both. Above and beyond this polarization was the Israeli Arab minority – 20 percent of the population – with identity problems of its own.[4]

POSTMODERNISM AND ISRAELI IDENTITY

Postmodernism has influenced, and continues to significantly influence, the modern Israeli identity. Though it is difficult to define, and postmodernists continually debate among themselves as to its real essence, a broad working definition is possible. Postmodernism is a philosophical and cultural movement, the core principle of which calls for a comprehensive dismissal of all "meta-narratives" of the modern world. Such narratives, it is argued within postmodernism, are regarded as "objective" – universally and eternally true. They thereby legitimize a prevailing body of knowledge, beliefs and practices, and marginalize others. Jean-François Lyotard, a leading thinker among postmodernists, is a sharp critic of what he terms "social totality." He insists on the necessity of "reflecting upon what is just or unjust…against the horizon of multiplicity or diversity." The world, say postmodernist followers of Lyotard, has become so fragmented and culturally diverse that it can no longer be viewed through the prism of the Enlightenment or modernity's monolithic worldview. Instead, postmodernism emphasizes a constantly fluid, multifaceted perspective and refuses to give preference to any particular narrative over any other.[5]

Recently, postmodernist scholars in a number of fields have also questioned whether one can objectively or scientifically determine the identity of peoples which, they insist, is in any case always changeable. "There are," suggests Stuart Hall, "at least two different ways of thinking about 'cultural identity.' The first position defines cultural identity in terms of one shared culture…, which people with a shared history and ancestry hold in common."[6] This "essentialist" position has informed most scholarly works on Jews and Judaism. Over the years, numerous scholars have continued to reflect on the very existence of Judaism and Jewish culture and sought to uncover their true essence. But a second postmodernist view argues that cultural identities are continually changing and evolving, and thus can never be described in any essentialist way. "Cultural identity" writes Hall, "…is a matter of 'becoming' as well as of 'being.' …It is not something which already exists transcending place, time, history, and culture. Cultural identities…like everything else which is historical…undergo constant transformation."[7]

Postmodernists have been increasingly emphasizing that changing cultural identities are inherently social constructs and that power and conflict are principal factors in this process. This can be seen in the way that cultural identities are very often consolidated by the exclusion of others. Jacques Derrida (of North African Jewish extraction) argued passionately that the only way to view a particular culture is by referring to the other culture against which it has defined itself.[8] Michel Foucault has written extensively about the countless ways in which others are excluded during cultural discourse and the attainment of knowledge and truth.[9] "To both Derrida and Foucault," observes Laurence J. Silberstein, "the process of identity formation is far from benign. Insofar as identity presupposes alterity, any effort by a group to establish the parameters of its own identity entails the exclusion and/or silencing of the voices of Others."[10]

Jewish scholars have, over a long period of time, explored the ways in which Jews have been depicted as "others" and their exclusion from dominant Christian and Islamic cultures. But it is only recently that scholars have taken up the question of the way Jewish identity has been formed by experiencing the same process.[11] The anthropologist Virginia Dominguez has taken a critical look at some of the ways in which Jews have shaped their cultural identity in Israel. In adopting postmodernist concepts of change, conflict and "otherness," Dominguez rejects the view of Jewish culture accepted by a majority of historians and social scientists. It is a view that emphasizes the importance of shared cultural values and common history, and considers Jewish nationhood (peoplehood) as a given. In Dominguez's view, Jewish nationhood is far from being "natural" and is actually a product of a continuing and endlessly changing and wide-ranging cultural process that objectifies and marginalizes others. Dominguez claims that for the Israeli mainstream the Jewish "other" is the Middle Eastern Jew or Arab; for all Israeli Jews the "other" is the Arab both inside and outside Israel. "I think the evidence points toward a dynamic interrelationship between selfhood and otherness in which selfhood is very dependent on the identification (or assumption) of otherness but in which, just as integrally, the boundaries between self and other – semantic as well as referential – are neither fixed nor determinate."[12]

The proliferation of identities in Israel has become an unmistakable phenomenon since the 1970s. Since that time, as Bar-On notes, Israeli society has become "increasingly segmented into a variety of cultural and ideological subgroups that coexist side by side and struggle for their independence, their worthiness and public conspicuousness." The hegemony of the pioneering, labor-oriented, Ashkenazi establishment is in a phase of retreat before a multicultural political system. Thus the old establishment became just one of many competing subgroups.[13] Baruch Kimmerling points out that a cluster of subgroups has formed and each one defines itself differently. The result is an emerging new Israeliness, both structurally and as a potential collective meta-identity.[14]

Not only has the homogeneity of Israeli society ended, but the very notion of homogeneity itself, shaped by the supremacy of a dominant cultural elite, is no longer part of the society's agenda. The sociologist David Ohana doubts "whether in principle, a positive collective identity may be sustained in a multicultural post-ideological society, which is torn by fundamental issues, devoid of any national consensus and a coalition of minorities." A new Israeli identity, writes Ohana, comprises "a mosaic of dreams, a reservoir of different longings, a web of memories."[15]

THE "NEW HISTORIANS" AND ISRAELI IDENTITY
The proliferation of so many competing subgroup identities is only one aspect of an evident identity crisis in Israel. Israelis are nowadays called on to decide where they stand not only in relation to these subgroups, but also with regard to sacred beliefs, values and conceptualizations of Israel's past. In other words, the continuing struggle to define Israeli identity always focuses on history because "a sense of common history – whether past sufferings and defeats or past victories and successes – tends to define the collective identity of groups, especially of nations."[16] There is a clear expression of such views in the heated debates on Israel's "New Historians" (Benny Morris, Avi Shlaim, Ilan Pappé and Tom Segev) who have questioned previously unchallengeable assumptions underlying the Zionist movement's attitudes vis-à-vis the Palestinian Arabs (especially during the 1948 war) and Israel's behavior toward the Arab world. According to the sociologist Uri Ram, this debate reflects

and elaborates on a struggle over the collective memory of Israel, a struggle that may herald potential changes in the definition of Israeli identity.[17] Indeed, the history of the Zionist-Arab conflict always had a significant influence on Israeli identity because this identity absorbed a series of "basic beliefs that were upheld for many years by most Israelis and constituted the way they perceived themselves and their position in the world."[18]

As the well-known Israeli writer and long-time Labor Zionist Aharon Megged put it, the New Historians set out to prove that "most of the certainties secured in our consciousness and experience are but lies.... All the beautifully formulated idioms in which we used to believe, and on which we and our children were raised for two to three generations, such as 'the redemption of the land,' 'the conquest of labor,' 'the ingathering of the Exiles,' 'defense' and so forth...are now depicted as hypocrisy and deceit, euphemisms for an ignominious conspiracy."[19]

At the center of revisionist depictions of Zionism lies its treatment of the Palestinian Arabs. Tensions between Arabs and Jews erupted immediately after the first wave of Zionist immigrants arrived in Palestine in the 1880s ("the First Aliyah").[20] But it was not until the eruption of murderous Arab riots in 1921 that Zionists fully realized the significance of the Jewish-Arab conflict for the Zionist movement.[21]

Zionists have regularly been blamed for having adopted the illusion that Palestine was a vacant land. During the nineteenth century there was indeed only a small minority among Hovevei Zion, people such as Rabbi Zvi Hirsch Kalischer, who spoke about the indigenous Arab population. Later on, Moses (Moshe) Leib Lilienblum and Ahad Ha'am added their voices to the subject. After visiting Eretz Israel in 1891, Ahad Ha'am issued a stern warning: Arabs were very much aware of Jewish settlement in the country and would act against it as soon as they felt threatened.[22] The Zionist educator Yitzhak Epstein was especially prophetic. At the Seventh Zionist Congress in the summer of 1905, he criticized the practice of replacing Arab workers with Jews, and maintained that Jewish settlers should offer the Arabs a partnership in developing the country. Epstein called for the ratification of a charter between the two Semitic peoples and emphasized the need to raise Arab standards of living by allowing them access to hospitals and schools without trying to make them converts to Judaism. These views were reiterated by Epstein in his famous article "*She'elah Ne'elmah*" (The Occult Question), published in the journal *Hashiloach* two years later.

The author Nechama Pohatchevsky responded to this in an article of her own titled "*She'elot Geluyot*" (Clear questions), in which she argued that no one could buy Arab friendship and that nothing would win over Arab consent to a Jewish presence in Palestine. She pointed out that many attempts had been made but to no avail. She reminded her readers that history is full of examples proving that the more the Jews tried to ingratiate themselves with other peoples, the more they were hated. She wondered whether the time had not come for Jews to at long last concern themselves with their own existence and survival.[23]

The arrival in Eretz Israel of the Russian Labor Zionists in the period after 1905, and their impact on events in the country, only worsened relations between Arabs and Jews. Stunned to discover that the Jewish agricultural sector was based on Arab labor, the socialist Zionists demanded that Arab workers be replaced by Jewish immigrants. They insisted that Jews and Jews alone were supposed to rebuild the Jewish homeland with their own hands. In so doing Jews would transform themselves and finally shed their occupational links to commerce. It is an irony of history, says Walter Laqueur, that "those who wanted close relations with the Arabs contributed, albeit knowingly, to the worsening of the conflict."[24]

Before the First World War there were attempts to reach a détente between the Jewish settlers and the indigenous population but none succeeded. At the time the Jewish population in the country numbered 84,000 within a total population of 700,000. Arabs became increasingly fearful of Zionist expansion and of Jewish land purchase from wealthy Arab notables who mostly lived outside of Palestine and who used to lease their lands to Arab cultivators. Arab nationalism had surfaced for the first time as a political force with the Young Turk Revolution in 1908; until then, the Ottoman sultan had quashed all signs of such nascent nationalism.[25] Though prominent Zionists (particularly from the socialist circles) persisted afterwards in painting the conflict in economic terms, it rapidly became apparent that this was a national conflict between two peoples occupying the same territory.

The First World War put an end to the Ottoman Empire. The victorious Allies redrew the map of the Middle East with Great Britain assuming control of Palestine. That happened a short time after the publication of the Balfour Declaration in November 1917 in which the British promised to support a Jewish homeland in Palestine. During this period, the Arab population of Palestine was led by two prominent and competing families: the more radical Al-Husseinis, and the relatively moderate Nashashibis. According to the historian Benny Morris, the Palestinian leaders were never willing to come to terms with any form of a Jewish state but seemed inclined to consider one form or another of confederation.[26]

In the mid-1930s the two families set up political parties of their own for the first time. But the rivalry between them was far from gentlemanly. In the end, the Husseini family and its followers, the more violent of the two factions, took control of Palestinian politics and launched assaults on the Jewish population. The first sign of things to come occurred in 1929, with the infamous massacre of Orthodox Jews who occupied a small area in the predominantly Arab town of Hebron. However, despite rising levels of Arab violence, Jewish immigration continued. In fact, it even increased in the wake of Hitler's rise to power in Germany in January 1933. The Yishuv boosted its preparedness for statehood and set up self-governing bodies, including the militia organization known as the Haganah. The Nazi threat prior to World War II accelerated the Yishuv's drive to ready itself for political independence, convinced that creating a haven for persecuted Jews would be the only way to ensure their survival. On November 29, 1947, when the UN's General Assembly voted in favor of partioning Palestine into two states, Jewish and Arab, the Haganah was more combat ready than the Palestinian Arab population and the Yishuv continued to relentlessly push ahead with its preparations for independence.

At the time of the UN partition resolution, the Arab population of Palestine was one and a quarter million and the Jews numbered six hundred thousand. The Arab population consisted mostly of poor,

illiterate peasants with only a small number of urban dwellers. This
population had grown during the mandatory period in part because of a
migration of Muslims (from Bosnia, Egypt and other Arab countries) that
took place following the First World War. Additional Arab immigrants
entered Palestine for economic reasons once the British mandate had
been established.[27]

At the time of the 1948 War of Independence there were seventeen
Arab cities and towns: Beersheba, Khan Yunis, Gaza, Hebron,
Bethlehem, Beit Jala, Ramallah, Ramle, Lod, Tulkarem, Qalqilya,
Nablus, Jenin, Beit She'an, Shefaram, Acre and Nazareth. In five other
cities – Jerusalem, Haifa, Tiberias, Safed and Jaffa – the populations
were mixed. In the period between December 1947 and May 1948 (the
civil-war phase of the War of Independence) there were Arab villages
and Jewish settlements that tried to reach local peace accords. More
than twenty Arab villages sent out feelers aimed at reaching mutual
nonviolence agreements, but the dynamic of warfare soon took over.[28]

During the Arab Revolt of 1936–1939 a significant number of the
dominant Husseini family left the country; many went to Germany and
actively supported the Nazis. The lack of a leadership was to prove
a major obstacle to the Palestinians when, on the day after the UN's
partition resolution, they engaged the Yishuv in a civil war. This
shortcoming, together with the disunity of the Arab population and
the lack of independent governing institutions that could organize a
national movement and control it, made the Arab Palestinian defeat in
the civil-war phase of 1948 a certainty.

Instead of developing functioning self-governing institutions
of their own, the Palestinians relied for these services on the British
administration and continued to do so until the end of the mandate in
May 1948. They went to war with the Jews when all they had were a few
mobile village militias and their efforts to acquire arms were frustrated
by the incessant rivalry between the Husseinis and Nashashibis. In
Benny Morris's view:

> The Palestinians (like the surrounding Arab states) had a
> socioeconomic elite with no tradition of public service or ethos of

contribution or sacrifice (typical was the almost complete absence of the sons of that elite among the fighters of 1936–1939 and 1948).... When war came, at their instigation, the Palestinians were unprepared.... The Palestinian militias performed moderately well, when they were on the offensive between late November 1947 and the end of March 1948...but once the Yishuv went over to the offensive, it was all over. From early April, the Haganah was able to concentrate forces and pick off Arab towns, villages and clusters of villages in one fell swoop; Arab villages failed to assist their neighbors, and clusters of villages didn't come to the aid of neighboring blocs of villages. Almost no villagers came to the aid of townspeople, and vice versa. In effect, each community was on its own.... The Yishuv had not fought off a "nation" but an assortment of regions, towns and villages. What this says about the Palestinian Arabs at the time as a "people" will also need to be confronted.[29]

The second half of Israel's War of Independence was a conventional war between the newly created state and the invading armies of the neighboring Arab countries. It was a war that led to the creation of approximately seven hundred thousand Palestinian refugees, a problem that remains unresolved to this very day and continues to be a burning issue in the post-Zionist discourse. Benny Morris was one of a number of New Historians to be published in Israel in the late 1980s and whose work quickly became the fulcrum of post-Zionism. When Morris's initial research on Palestinian refugees was published in English in 1987,[30] and it became known that in his view the Israelis had actively contributed to the creation of the refugee problem, Morris was quickly accused of being an anti-Zionist. He had lifted a curtain that Israelis had declined to look behind for years in an ongoing refusal to accept any responsibility for the refugees. Moreover, the publication of Morris's book coincided with the eruption of the first Palestinian *intifada*, an event that in and of itself led many Israelis to rethink hitherto sacrosanct viewpoints and re-examine Israeli history in a more critical way.

That is not to say, however, that Israelis had not previously grappled with the Palestinian issue. At the end of the 1948 war, S. Yizhar, a native-born Israeli writer published a short story that rocked the country and unleashed a wave of angry responses. For the first time, *Sippur Hirbat Hiza* (The story of Hirbat Hiza) brought to light the struggle for a new Jewish-Israeli identity in a young republic that had just begun to renew its links to the Jews' past as a persecuted people. The Israeli struggle now involved an attempt to integrate this history of oppression within a new moral code while facing up to such complex issues as self-government and the determination to survive.

Hirbat Hiza describes the expulsion by a platoon of Israeli soldiers of the residents of an imaginary Arab village toward the end of the War of Independence. Most of the residents escaped from the village before the Israeli soldiers entered, leaving only women, children and the old behind them. Yizhar depicts the soldiers as lacking any sense of empathy and apathetically obeying every order to "burn–blow up–detain–load on trucks–expel." When one of the soldiers complains to his commander about the treatment of the villagers, the officer tells him that new Jewish immigrants will quickly settle the place and till the soil, and everything will come right.[31]

In writing *Hirbat Hiza*, Yizhar expressed his clear disillusionment with his own moral failings during the war. "I was never in the Diaspora," he declares, "...but I was taught about it and reminded of it over and over again wherever I went, in every book and newspaper and in every place: exile.... What have we done here today? We, the Jews, have driven others into exile." Yizhar's writings were criticized but he was never called a post-Zionist. He was a Sabra, born and bred in the country and raised to believe in the Zionist dream of Jewish political independence. Yet he admitted to being shocked by the dilemmas faced by his young country as the Zionist dream of independence was turned into a reality that continually demanded sacrifices and moral compromises.

In fact, Yizhar was trapped between two worlds and ideologies – a contradiction that continues to animate the ongoing effort to create an Israeli national identity. He was raised in the prestate period on humanistic ideals and basic civil rights and truly believed that Jews and

Arabs could live together in dignity on the basis of a mutual commitment to create a better society while at the same time adhering to the Jewish entitlement to Eretz Israel. Indeed, his mostly friendly relations with his Arab neighbors strengthened his staunch optimism that the national conflict between Jews and Arabs could be peacefully resolved. He did not foresee that the Arabs would wage war in order to block the decision on partition; he did not anticipate the Palestinian exile that was to result from the war; and he struggled with the painful postwar reality which he believed to be justifiable even though he was unable to ignore the fact that this reality undermined his own fundamental moral code. This struggle continues to be evident in Israeli society even today.

Notwithstanding previous attempts at dealing with this issue, Morris's research of 1987 (revised in a second edition published in 2004)[32] proved to be a major watershed in the historiography of the Israel-Palestine conflict. This was the first comprehensive scholarly inquiry into the problem of the Palestinian refugees based on Israeli archives opened to researchers only a short while earlier.[33] From the 1980s onward, post-Zionist research was characterized by a conspicuous imbalance in the availability of primary sources: there were more and more revelations from documents found in Israeli archives, while from the other side there was no new information at all. There are no Palestinian Arab archives, and the Arab states involved in the Israeli War of Independence refused to open their archives to researchers because, among other things, they regarded their defeat in the war as a "national catastrophe" about which the less said the better.[34]

Morris's research discredited the long-accepted Israeli version of events according to which the Palestinians left their homes of their own free will or in response to the urgings of their own leaders.[35] At the same time, Morris's findings rebut the long-held Arab version of events according to which the flight of refugees from Israeli territory was the result of a preconceived Israeli strategy to "transfer" the Palestinian Arabs out of Israel.[36] The Zionist historians Shabtai Teveth and Anita Shapira adamantly claim that "transfer" was never a cornerstone of Zionist ideology,[37] a view confirmed by none other than Baruch Kimmerling, the leading post-Zionist sociologist. The occasional "abstract thought" about a transfer of Palestinians, Kimmerling admits, was not the reason for their departure from Israel's territory.[38] Rather, Morris concludes, this exodus was "essentially a result of the war."[39]

More specifically, the Palestinian exodus came in four phases. Phase one (December 1947 to March 1948) saw as many as seventy-five thousand upper- and middle-class Palestinians, predominantly from the mixed Arab-Jewish urban populations, fleeing the civil-war battle zones or sending their families abroad or to the area which, in time, would be called the West Bank. To quote Kimmerling and Joel S. Migdal:

> The week after the vote [on partition in the General Assembly of the UN] introduced another motif that would become familiar – the migration of Palestinians from their homes to places where they hoped they would be safer. Arabs from neighborhoods in Haifa and Jaffa were the first to look for a place of refuge until the fury abated. On the second day of fighting, a Haganah intelligence source reported on events in Jaffa's northern suburbs: "Empty carts are seen entering. Then carts loaded with belongings are seen leaving." Although Benny Morris notes that "abandoning one's home, and thus breaking a major psychological barrier, in the final analysis paved the way for the abandonment of a village or city and ultimately of the country," such barriers may not, in fact, have existed at all. As was seen in the course of the uprising of 1936–1939, the Palestinians had already created a highly mobile society that reflected frequent communal and economic crises. Moving to safe ground – particularly to home villages far away from areas of dense Jewish settlement – was a fixed pattern of behavior among workers in cities and on citrus plantations. This resembled the custom of the community's notables and business people to seek more peaceful places abroad in which they could reside....
>
> Beginning in December 1947...as militiamen on both sides tried to improve their positions, those on the fringes of neighborhoods and in isolated settlements came under heavy attack. Palestinians caught in the cross fire began seeking refuge,

as did Arabs living in predominantly Jewish neighborhoods. This resulted in two waves of displacement. Many wealthy citizens and others with the means at their disposal – mostly leaders from among the ranks of notables – found refuge abroad. Their flight from the most beleaguered cities with the densest Jewish populations – Jaffa (on the Tel Aviv border), Haifa and Jerusalem, landed them mainly in Lebanon, Egypt and Trans-Jordan. This group included a disproportionate number of Arab Christians – reawakening the Muslim suspicion that the Christians were not as committed as they were to the national struggle. The second wave consisted of the upper and middle classes, as well as many villagers from the Jerusalem area and the coastal plain, who tried to return to their villages or to reach wholly Arab populated cities such as Nazareth and Nablus....

Despite the opposition of the remnants of the Palestinian leadership – who from time to time consented only to the temporary evacuation of women, elderly men and children – the mass exodus of entire Arab families continued. It was also maintained in the absence, at this juncture, of a Zionist policy of forcibly expelling or evacuating Arabs, though instances of villages being intimidated did apparently accelerate the process. In March [1948] isolated but ominous forcible expulsions began.[40]

This exodus resulted in the closure of schools, clinics and hospitals, businesses and offices. That in turn led to rising unemployment and impoverishment among Palestinians – two additional factors responsible for the movement of the Palestinian population during this period.[41]

The second phase of the Palestinian exodus took place between April and June 1948. During this period there was a mass flight of 250,000–300,000 Palestinians from urban and rural areas that had fallen into the hands of the Israeli forces. At this point in time, the Haganah had began to implement "Plan Dalet" (plan D), a military strategy that was intended to defend the territory of the future Jewish state and remove all hostile elements from these areas. "While Plan Dalet...was not initially and directly designed for the purpose of expelling the Palestinians...

it gave field officers the freedom to root out and destroy clusters of hostile villages or forces that controlled vital access routes. But it was not this part of the plan that led to the massive exodus of April, May and June. Many Arabs fled the chaos and insecurity that engulfed the areas of intense fighting even before the Haganah commanders had to make those decisions."[42]

One after the other, the Arab neighborhoods of Haifa, Tiberias, Safed and Jaffa fell between April 18 and May 10. The flight from the larger cities created a wave of hysteria in the villages around them. The panic was exacerbated on April 9 by the military actions of Etzel and Lehi in the village of Deir Yassin in the approaches to Jerusalem. The number of Arabs killed in this action was at first greatly inflated. It remained a controversial issue with estimates of the number killed ranging between fifty and one hundred. Though the Haganah and the Yishuv's leadership strongly condemned the action, the immediate reportage of the incident in the Arab press was frenzied.[43] Haganah documents describe a "psychosis of flight" that had not been anticipated by the Jewish leadership; indeed, Jewish leaders were so taken aback by the exodus that many mistakenly believed that the mass flight had been planned in advance by the Arab leaders.[44] As the Zionist historian Yoav Gelber has noted: "Here and there Jews who had local contacts with Arabs tried to stop the exodus and persuade their friends to stay put…. In the beginning of May, at the height of the exodus, a broadcast in Arabic from Haganah's radio station called on the Arab population 'not to be afraid and not to flee. Do not cause yourselves hardship, humiliation and suffering. We are not like your extremist leaders preparing to throw you into the sea as they are planning to do to us.'"[45]

In the third phase, a ten-day period between the two ceasefires of July 1948, Israeli commanders compelled more than one hundred thousand Palestinians to move into those parts of the country that were in the hands of the Arab armies. Occasionally the Arabs were forcefully driven to cross the lines. Cities, towns and villages behind the line of Israeli forces fighting the Egyptian army and the Jordanian Arab Legion were seen as particularly dangerous for Israel because of the fear that their residents might attack Israeli forces from the rear. During this period, 60,000 Arabs from Lod and Ramle were exiled; in the bloodiest battle of the war 250 Arabs were killed in Lod.[46]

In the fourth phase (October–November 1948) Israeli forces expelled up to two hundred thousand Palestinians. As Yoav Gelber has written:

> In October 1948, the Israel Defense Forces (IDF) actively accelerated the flight. The *fellaheen* often held on to their villages or remained close by to them…. Unlike earlier escapees, they knew that fleeing would not be a temporary matter and would not save them from suffering. They also knew about the living conditions of the refugees in their own areas and beyond the front lines. Their awareness of the situation in Nazareth [whose Arab residents had been allowed to remain] lessened the fear that what had happened in Deir Yassin would be repeated. As a result there were numerous confrontations between Israeli soldiers and Arab civilians…. IDF soldiers forcibly drove them across enemy lines.

The relatively large number of atrocities in the Negev and the Galilee during the month of October 1948 requires an explanation. Blaming them on poor discipline doesn't work since the IDF's standards in this area actually rose with the passage of time. Given the sporadic and isolated nature of these incidents, and the lack of any definitive directives and clear orders to the forces involved, they cannot be said to be the outcome of some new policy. Since there were no authoritative instructions to the contrary, it is possible that unruly behavior by some IDF soldiers might have added fuel to the fire but that wasn't what ignited it.

Animosity toward the Palestinians – blaming them for the ongoing war – became more and more bitter as the fighting continued. At this stage of the campaign, the proportion of Holocaust survivors who arrived in Israel and were mobilized was greater than was previously the case. Many soldiers who arrived from Europe after World War II regarded the brutal behavior of the Red Army toward German civilians – whether they had themselves witnessed it or merely been told about it after the event – as a model for treating the civilian population of an enemy that was responsible for the war.[47] Anita Shapira points out that the Israeli expulsion of some of the Palestinian refugees stemmed from policies that became apparent on both sides of the divide.

On both sides, Arab and Jewish, there was a composite of flight and expulsion. Jews fled in fear from mixed neighborhoods such as the border areas between Tel Aviv and Jaffa and even from within Jaffa itself. There were some ten thousand Jewish refugees in the early stages of the war. Gush Etzion, on the road between Bethlehem and Hebron, was captured by the Arab Legion and local Palestinian forces; the inhabitants were killed or taken prisoner and carried across the Jordan. Their settlements were completely demolished. The settlements of Neve Yaakov and Atarot, north of Jerusalem, were also captured and totally obliterated. All the residents of the Jewish Quarter in the Old City in Jerusalem, conquered by local forces with the aid of the Arab Legion, were taken captive. No Jew was allowed to return to settle in the Old City – not even the ultra-Orthodox who detested Zionism and were prepared to live under Arab rule.[48]

In his latest research on the War of Independence, Benny Morris agrees with Shapira's assessment. The Palestinian refugee problem, concludes Morris, "was in part a product of expulsionist tendencies in the ideologies of both sides in the conflict.... Among the Zionists, it was a minor and secondary element. Though important Zionist leaders such as Ben-Gurion and Chaim Weizmann occasionally took to the idea and talked about it, it was not part of the original Zionist ideology and usually emerged only in response to some Arab act of violence... Zionist thought that supported expulsion stemmed...in part from the expulsionist and murderous thinking and behavior of Arabs and European Christians.... In the course of the 1948 war, clearly perceived by everyone on the Jewish side as an existential struggle, transfer never was part of accepted or declared Zionist policy even though there were expulsions and even though during the first months of the war there was an atmosphere that in time to come would be called ethnic cleansing."[49]

In July 1948, the Israeli government reached a fateful decision to prevent the refugees' return to their homes inside Israel. The decision was not sudden. It was the result of a process lasting several months. Arab states such as Jordan applied increasing pressure in demanding the repatriation of the refugees. However, to the Israelis it became apparent that such a move in the midst of a war would be dangerous not only for the Jews but also for the Arabs themselves, because of the possibility that they could become targets for acts of revenge. Ben-Gurion's conclusion was that the Jews had to provide the Arabs remaining in Israel with humane and civil equality but that the Jews need not be concerned with the return to their homes of those who had fled.[50]

The political pressure to allow the refugees' return continued to increase. The UN emissary Count Bernadotte called for their repatriation but the government of Israel stood its ground. The Israeli foreign minister Moshe Sharett, who was in favor of financial compensation for the refugees and humanitarian aid in their resettlement after the war, wrote to tell Bernadotte that Israel was not ignoring the distress of the Arabs. The Jewish nation had suffered too much from similar ordeals for it to be indifferent to the hardship of others. Israel, however, could not agree to the re-entry of the refugees into its territory.[51]

On several occasions in 1949, Israel agreed to return one hundred thousand refugees to their homes. While insisting that Israel had not intentionally expelled the Palestinians, Ben-Gurion reiterated that it was desirable that the refugees be resettled in the surrounding Arab states. At the same time he didn't foreclose the possibility that Israel would contribute to the solution by settling a part of them within its territory.[52] The Arab leaders, however, rejected the idea of a partial return of the refugees to Israel.

Moreover, objective circumstances ensured that a full or even a partial return of the refugees would soon prove to be an impossibility. Among other things, the massive influx of Jewish refugees and penniless Holocaust survivors doubled the Jewish population of the fledgling state and overwhelmed the state's institutions during the first years of independence. This created an urgent need to make use of the ready supply of land, jobs and housing that had been abandoned by the Arabs. By mid-1949 the government had wiped hundreds of Arab villages that had been emptied of their inhabitants off the map, and handed over their lands to new Jewish settlements. These settlements were under pressure to greatly increase their agricultural output so as to feed the flood of new immigrants.

The left-wing party Mapam didn't hide its opposition to these methods but their moral qualms weren't a barrier to them remaining in the provisional government led by Ben-Gurion until the end of its term in March 1949. Moreover, their refusal until 1955 to join the governing coalition was not connected to this issue. Essentially, Mapam was faced with ideological dilemmas that continue to plague left-leaning Zionist political parties to this very day. The party had exalted the need for Arab-Jewish coexistence yet at the same time established kibbutzim on abandoned Arab land. To ease the minds of Mapam's leadership, Ben-Gurion instructed the IDF's General Staff to issue the following guidelines on the treatment of the Arab population: In periods when there was no actual fighting, it was forbidden to destroy, burn or demolish Arab settlements; expel Arab inhabitants from villages, neighborhoods and cities; or uproot inhabitants from their places without special permission or explicit orders from the defense minister in each specific case. Anyone violating this order was to be put on trial.

Over 150,000 Palestinian Arabs (among them Muslims, Christians and Druze) remained within Israeli territory at the end of the War of Independence. With the exception of a short-lived Syrian proposal in 1949, Arab countries have consistently refused to resettle the refugees and have insisted that there will be no peace agreement without there being, first of all, a solution to the predicament of the refugees. The decisive reason for the creation of the refugee problem was the Arab refusal to accept the UN partition resolution of 1947. Had the Palestinian Arabs and Arab states accepted the resolution instead of waging war the course of history throughout the Middle East would have been entirely different.

Israel's victory in 1948 and in subsequent wars had a major impact on Israeli identity. Israelis began to view their identity as an expression of the embracement of force and the rejection of Jewish victimhood. They proudly saw themselves as representing the polar opposite of the discriminated against and downtrodden Jew; they were the vanquishers, not the vanquished; the persecutors, not the persecuted; the killers, not the killed. In opposition to this view there is a growing postmodern Israeli identity that is once more connecting to the world's oppressed peoples and distancing itself from the subjugation of the Palestinian people. The depiction of Israel as an entity born in sin has led to a tendency among various Israelis and Diaspora Jews to reject solidarity with Israel as an expression of Jewish identity.

A particular brand of historiographical and sociological analysis has appeared on the scene since the failure of the Oslo peace process in 2000 (at the Clinton-convened Camp David conference between Ehud Barak and Yasser Arafat). This analysis transcends the agenda of the New Historians: its purpose is to correct what it regards as factually erroneous perceptions of the Israeli-Arab conflict; this critique seeks to completely alter the "Zionist ethos and Israeli identity themselves." The roots of failed peace efforts and the continuing bloodshed, it is argued in these studies, are embedded in the fundamental cultural flaws of the Zionist project itself, flaws that must be confronted and put right.[53] This analysis, according to Adi Ophir, sets out to question both the Israeli-Jewish identity as well as the way in which that identity has been achieved. The analysis undermines the capacity of Zionist ideology to continue to construct and disseminate the Israeli-Jewish identity and denies the very validity of that identity.[54]

Motti Golani's autobiographical study *Milchamot lo korot me'atzman* (Wars don't just happen) begins with the provocative fundamental assumption that since its inception the Zionist movement has chosen force and power as the preferred means of achieving its aims. Furthermore, over the years, this choice has evolved into an all-encompassing militarized ethos that has effectively corrupted Israeli culture. The use of violence, argues Golani, was an integral part of the Zionist choice. That this was so was already clear in the 1930s. Although the prestate Zionist movement employed force hesitantly, the State of Israel since its founding has relished the use of force and has done so in ways that were not necessary from a rational or functional point of view. As a result, force has become a basic component of the Israeli ethos and collective identity.[55]

Yona Hadari's book, *Mashiach rachuv al tank* (Messiah rides a tank), examines a large range of works, written by scholars, authors, poets, journalists and political figures. These, claims Hadari, are representative of what she terms "public thinking" in Israel in which she discerns a clear pattern. In between the major wars (1956, 1967 and 1973), Israeli society was permeated by a pervasive pessimism, a sense of malaise and a loss of idealism that could only be shed by engaging in war. The early "realistic utopia" of the prestate pioneers had in fact given way to a militaristic public ethos that is personified by the image of the "messianic soldier" searching for a new utopia that is "messianic, secular but devout." In Hadari's view, Israel experiences an "eroticization of war" and is controlled by the image of the "fighting soldier as the lover of the land," whose "combative masculine romanticism" connects manhood with nationalism. Israel identity, Hadari concludes, has become inseparable from war and conquest.[56]

The basic argument in Idith Zertal's *Israel's Holocaust and the Politics of Nationhood* is that death and soldiers killed in combat have become the core components of collective Israeli identity. "The Holocaust and its millions of dead have been ever-present in Israel from the day of its establishment…in legislation, orations, ceremonies, courtrooms, schools, in the press, poetry, gravestone inscriptions, monuments, memorial books."[57] The Holocaust, argues Zertal, has served to justify not only the creation of a Jewish state but also its accumulation and employment of military might. The Holocaust produced "a new, or new-old, myth of destruction and redemption; of powerlessness and empowerment that was removed from both the historical and the political."[58]

These studies went beyond the boundaries of the original New Historians and their attack on particular aspects or periods of the Israeli collective memory. In contrast to such writings, these works have set out to challenge the totality of Israeli identity. Golani and Hadari focus on the cultural and moral traits that in their view have disrupted the Zionist project but do not challenge the project itself. Not so with Zertal, who seems to question the moral justification of Zionism as a whole.[59] Zertal is part of a clear trend of post-Zionist critiques that will be the subject of the following chapter.

POST-ZIONISM

P ost-Zionism is hard to define. It is a concept that encompasses a range of sometimes contradictory viewpoints and includes advocates who differ among themselves as to what precisely they are supporting. And yet it is still possible to confidently say that post-Zionism represents an ideological and cultural approach that seeks to strip Israel of its Jewish and Zionist characteristics.[1]

At the heart of post-Zionism is the thesis that Israel has to develop into a state whose institutions are oriented to the universal values of a liberal democracy whose citizenry shares a common civil identity without favoring one ethnic group over others. Post-Zionists argue that the cornerstone of Zionism is that Israel is a Jewish ethnic state founded in order to resolve the anomaly of the Jewish people and has to remain so if it is not to lose its raison d'être. This basic premise, say the post-Zionists, is incompatible with liberal democracy. In their view Israel can be either Jewish or democratic, but not both.

Zionists completely reject this proposition. The preference given to Israel's Jewish citizens, claim the Zionists, does not necessarily preclude it from being a democracy or acting fairly toward its Arab national minority. In this sense, they argue, Israel is no different than any other nation-state whose national identity includes an ethnic component. Israel's existence merely "normalizes" Jews by enabling them to be part of the common global process of incorporating ethnic identity within the fabric of a state. To this post-Zionists respond by saying that this was indeed the case among most democratic nation-states of the nineteenth century but is certainly not so today. Notwithstanding the exception of Yugoslavia, they argue, the emergence of multiculturalism and the politics of recognition led most liberal democracies to adopt more "civic" and "post-national" models of state identity.[2]

The historian Yosef Gorny has identified two forms of post-Zionism – one negative, the other positive. Moreover, he does so while recognizing the lack of uniformity among post-Zionists so that at times they do not slot into either of these categories or, alternatively, conform to parts of both. Negative post-Zionists, Gorny suggests, are in essence anti-Zionists because they reject the legitimacy or the historical necessity of Zionism as a Jewish national movement. In their view a liberal democracy can only come about following the total uprooting of Zionism, which they regard as colonialist and racist by its very nature. Positive post-Zionists, who are often labeled non-Zionists or a-Zionists, do not necessarily contest Zionism's historical role. However, they think that the movement has already achieved its basic objectives of establishing a Jewish state with a Jewish majority, a flourishing Hebrew culture, a highly developed economy and a mighty defense force. Given these facts, it is argued, Israel must now advance to the post-Zionist or post-ideological stage of development in which Jewish primacy is reined in and the symbols of a Jewish state are discarded.[3]

NEGATIVE POST-ZIONISM
According to the Israeli sociologist Uri Ram, negative post-Zionism includes elements of both postmodernism and post-colonialism. The postmodern approach does not regard post-Zionism as the logical outcome of a realized or developed form of Jewish nationalism because it doesn't view nationalism as a natural expression of peoplehood. Instead, postmodernists maintain, nationalism inevitably oppresses nations because it attempts to impose an artificial unique identity over peoples whose identities are constantly changing and shifting. Therefore, nationalism needs to be replaced by a multicultural "discourse" that combines differences and otherness.[4] A "recurring theme" among post-

Zionists of this stripe is "the need to open spaces for the voices of those who have been designated as the Other in Israeli society, including Diaspora Jews...."[5]

According to Ram, in addition to this identity-centered approach à la Foucault, postmodernist post-Zionism also includes a citizen-oriented approach as formulated by Jurgen Habermas that differentiates between ethnic and territorial nationalism.[6] This perspective rejects an ethnic Jewish state in favor of one that "represents a post-national concept of Israeli citizenship, or even of Israeli constitutional nationalism, de-linked from the Jewish (or any other) communal belonging."[7] Both the Foucauldian and Habermasian varieties of postmodernism focus on drawing a firm line between Jewish and Israeli identity. The former concentrates on maintaining autonomous Jewish identities in the Diaspora whereas the latter focuses on an all-inclusive autonomous Israeli identity that will confer legitimacy on a liberal-democratic Israeli state.[8]

The post-colonial approach views Zionism as an inherently Western phenomenon and clearly distinguishable from an Eastern post-Zionism that combines Arab-Palestinian and Jewish Eastern (Oriental) identities. Much influenced by Edward Said's magnus opus *Orientalism*, this approach reviles Zionism as a colonialist movement consisting entirely of white European Ashkenazi Jews who oppressed not only the native Palestinian Arabs but also Middle Eastern Jews (Mizrachim) – described by Yehouda Shenhav as "Arab Jews." Those holding such views envision a new post-nationalist solution that turns Palestinian Arab and Jewish Middle Eastern identities into a single hybrid identity[9] – a vision, as Ram points out, that is not shared by today's Palestinian Arab population. "Palestinians in Israel," writes Ram, "usually speak from a national point of view, rather than from a post-national one. Post-nationalism seems to be the privilege of well-established nations."[10]

The question of Zionism as an offshoot of colonialism (dealt with in detail in the following chapter) is the principal argument advanced by most negative post-Zionists. From the early 1980s, the New Sociologists – including Gershon Shafir, Baruch Kimmerling, Uri Ram,

Amir Ben-Porat and Ronen Shamir – depicted the Zionist movement as a classic colonial invader of a third-world country.[11] Ilan Pappé set himself apart from other New Historians (Benny Morris, Avi Shlaim, Tom Segev, Zeev Sternhell and Simha Flapan) by making the equation between Zionism and colonialism the cornerstone of his work.[12] Pappé, undoubtedly the most provocative and controversial of all these historians, utterly rejects "positivist" historical approaches that attempt to reach an objective truth based on empirical research. Instead, he adopts a relativist approach that, by design, rejects the monopolization of knowledge by those in power. "My leanings are clearly apparent," he writes, "despite the desire of my colleagues that I stick to facts and the 'truth' as I reconstruct the reality of the past, I view every such reconstruction as arrogant and impudent. I admit that my sympathy is with the colonized not the colonizer; that I support the conquered not the conquerors."[13] On the basis of his regarding Zionism as "both a national movement and a colonial project," Pappé calls for the dismantling of the Jewish state in favor of resolving the Israeli-Palestinian conflict by the establishment of a binational state.[14]

This approach places Pappé to the right of more and more negative post-Zionists who reject the very idea of Zionism being "a national movement that is competing with another, Palestinian, national movement, over its claim to the same territory."[15] In their view, Zionism is not simply one of a variety of nationalisms that include elements of exclusionary racism and must now rise to another level in the new multicultural world. Rather, "Zionism is often understood to be essentially different from all other nationalisms – as nothing at all but a mode of exclusion."[16] Nuances and contradictions in the historical record, suggests David Hirsh, do not generally fit in with this more radical way of thinking which tends to view Zionism in one-dimensional terms and equates its very nature with racism, Nazism or apartheid. "Left anti-Zionism is often adopted by people who consider themselves to be anti-essentialist yet it operates with a methodology that understands events as little more than the manifestations of Israel's racist, colonialist and totalitarian essences."[17]

Negative post-Zionism is part of a continuum of Jewish anti-

Zionism that was prevalent throughout the first half of the twentieth
century. This phenomenon has been well described by Anthony Julius:

> There have always been distinct strands in the Jewish objection
> to Zionism. It has been regarded as inconsistent with Jewish
> teaching (the *"religious objection"*), with Jews' obligations to
> their countries of citizenship ("the *patriotic objection*"), and with
> projects of universal emancipation both/either from capitalism
> (*"the leftist objection"*) and/or ethnic or religious particularism
> (*"the liberal objection"*).
>
> In the pre-1948 period, every one of these objections counted
> for a great deal. The religious objection existed in both Orthodox
> and Reform or Liberal versions. The patriotic objection, which
> was often advanced in tandem with the religious one, was made by
> substantial fractions of the Jewish communities of most Western
> European nations and of the United States. Indeed, antipathy to
> Zionism was one of the few positions…around which, in the early
> 1900s, most of American Jewry could rally.[18]

Western Jewry's opposition to Zionism remained very strong up until the
Holocaust and the establishment of the State of Israel. Since then, Jewish
anti-Zionism has weakened for a number of reasons. Most followers of
the "religious objection" were pacified when the non-Zionist religious
parties reached a modus vivendi with the new state; the "patriotic
objectors" changed their minds in light of the ever-increasing ability of
Diaspora Jews to support Israel without appearing to be unpatriotic to
their countries of domicile; finally, in the wake of the Holocaust, those
who subscribed to the "liberal" or "leftist" objection understood how
unrealistic it was to rely on non-Jewish or international solidarity.[19] As
Isaac Deutscher, who had lived his entire life in the anti-Zionist Yiddish-
speaking milieu of the Jewish internationalist left in Europe, declared in
1954: "I have, of course, long since abandoned my anti-Zionism, which
was based on a confidence in the European labour movement, or, more
broadly, in European society and civilisation, which that society and
civilisation have not justified."[20]

The determined anti-Zionists faded into the background of the post–

World War II Jewish community in the Diaspora. There they remained, says Anthony Julius, until around 1989 when

> the socialist project was all but abandoned and the radical transformation of society was ruled out of question. And it is at this moment that contemporary Jewish anti-Zionism emerges (though there were early intimations of its emergence in certain positions taken by Diaspora Jews on the 1982 Lebanon War). The leftist objections wither, while the religious objection is revived – though in radically reformulated terms. This new Jewish anti-Zionism inaugurates a return for many Jews to some kind of Jewish identity.[21]

Whereas earlier Jewish universalists embraced a form of cosmopolitanism that erased all semblance of a Jewish identity, these "new" universalists reconnected to a rejuvenated Jewish identity based on cosmopolitanism. They regard universalism and internationalism as fundamental Jewish characteristics.[22] Authentic Jewishness devoid of all the "trappings of linguistic, religious, and national identity" is, according to the British anti-Zionist Jacqueline Rose, "a striking self-definition of a modern secular Jew."[23] In the opinion of Rose and all who share her view, Jewish nationalism, indeed Jewish particularism as a whole, debases and warps authentic Jewishness.[24] This being so, Jews must aspire to sustain the Jewish trait of possessing no Jewish characteristics whatsoever. This aspiration was already fittingly described at the turn of the twentieth century by the Austrian Jewish writer Karl Kraus: "Through dissolution to redemption!"[25] Jews, wrote Kraus, must disband their petty particularism, be cleansed of "group and ethnic loyalty,"[26] and return once more to being the prototypes of a pure humanity. "Israel is a test of their commitment to a cosmopolitan identity," claims Anthony Julius. "Once, it was a test of their patriotism; now, it is a test of their freedom from all patriotisms – all loyalties smaller than to an indivisible human race."[27]

    Moreover, these new anti-Zionists have reformulated the "religious objection" of earlier generations and regard the abandonment of Israel as part of their unending pursuit of justice. The founding statement of the British anti-Zionist group Independent Jewish Voices calls for a return to the "tradition of Jewish support for universal freedoms, human rights and social justice.... Judaism means nothing if it does not mean social justice."[28] "Israel's actions," declared a Jewish group supporting a boycott of Israel, "betray Jewish ethical traditions."[29] Loyalty to Judaism, according to this group, requires a renunciation of Zionism and an end to Israel's centrality in post–World War II Jewish identity.

This new generation of Jewish anti-Zionists in the Diaspora has its ideological partners within Israel who, some time ago, created a minuscule movement. In 1962 two former members of the Israeli Communist Party (Maki), Moshe Machover and Akiva Orr, founded Matzpen (Compass). This voice could be heard in Israel up until the 1980s.[30] The cornerstone of Matzpen's anti-Zionism was the denial of Jewish peoplehood. In Akiva Orr's view, "the term 'Jew' is inseparable from a particular religious practice." A secular Jewish identity, insists Orr, has no meaning and is illegitimate.

The denial of Jewish peoplehood is also the position of Tel Aviv University historian Shlomo Sand. Sand rejects the "mythical view" held by ideological Zionists according to which the Jewish people have a common origin in an ancient "nation-race." Sand maintains that the Jews of our era are mostly the progeny of Russian, European and African converts to Judaism. The failure to properly understand this fact, adds Sand, has led to truly racist thinking.[31] Such ideas are common among the bulk of negative post-Zionists. As noted in a 1997 discussion paper on post-Zionism drawn up jointly by a group of Israeli and Diaspora Jews, "perhaps the most dangerous implication of post-Zionism is its denial of Jewish peoplehood."[32]

Similarly, the new anti-Zionists tend to dismiss contemporary European and Arab anti-Semitism as a trivial phenomenon and attribute any eruption of anti-Jewish hostility solely to Israel's sins.[33] Perhaps the most infamous proponent of these ideas is Gilad Atzmon. "Antisemitism" Atzmon claims, "is a spin...a myth...there is no such thing as antisemitism."[34] The trivialization of anti-Semitism or its denial apparently goes hand in hand with a tendency to avoid associating ideologies with the historical reality of the Holocaust. As David Hirsh sees it, contemporary anti-Zionists think that they are following in the footsteps of the Jewish anti-Zionist tradition that preceded World War II, but they have

> difficulty relating its tradition to the material, historical events of the twentieth century. What happened was that the perspectives of the European Jewish anti-Zionists were not only politically defeated by Nazism (not by "Zionism") but most of the anti-Zionists were also killed by Nazis. Jewish life and culture over large parts of Europe was removed.... It would surely be incomplete to understand events as the actualization of an unbroken thread of ideas and to neglect the huge material transformation that gave an entirely new context to those ideas.[35]

POSITIVE POST-ZIONISM

As already said, positive post-Zionists are basically non-Zionists who argue that "Zionism has done its job, with notable success, and that Israel must now move on to the next stage," becoming a post-ideological liberal-democratic state of all its citizens.[36] This process is frequently described as the "normalization" of Israel. The historian Robert Wistrich has said that this normalization appears to him to be "a very understandable human wish: an end to ceaseless sacrifice, to the kind of demands that living in Israel places on citizens, whether in terms of taxation or the number of days served in the army each year; an end to the levels of stress and anxiety."[37]

The post-ideological perspective, notes Uri Ram, sees Zionism "as a scaffold, which turns redundant after the building is accomplished." Similarly, in his famous essay *In Praise of Normalcy* A. B. Yehoshua likened Zionism to a climber, who ceases to be a climber once he scales the mountain. One can describe this as the most Zionist approach to post-Zionism or even as a Ben-Gurionist approach to this matter given its similarity to the position adopted by Israel's first prime minister vis-à-vis the Jewish Agency when he argued that with the establishment of the state the agency's role had ended.[38]

In Ram's view, post-Zionism of this sort represents an Israeli version of Daniel Bell's "end of ideology" thesis, noting also that it is in line with S. N. Eisenstadt's theory about the breakdown of the dominant elite's "original mold." "Eisenstadt may be thus termed a 'cognitive post-Zionist,' as distinct from a normative one, i.e., someone who recognizes the post-Zionist situation, even without being happy with it. A number of Israel's veteran Zionist intellectuals share this position with him."[39] It is an approach that emphasizes the natural evolution of "historical phases" in the process of nation building: nations naturally transition from an early "stormy nationalism" to a more mature and liberal "banal nationalism."[40] In the words of the Israeli journalist Amos Elon, "there is a need to move ahead to a more Western, more pluralistic, less ideological form of patriotism and citizenship. One looks with envy at the United States, where patriotism is centered on the constitution; naturalization is conferred by a judge in a court of law; identity is defined politically and is based on law, not on history, culture, race, religion, nationality or language."[41]

Laurence J. Silberstein adopted a broader definition of post-Zionism. In his view it is a "term applied to a current set of critical positions that problematize Zionist discourse, and the historical narratives and social and cultural representations that it produced."[42] It would seem that this definition includes Israel's New Historians who question long-held sacred Zionist positions regarding the War of Independence and Israel's conflict with the Arab world. For example, Meyrav Wurmser argues that these historians were "early post-Zionists" because they "challenged mainstream Zionist historiography as ideologically biased in employing research to prove the moral validity of the Zionist claims." Wurmser notes that post-Zionists do not make do with calling for Israel to withdraw to its pre-1967 borders but also question the "very existence of the state." In her view, those New Historians who favor a two-state solution and support Israel's right to exist must nonetheless be considered part of the continuum of post-Zionists because their purpose is to undermine Zionism's moral standing.[43]

Benny Morris, the most prominent and most prolific of the New Historians, utterly rejects Wurmser's argument. "I have never considered myself a post-Zionist. I am and always will be a Zionist,"

Morris insisted in an interview with the author. Asked what, in his view, Zionist identity now entails, his response was that to be a Zionist today meant to "maintain the struggle for the continued existence of the Jewish state."[44] Zeev Sternhell, whose research questioned many of the basic assumptions made by Labor Zionism in the course of its history, has likewise never challenged the historical necessity of Zionism or of Jewish settlement in Eretz Israel. Indeed, the noted Arab historian Edward Said wrote of his frustration with the "profound contradiction, bordering on schizophrenia" exhibited by Morris and Sternhell in refusing to draw the logical conclusion that necessarily flows from their own research.[45]

Similar ambiguities are evident in the support of certain post-Zionists or anti-Zionists for a two-state solution to the Arab-Israeli conflict.[46] The classic case in point is that of Noam Chomsky, a sort of icon in the eyes of left-wing and anti-Zionist critics of Israel. A member of the socialist Hashomer Hatzair movement in the 1940s, Chomsky enthusiastically embraced the movement's espousal, until 1948, of a binational state. "I was part of the Zionist movement," said Chomsky, "in fact, a Zionist youth leader, but I was opposed to a Jewish state, and that was part of the Zionist movement at the time. It was not the main part, but it was considered within the umbrella, so I could be an activist Zionist youth leader – the main thing in my life as a teenager – but opposed to a Jewish state, up until 1948." However, once Israel was established, Chomsky didn't challenge its existence and even lived and worked for a few months in Kibbutz Hazore'a – limiting himself, so he has said, to "eliminating the highly discriminatory elements internal to Israel, and of course opposing foreign conquest." After the Israeli victory in 1967 he was sure that Israel had been given "a fantastic opportunity" to advance toward peace with Egypt and Jordan "which basically agreed to peace within a couple of years" and to progress within Israel, the West Bank and Gaza "towards a kind of federal bi-nationalism, so two federalist units, kind of like Belgium in a way. One of them basically Jewish, the other basically Arab. Each would internally be discriminatory, there is no way of avoiding that, but that would be compensated by the fact that there is a paired society, and then they could become integrated." However, after the 1973 war, Chomsky abandoned his support of binationalism and backed the "international consensus" of a two-state solution with only a limited right for Palestinian refugees to return to Israel. "The only feasible settlement now," he declared in 2004, "is through the international consensus: a two-state settlement or something like it, on or near the international border."[47]

IMPLICATIONS OF POST-ZIONISM FOR THE DIASPORA

While negative post-Zionists have an ideological objection to the idea of a link between Israel and the Diaspora, positive post-Zionists object to such a connection primarily for practical reasons, arguing that it affects the standard of living and quality of life of Israel's citizens. In their persistent efforts to normalize their lives, Israelis instinctively distance themselves from the Diaspora and have a preference for "Israeliness" rather than "Jewishness" as an identity. As Danny Ben-Moshe points out, this is confirmed by empirical data.

> Asked in 1996 "How do you perceive yourself, firstly as an Israeli or firstly as a Jew?" 47.84 percent of trainee teachers for state secular schools replied that they saw themselves first and foremost as Jews, while the percentage of trainee teachers for state religious schools who answered in this way was 99.06. Similarly, 52.1 percent of teacher students for secular state schools, but only 0.94 percent of their counterparts training for state run religious schools, declared that their Israeliness took precedence over their Jewishness. This led researcher Dr. Yair Auron to conclude that national Jewish identity and attitudes towards the Jewish people in the past and present is a "vulnerable point in Jewish national identity and education of non-religious youth...who do not consider themselves in a deep, meaningful sense to be part of the Jewish people."[48]

This matter is also evident in the significant unwillingness of Israelis to support continued Jewish immigration to Israel or to make personal sacrifices for such immigration. In the 1990s, in response to the mass immigration from the former Soviet Union that began in 1989, many

Israelis exhibited a growing hostility, or at least an indifference, toward Diaspora Jewry. A poll conducted in June 1997 found that a third of Israelis "feared" the immigrants; more than 40 percent thought that the government was giving them too much, and 63 percent opposed the mass immigration from the former Soviet Union. Research by the Jewish Agency in 1994 revealed that no less than 51 percent of Israelis thought that Israel didn't need to take in more new immigrants.[49] Such anti-immigration feelings were also reflected in the views of Israel's environmental movement, which claimed that there was a clear conflict between immigration and the protection of Israel's environment. This led to a call in an Israeli nature journal for restricting immigration into the country.[50]

The Law of Return, described at the time by A. B. Yehoshua as "the moral foundation of Zionism"[51] has become the main target of both positive and negative post-Zionists. As Amos Elon concluded in 1996: "If the target that the Zionists have set themselves is to be accomplished soon, it could be argued that the Law of Return, as a form of 'affirmative action,' has also become redundant."[52] In line with this, Professor Asa Kasher, responsible for what has been dubbed a post-Zionist revision of the Israel Defense Forces' code of ethics, has said that henceforth Jews wanting to immigrate to Israel should be dealt with in the same way as requests for citizenship are processed in any other country.[53] Post-Zionists recognize the unlikelihood of an immediate complete severance from the Diaspora and suggest that Israel should promise to provide temporary refuge for Jews in danger. Kasher himself has proposed limiting the automatic right to Israeli citizenship to Jewish refugees who are oppressed in their native countries just for being Jews.[54] According to Danny Ben-Moshe, a revision of the Law of Return with such an insurance policy may, in fact, not be opposed by the American Jewish establishment. That, at least, is what he was told by Carl Sheingold, a senior analyst at the Council of Jewish Federations of New York who, in 1997, said that such a provision in Israeli law for Jewish refugees may make the cancellation of the Law of Return an acceptable proposition.[55]

Ben-Moshe argues that the failure of the Oslo process and the eruption of Palestinian violence in the second *intifada* in September 2000 have set this process back significantly and "led to a reinforcement of Israeli-Diaspora ties." But he adds that it would be reasonable to assume that this may prove to be only a temporary pause in the process and that the post-Zionist tendencies of Israelis in their daily lives would remanifest.[56]

In the meantime, however, it would appear that the rise of international terrorism and increasing existential fears in Israel have convinced and continue to convince more and more Israelis of their inability to be "normal." As a current joke in Israel has it, "Before 9/11 people in Israel said that they hoped Israel would start being just like the rest of the world, and after 9/11 it turns out that the rest of the world was becoming just like Israel."[57]

CHAPTER 10

ZIONISM: A PRODUCT OF COLONIALISM AND IMPERIALISM?

T he increasing tendency of liberal-progressive Jews and Israelis to distance themselves from Zionism and Israel, if not to expressly reject them, reflects a fundamental shift in Jewish identity. In growing numbers, Jews and Israelis refuse to be identified with the Jewish state seen by many in the world as having been "born in sin" and up to its neck in the systematic oppression of indigenous Palestinians. As one left-wing American Jew asked in anger "How have the Jews, immemorially associated with suffering and high moral purpose, become identified with a nation-state loathed around the world for its oppressiveness toward a subjugated indigenous people?"[1] This tendency has been reinforced by the increasing link being made in academic circles connecting Zionism and Israel with Western colonialism and imperialism.

Equating Israel and colonialism is not a new phenomenon. The first significant attempt at this was made by the French-Jewish historian, sociologist and Orientalist Maxime Rodinson in a celebrated 1967 article in Jean-Paul Sartre's journal *Les Temps Modernes.*[2] The major thesis of this article was published several years later in book form under the title *Israel: A Colonial-Settler State?*[3] This book quickly became one of the new left's standard texts promoting the delegitimization of Israel at a time when mainstream progressive circles had not yet embraced the Palestinian cause.

The establishment of Israel, Rodinson argued, "is the culmination of a process that fits perfectly into the great European-American movement of expansion in the nineteenth and twentieth centuries whose aim was to settle new inhabitants among other peoples or to dominate them economically and politically.... It is obvious that this was a colonial process with its own particular characteristics as well as many other additional traits."[4] While every colonial process is distinguishable by its own unique features, Rodinson argued, all situations in which occupation and persisting domination are combined can be defined as colonialist.[5]

Rodinson acknowledges that Jews who immigrated to Palestine had no imperialist motives and that their choice of country was not necessarily either colonialist or imperialist. "The element that made it possible to connect these aspirations of Jewish shopkeepers, peddlers, craftsmen, and intellectuals in Russia and elsewhere to the conceptual orbit of imperialism was one small detail that seemed to be of no importance: the existence in Palestine of another people."[6] The Jews, therefore, had no choice other than to seek the protection of an imperialist power to overcome the opposition of the indigenous population. It was the protection provided by imperial Britain that was to prove decisive in the process of establishing the Jewish state.

> The demand that independence be granted to the Yishuv only became conceivable in 1943 when the number of Jews in Palestine had reached 539,000 or 31.5 percent of the population as a whole. In 1922 [when the British were granted the Mandate by the League of Nations] they had been only 11 percent. The massive increase was only possible due to the protection of the British.... Mass Jewish immigration would have been inconceivable within an independent Arab state free from external pressures. During the period of the British mandate Zionist leaders were well aware of this and therefore called for the strengthening of the British police force in the country and opposed the creation of

any representative body that might, however slightly, reduce the authority of the British High Commissioner.[7]

In other words, mass Jewish immigration into Eretz Israel only became possible as the result of the forcible domination of the indigenous population following Britain's colonialist-imperialist occupation of the country.

According to Rodinson, the fact that the Jews did not exploit the Palestinian population is of no significance. This, he argued, is because even "if direct exploitation of the native population occurs frequently in the colonial world, it is not necessarily a constant characteristic of that world. Thus, for example, only in exceptional circumstances did the British settlers who colonized the territory that was to become the United States enslave members of the indigenous American Indian population."[8] In Rodinson's view, the Jewish settlement in Palestine is "colonialist" not because of its exploitation of the indigenous population but because of its domination of that populace.

Nor is it important to Rodinson's argument that the Jewish settlers rebelled against British rule after World War II. There was no alternative to such a rebellion from the moment Britain changed its policy in 1939 abandoning its support of unrestricted Jewish immigration and an eventual Jewish majority in Eretz Israel. But the rebellion, Rodinson suggests, was not inherently anti-imperialist or anti-colonialist; rather it has to be seen as a colonist rebellion against the mother country even though that is not where the settlers originally came from. Colonists, Rodinson adds, can be regarded as settlers even if their country of origin is not the mother country.[9]

Moreover, even the fact that the Zionists purchased the lands on which they settled during the mandatory period, and often bought the least fertile plots, does not absolve them from being classified as colonists. The "brutal confiscation of land," argues Rodinson, "is in no sense a fundamental characteristic of colonization. In fact, all over the world the purchase of land for settlement was accomplished more often than not by ostensibly legal transactions rather than by force.... In British Africa, for example, confiscation of land was a fairly rare occurrence.

Great Britain did not settle British colonists on lands belonging to Hindu peasants. And there are many more such examples, yet in all of them there is no doubt that we are talking about colonialism."[10]

Rodinson's aspiration was to achieve a reconciliation between Arabs and Jews. His hope was that once Israel had compensated the Palestinian refugees, the Arabs would adjust to the situation and accept Israel's existence. Only upon such acceptance, he argued, Israel would cease to be a "colonial" phenomenon.[11]

Rodinson's colonial model has been taken up by a number of Israeli post-Zionist scholars.[12] In their view, Israeli thinking has, for some time, suffered from mistakenly emphasizing Jewish history and Jewish nationalism (the "Zionist-centric" approach) or stressing the specific uniqueness of the history of Eretz Israel (the "Palestine-centric" approach). Such narrow and biased approaches, it is argued, often mislead scholars and result in their being influenced by subjective unscientific considerations (such as viewing genocidal anti-Semitism as a justification of Zionism). Instead, researchers should be using "concepts derived from theory and tools used in comparative research." This would enable objective presentation of Jewish immigration to Palestine in the context of universal patterns of immigration and settlement. It could be demonstrated definitively that Zionist settlement in Eretz Israel was no different from European colonial settlement in such places as South Africa and Algeria.[13] In 1983, Baruch Kimmerling, a sociologist at the Hebrew University of Jerusalem, became the first Israeli academic to compare Zionist settlement with colonial settlements in the United States, Africa, Australia and other parts of the world, thereby branding Zionism a colonialist movement. Kimmerling deliberately avoided discussing the moral right of Jewish immigrants to settle or establish a national state in Eretz Israel – insisting that such justifications of Zionist settlement belonged to "the realm of philosophy, international law, ideology, theology, or political science."[14]

Yet another Israeli sociologist, Gershon Shafir, broadened and elaborated on Kimmerling's colonial model. Shafir acknowledges that Zionism was "a variety of Eastern European nationalism, that is, an ethnic movement in search of a state." However, like Kimmerling,

Shafir thinks that the best way of understanding Israel and Zionism is by comparing it with other European colonial-settler societies that clashed with indigenous populations. Shafir rejects "inward-looking" historicist interpretations of Jewish history that seek to provide an explanation of Zionist values and ideology. According to Shafir, it is the conflict with the Palestinian people that has, in fact, been the most decisive element in shaping Zionism and in the creation of a collective Israeli identity.[15] Shafir focuses on the implications of Zionist settlement for Palestinian society, rather than on the causes or motivation of the settlers for being there.[16]

Unlike Rodinson, Shafir accepts that Zionism does not exactly correspond to European colonial models given that it lacked a metropolis (mother country), had a clear national character of its own and was not interested in capitalistic expansion. Nonetheless he insists that since Zionism's aim was "the creation of a homogeneous settler-immigrant population" its place is firmly within the colonial camp.[17] In Shafir's view one must, therefore, look at every aspect of Zionist activity through the prism of colonialism. Thus he claims, for example, that Zionists' real motive in modernizing Eretz Israel and encouraging Jewish labor was not to normalize the Jewish society's economy there (as the promoters of Jewish Enlightenment had attempted to do in Europe), but rather to dispossess the indigenous Arab inhabitants. This is the context, according to Shafir, in which even the most progressive aspects of Zionist activity, such as the creation of kibbutzim, must be viewed.[18]

Critics of the "Zionism is colonialism" thesis base their reservations on a number of grounds. This detached comparative model, say some left-wing or progressive Zionists, ignores the motives of the Zionist settlers. It coolly analyses the "how" of Zionist settlement but refuses to explore its "why." To do so requires one to shed all sense of empathy for the plight of the Jewish people in the Diaspora, a plight that has become so anchored in Jewish identity. These critics assign a moral relevance to the motives for Jewish settlement. It is, of course, perfectly reasonable to argue that the motives of a benevolent dictator do not in any way justify the dictator's use of force to strip his people of their freedom.[19]

There is only one moral justification, says A. B. Yehoshua, for entering a country by force and against the wishes of the indigenous population: that it is the invader's only hope of survival. In Yehoshua's view, survival entails not only refuge from persecution, something which at times was offered to European Jewry in places other than Palestine, but also political sovereignty.

In the modern age, especially since the "Spring of Nations" of 1848, national consciousness began to crystallize to the point that an independent sovereign framework became the necessary condition for the survival of every people. As more and more nations gained sovereignty and declared their independence, the need to achieve such independence became increasingly pressing for those nations that were not yet sovereign. As long as there were still multinational empires united under either a monarchy or the church, various nations were able to waive the need for an independent state. But as soon as the state, as such, became an instrument of national unity with a powerful, secular, framework, every nationality was forced to opt for self-determination in order to ensure its survival. At the end of the nineteenth century, many nations lived within the boundaries of their historical homeland but had not yet reached the stage of self-determination; the independence of these nations became vitally important.

But there were two or three nations that found themselves in an even more grievous situation. They not only lacked sovereignty, but a homeland as well. I shall not go into a detailed historical explanation of why peoples such as the Armenians, the Gypsies and the Jews wandered the world for hundreds of years without having a homeland in which they could live as the majority, but suffice it to say that in the modern world of nationalism the situation of a people without a homeland becomes extremely dangerous. Firstly, this is because the lack of sovereignty deprives a people of the ability to defend itself and take responsibility for its fate. Moreover, being dispersed among other nations greatly increases the potential areas of friction with other peoples. Finally, the fact that a nation's members are not concentrated within a particular territory means that it does not even possess the territorial power of a minority living in the midst of a majority. A people without a homeland is not a minority but an alien group. From an existential perspective, the difference between these two categories is significant.

A. B. Yehoshua thus asserts:

> Absolute proof of how dangerous this situation is was provided in the course of the twentieth century by the holocaust of the Armenians during the First World War as well as by the holocausts of the Jews and Gypsies in World War II.... The right of survival, a constant refrain throughout Jewish history but tested to its ultimate with the creation of secular national states, gave the Jewish people (as it did the few other peoples without a homeland) the moral right to seize, even by force, a part of any other country in the world in which it could establish a sovereign state of its own.[20]

The Israeli writer Amos Oz also relates to this issue and suggests a useful metaphor. In his view, the Zionist right to the land can be compared to that of a drowning man who grabs the only available raft even if it means crowding those already sitting on it to make room for himself, provided that all he asks of them is to accommodate him and does not demand that they get off the raft or drown in the sea. The version of Zionism that wants a part of the land has morality on its side; the Zionism that demands that the Palestinians relinquish their identity and give up the whole country has no moral justification.[21]

The "raft," Oz suggests, symbolizes not only a place of refuge but also political sovereignty. He indeed recognizes that as a secular atheistic Jew he cannot use the analogy of the "drowning man" to justify settlement by force in Eretz Israel rather than in some other place on earth. And yet he considers this specific territory as crucial to the argument. Why here of all places? he asks. His answer is that it is to here and only to here that the Jews could have gone to establish their independence. In no other territory could Jewish independence have been established because here is the focal point of all their yearnings.[22]

In any event, Oz, Yehoshua and other progressive Zionists recognize that the "rightness" of Zionism doesn't mitigate the Palestinian outrage at the historical injustice that they believe Zionism has inflicted upon them; hence the view of the progressive Zionists that this is a tragic clash between two opposing rights and their hope that reconciliation and Palestinian independence will help find a remedy for the consequences of this conflict. A champion of this viewpoint is the Israeli peace activist Uri Avnery who has written:

> The burning desire of the founding fathers of this movement was to save the Jews of Europe, where the dark clouds of hatred for the Jews were gathering. In Eastern Europe, pogroms were raging, and all over Europe there were signs of the process that would eventually lead to the terrible Holocaust, in which six million Jews perished.
>
> This basic aim attached itself to the profound devotion of the Jews, throughout the generations, to the country in which the Bible, the defining text of our people, was written, and to the city of Jerusalem, towards which the Jews have turned for thousands of years in their prayers.
>
> The Zionist fathers who came to this country were pioneers who carried in their hearts the most lofty ideals. They believed in national liberation, freedom, justice and equality. We are proud of them. They certainly did not dream of committing an injustice of historic dimensions.
>
> ALL THIS does not justify what happened afterwards. The creation of the Jewish national home in this country has involved a profound injustice to you, the people who lived here for generations....
>
> We cannot ignore anymore the fact that for 60 years of conflict and war, you have been prevented from realizing your natural right to independence in your own free national state.... For all this, we owe you an apology.[23]

Oz and Avnery touch on the critics' second objection to the "Zionism is colonialism" theory. The Jews, they point out, didn't settle in some randomly chosen country for exploitation; essentially they were motivated by the idea of a return to their homeland. For this they were willing to make every conceivable material sacrifice. "From the perspective of the individual," Ran Aharonson argues, "the Jewish immigrant-settler reaching Eretz Israel, saw himself as returning to his one and only ancestral homeland – without minding its impoverished state and with only low expectations, if any, of improving his personal economic conditions. Thus, the Jewish settlement in Eretz Israel differs from all other known immigrant settlements. For example, the English migrant set sail for Australia without there being any ideological or national link to the country of his destination. This was even more so if viewed from a collective perspective: Jewish settlement in Eretz Israel is a unique example of a dispersed people returning to its historical territory."[24]

A major voice emphasizing the historical Jewish link to Eretz Israel was that of Samuel (Shmuel) Katz – a writer, historian and journalist, close to Jabotinsky and Begin and a member of Israel's Knesset. His central thesis was that "the Jews were never a people without a homeland."[25] Throughout their years in the Diaspora, said Katz, the Jewish people maintained an unwavering connection with Eretz Israel and never stopped dreaming of their return to that land. Jews regularly referred to their lost land in their daily prayers, in all their religious holiday ceremonies and in their life-cycle rituals. Despite their incessant wanderings from country to country and from one climate to another, they continued to celebrate all the holidays according to seasonal changes in Eretz Israel. Across the generations, that country was referred to by Jews simply as Ha'aretz (The Land) to denote their natural and self-evident connection to this territory.[26]

Samuel Katz also maintained that the continuity of Jewish life in Eretz Israel was beyond doubt. As evidence of this he cites the distinguished Christian scholar James Parkes: "The Zionists' real title deeds," Parkes claimed, "were written by...the heroic endurance of those who had maintained a Jewish presence in the Land all through the centuries, and in spite of every discouragement."[27] Katz methodically traces the Jewish presence in Eretz Israel from the time of the destruction of the Second Temple and the Roman suppression of Jewish political independence in Eretz Israel. Jewish wanderings from country to country, according to Katz, did not begin until the crushing of the Bar

Kochba revolt of 135 CE in which no less than 580,000 Jews perished and 985 Jewish villages were destroyed.[28] Only then did the Romans succeed in putting an end to Jewish political independence in Eretz Israel. It was then that the Roman emperor Hadrian changed the name of Jerusalem to Aelia Capitolina, building a Roman colony of this name over the ruins of Jerusalem. He also changed the name of the Judean province by combining it with the Syrian province into the larger Syria-Palaestina province.

Nonetheless, Jewish life in the country continued (even though the center moved from Jerusalem to the Galilee) and Jewish spiritual creativity blossomed. The Mishnah, a compilation of orally transmitted Jewish law, was completed in Eretz Israel in the year 200 CE. A supplement to the Mishnah and the Jerusalem Talmud followed and were completed at the beginning of the fifth century CE.

The Roman Empire, which embraced Christianity in the fourth century, was determined not to allow Jewish political independence in Eretz Israel, in part as a punishment for the Jews having rejected Christ. But the Jewish community that remained in Eretz Israel refused to give up on the idea of a Jewish national homeland. A further revolt that erupted in 351 CE was brutally crushed after a year of fighting but managed to establish a continuing pattern of Jewish allegiance to Eretz Israel.

The hope of restoring Jewish independence in the homeland led the Jews to assist the Persian invasion of Palestine in 614 CE and fight alongside the forces of the Persian army. The Jews continued to maintain a presence in Eretz Israel over the course of some 450 years of Muslim rule that began in 640 CE and fought with the Arabs against the invading Crusaders. During the period of Crusader rule, the number of Jews in the country declined but a presence was nonetheless maintained throughout. There is historical evidence of their continued presence following the Mongol invasion of the country in 1260, as well as after the defeat of the Mongols by the Mamluks, who invaded from Egypt in the same year and ruled the country until 1516.[29] With the conquest of the country in 1516 by the Ottomans, the Jewish community began to flourish and though their numbers fluctuated, a continuous presence was maintained until the beginning of the Zionist settlement at the end of the nineteenth century.

A third criticism of the comparative model focuses on the mistaken deductive linkage that is made between the historical background that led to Zionist settlement in Eretz Israel and the events that gave rise to the various European colonial-settler communities in North America, South Africa, Algeria and other places. The latter came from developed nations central to the development of commercial, and later on, industrial capitalism; in contrast, almost all the Zionists who emigrated to Eretz Israel were from developing countries, firstly from eastern Europe and later from the Middle East itself. These were countries experiencing the systematic disintegration of their traditionalist societies under the assault of Western economic penetration. This disintegration undermined the social order in the rapidly changing societies as a result of the sudden disappearance of the old ways of life. More often than not the first victims of this process of disintegration were the nonindigenous minorities: they became the lightning rods for the social agitation surrounding them.[30]

The vulnerable nonindigenous minorities included Jews in eastern Europe and the Middle East, Indians in Africa, and ethnic Chinese in Southeast Asia and Indonesia. All these minorities functioned as entrepreneurial middlemen; they were an alternative to a middle class in neofeudal or premodern agricultural societies whose feudal landlords preferred nonindigenous minorities to a nascent native middle class. But as soon as the economic penetration of Western powers forced these societies to modernize and develop their economies along capitalist lines, the nonindigenous minorities were considered superfluous. A mass of displaced eastern European peasants lost their livelihoods because of the inflow of cheap Western imports. In consequence, they flooded cities and towns with substantial Jewish populations near their disintegrating communities and became the bedrock of various xenophobic nationalist movements seeking to replace Jewish entrepreneurs with people from the indigenous majority. Thus, whereas European settlers were the beneficiaries of Western European colonialist economic expansion, the Jews were unquestionably its victims.[31]

A similar situation developed in the Middle East, the main source of immigration to Israel after 1948. The creation of Israel may have exacerbated a rapidly deteriorating situation but was not the cause of it. Jews, and other minorities in the Middle East were quicker to abandon their traditional way of life than were the Muslims. They adopted Western ways and developed contacts abroad. A new bourgeoisie sprouted, made up of minorities that included Greeks, Armenians, various other Christian sects and Jews. Their position as middlemen, their economic success and their links with the West provoked hostility toward them from within the Muslim majority. They were therefore forced to rely on the protection of foreign governments which still further estranged them from the majority.

When Arab societies embarked on a process of modernization and embraced a xenophobic nationalism that aimed at ending minority "privileges," the Jews, together with a number of other ethnic minorities, found themselves being pushed to the sidelines. It was in Iraq that the entrepreneurial minorities suffered most from these developments. There, the Arab majority repeatedly and savagely attacked the Kurds and Assyrians. One of the peaks of this brutality was the infamous massacre of the Assyrians by the Iraqi army in 1933. By the mid-1940s the position of all minorities in the Arab states of the Middle East had become increasingly insecure.[32]

These developments led, in general, to minorities being driven from their homes. They were forced to look elsewhere for both security and livelihoods. Being compelled to settle in another place almost always required cooperation of some kind with countries powerful enough to be able to help them emigrate. The "solution" in the case of the Armenians was to remove them from their homes and repatriate them to an autonomous Armenian state in the Soviet Union. A similar procedure of "dispossession and resettlement" was also to be the fate of the East Indians in Uganda and the ethnic Chinese in Indochina. But in all these instances the persecuted minorities had, at least in theory, somewhere to return to. In complete contrast to this, the Jews had to re-establish their homeland which, inevitably, led to the dispossession of others.

The forcible dispossession of persecuted minorities leads us to the fourth objection posed by the critics of the model that equates Zionism with colonialism. Ran Aharonson points out that historical geographers consistently draw a distinction between two very different phenomena: colonization and colonialism. "Colonization is fundamentally a geographic phenomenon, whose essence is emigration to a new country and the establishment there of immigrant settlements that differ from the existing settlements in that country. Colonialism, on the other hand, is a political and economic phenomenon, the essence of which is the imposition of one country's control over a territory and a population beyond its own borders and their exploitation for the benefit of the conqueror."[33]

There are cases, says Aharonson, of colonization that does not involve colonialism. Examples of this are the migration of Jews from eastern Europe to Argentina with the aid of philanthropic organizations, or the spontaneous mass migration of Italians to Tunisia that occurred without governmental support or sponsorship. Similarly there are cases of colonialism without colonization, such as Belgian control over, and activity in, the Congo, the French in Morocco or the British in Sudan. These countries established colonial regimes without creating settlements of Belgian, French or British nationals. There are also cases of colonization within colonialism, where certain groups of people (the Dutch in South Africa, Germans in Australia and Ukrainians in Canada) migrated to Western colonies to set up their own settlements without obtaining the support of the colonial government. Finally, there are instances of colonization through colonialism such as "the settling of the French in French Algeria, of the Italians in Italian Libya, or of the Germans in the areas of Poland annexed by Germany; in all these cases the process of populating the conquered areas was an instrument of the foreign regime."[34]

Proponents of the comparative model who link Zionism to all other colonial projects fail to distinguish between these four categories; indeed their reductive methodology ignores the fundamental differences between colonization and colonialism and in many instances uses the two terms interchangeably as if they are synonymous. As a result, they fail to place Zionism where it rightfully belongs: in the category of colonization without colonialism.[35]

Not only did the explicit components of colonialism (conquest, economic exploitation, domination of the centers of power) not exist at the beginning of Zionist activity in the country, very few of the characteristics associated with "exploitative settlement" can be found either. Such settlement relies on privileges granted by the ruling power, and the focus of the settlers and their supporters is the exploitation of local natural and human resources for the sake of monetary gain. Neither of these characterized Jewish settlement in Eretz Israel during the Ottoman period. On the other hand, research shows that Jewish settlement in Eretz Israel at that time fitted in many respects with the model of "settlement of population" (*colonization de peuplement*) which should be categorized as colonization without colonialism.[36]

Aharonson does concede, however, that "Zionist settlement during the British Mandate bore the hallmarks of colonization within colonialism"[37] – a fact that somewhat complicates the picture but doesn't change his thesis that there is no basis for categorizing Zionist settlement as colonialism.

These important qualifications notwithstanding, it remains the case that a certain view of Israel's aggressive actions after 1948 reinforces a growing alienation from Israel among some Jews. This is no doubt aided and abetted by the enduring and widely held idea that Zionism, Israel and Western imperialism are as one. Boaz Evron, a former member of the Canaanite movement, and latterly one of the leading lights of post-Zionism, readily admits that the Zionist movement was indeed guilty of "colluding with imperialism." But he insists on putting things in their "proper context." "Everybody in the Middle East, Jew and Arab, was connected at one time or another with imperialistic powers. All movements of national liberation sought the support of the big powers and those who failed to attract such support, Biafra for example, were generally doomed to failure. And big powers are also, by definition, imperialistic if, indeed, they extend their influence beyond their national boundaries, as they always do. If they didn't they would have no active interest in aiding such movements; they will not aid national liberation movements unless such movements, in some way, serve their own self-interests. This is elementary politics." Moreover adds Evron, many fail to remember a key fact about the Arab-Israel conflict: "The imperialists…were always more interested in allying themselves with the Arabs than with the Jews, because of the incomparably greater resources of the Arabs in terms of land, population and mineral wealth. This is the reason why Western oil companies are unambiguously pro-Arab. The fact of Israel's development and survival becomes even more impressive considering that the imperialists generally opposed Israel."[38]

Yet it would appear that the critics of revisionist post-Zionism are losing the argument against an increasing tendency to delegitimize Israel and Zionism in academic circles throughout the Western world. This is having a profound impact on Jewish identity among those with progressive and liberal views both in Israel and among Diaspora Jewry. It would seem that there is a growing consensus among those who distance themselves from the "violent Israeli hooligan" and identify with the oppressed Palestinian "underdog," as is reflected by the words of the left-wing Jewish American cited at the beginning of this chapter. "Jews were supposed to know better, to be better," he lamented. "Suffering persecution and being eternally on the margins of Europe were supposed to have made Jews more morally developed."[39]

In ever-growing numbers, Jews seem to think that the concept of Jewish identity has come full circle. Jewish powerlessness and the marginalization of the Jewish people before and during the Holocaust were, at one time, widely seen as painful cautionary tales that must "never again" be repeated. Today, past Jewish powerlessness and the marginalization of Jews in the not very distant past are being viewed as qualifying Jews and even obliging them to once again identify with the powerless and the marginalized.

CHAPTER 11

JEWISH SOVEREIGNTY AND DEMOCRACY

Israel's character and the question of its identity have been the source of profound controversy since its establishment as a state. A liberal democratic state? A Jewish state? A democratic state of all its citizens or an ethnic Israeli-Jewish state? Each of these possible options arouses sharp disagreements. There are those who oppose rigid definitions and the differing realities they lead to, insisting that the country's national identity is continually evolving. Others seek stability by an adherence to a rigorous and impenetrable delineation of Israeli identity.

The sociologist Sammy Smooha claims that Israel, as a sociological concept, is a novelty – an "ethnic democracy." According to Smooha:

> The current literature on comparative politics distinguishes three types of democracy: Liberal, consociational, and *Herrenvolk* [the democracy of a master race]....
>
> In a *liberal democracy*, such as the United States, ethnicity is privatized. The state does not legislate or intervene in ethnic cleavages, but forges a homogeneous nation-state by setting up uniform language, identity, nationalism, and national institutions for its citizens....
>
> In a *consociational democracy*, such as Belgium, ethnicity is accepted as a major principle in the organization of the state.

Individuals are judged on merit and accorded civil and political rights, but ethnic groups are also officially recognized and granted certain rights, such as control over education and allocation of public posts on a proportional basis. The state is not identified with any one of the constituent groups and tries to reconcile the differences between them. Ethnicity is thus institutionalized and ethnic identities and institutions are usually kept separate....

In *Herrenvolk democracy*, democracy is confined to the master race or group and is forcibly denied to other groups.[1]

According to Smooha, there is general consensus among scholars that a master race democracy does not in fact qualify to be defined as a democracy. On the other hand, ethnic democracy institutionalizes the control of the majority ethnic group over the state, grants civil and political rights to individuals, and ostensibly bestows collective rights to minorities. Such a construct can therefore be said to be "located somewhere in the democratic section of the democracy-non-democracy continuum."[2]

In an ethnic democracy such as Israel (or Canada between 1867 and the Quiet Revolution of the 1960s, Northern Ireland from 1921 to 1972, Poland from 1918 to 1939, and Malaysia since the early 1970s) the state, inspired by ethnic nationalism, is identified with a "core ethnic nation" and not with its citizens. It strives to create a homogeneous nation-state for the majority ethnicity. It encourages this majority to develop its culture, language, economy and demographic dominance, and treats minorities as second-class citizens who are to be feared as a threat, kept under the control of the state, and excluded from exercising institutional power. But at the same time the state grants these minorities the right to vote and enables them to work peacefully toward improving their civil rights.[3] Accordingly, says Smooha, one has to distinguish between ethnic democracies and nondemocratic "ethnic states" such as Syria, Iraq before 2003, Ethiopia and Burma. On the other hand, Israel, "often considered to be a unique case," can serve as a model of a viable ethnic democracy for those ethnic states that were established on the ruins of the Soviet bloc.[4]

The post-Zionist geographer, Oren Yiftachel, rejects Smooha's analysis and claims that Israel is an ethnocratic state in the sense that it seeks to further strengthen the position of one ethnic group at the expense of another. He unflatteringly compares Israel to Estonia, another ethnocratic state, and to Greece and its attempt to eradicate the influence of its Turkish minority.[5] Smooha's response is that the comparison with Estonia is factually inaccurate because Estonia does not grant its Russian minority citizenship rights whereas Israel does grant such rights to its Arab minority. Israel, he admits, will never be a liberal democracy, since it assigns its Jewish majority a "certain advantage." But any attempt to change Israel's Zionist character, Smooha argues, would inevitably lead to an impasse because the Jewish majority will never accept such change. Instead, he argues, all those who seek Arab-Jewish reconciliation should focus on improving and reenforcing Israel's democratic makeup and tempering Jewish dominance without dismantling the Jewish state. This is a process that has gained momentum as the state has matured and, so Smooha hopes, peace would further bolster this trend.[6]

Shulamit Aloni, a former member of Knesset and government minister, does not share Smooha's optimism. Israel, she claims, has become a highly discriminatory ethnocratic state. This was not always the case in the period prior to the establishment of the state, says Aloni. Under Ottoman rule, the *millet* system ensured representation and autonomy to many of the religious and ethnic groups living in Eretz Israel under the Sultan's rule. Aloni stresses the liberal character of the *millet* system that not only recognized all the religious ethnic groups but also left them with the choice of whether or not to participate in the system. Every religious-ethnic group was given juridical authority in matters involving religion whereas civil matters that affected all groups were dealt with in civil courts. When the British mandate was established in 1922, the leadership of the prestate Yishuv chose to persist with the *millet* system. The Jewish leadership took advantage of the autonomy that the system provided in order to develop prestate civil institutions. Yet at the same time this was also the means of laying the foundations for future religious control.[7]

In 1953, says Aloni, the religious parties in Israel's Knesset succeeded in applying sufficient political pressure to ensure the introduction of a new system. Since then, it has been enshrined in the country's law that all Jews living in Israel were to be regarded as a closed religious society subject to the authority of the state-appointed chief rabbinate. This legislation has its roots in the months preceding the formulation of the partition plan and the vote at the UN General Assembly (November 29, 1947), when the Yishuv was engaged in an intense diplomatic struggle to secure the required vote. The leaders of the ultra-Orthodox anti-Zionist Agudat Israel party took advantage of the Yishuv's plight by presenting Ben-Gurion with an ultimatum: if a "religious settlement" as to how life was to be organized in the planned Jewish state was not reached, they would publicly demonstrate against the establishment of a Jewish state and work to prevent a positive outcome in the General Assembly. Fearing violent Orthodox protests and the defeat of the partition resolution at the UN, Ben-Gurion succumbed to the blackmail of the Orthodox. As a result a "status-quo" agreement was signed that gave the Orthodox community an independent educational system funded by the state, an exclusive say in all matters concerning the observance of the Sabbath and *kashrut* and control of family law (marriage and divorce) in Israel's Jewish community.

As Aloni points out, the agreement included the important qualification that freedom of religion would be honored in the new state and that there was no intention of creating a Jewish theocracy. Nonetheless, to this day, Israeli laws relating to personal status and freedom of religion contradict basic liberal principles. Among other consequences, this situation is the source of tension with Jewish communities in the Diaspora. For example, Israel's population registry law does not permit Jews to simply register themselves as Israeli citizens and no more, but compels them to register as Israeli citizens of Jewish nationality. This is very different from the position in the Diaspora where the national and religious affiliation of Jews (and all other minority groups) is entirely a matter of personal choice.[8]

Over the years, Aloni explains, innumerable attempts have been made to formulate a written constitution. Those in favor claim that it is a necessary condition for guaranteeing individual and ethnic rights in the country. But fear of the response of the Orthodox community has time and again frustrated these initiatives. Aloni bitterly laments the opportunity that was missed to set up a liberal civil system of governance when the state was first established. "It seems that there were opportunities to build the exemplary society we had dreamed of," she writes, "a society in which the individual mattered, a genuinely democratic society, free of racism, of hatred of the other, of past fears, and free of a self-image of the ultimate victim for whom everything is permissible.... I want to be 'Israeli,' I don't want religion imposed on me by rabbis. Culture – yes. History – yes. Religion and rabbis – no!"[9]

The "new sociologist" Baruch Kimmerling has expressed views similar to those of Yiftachel and Aloni. Kimmerling asserts that the term "democracy" has been variously defined and interpreted; many democratic systems differ from each other and there are no axiomatic definitions of the term. But one cannot classify a state as democratic unless it conforms to five essential criteria: that it conducts periodic free elections; that the sovereignty of the nation be in the hands of an elected legislature; that there be equal citizenship and an equality that includes citizens' rights; that there be a system of universal and egalitarian suffrage; and that the civil and human rights of the minority be protected against the tyranny of the majority. Conditions in Israel led Kimmerling to the conclusion that "it is easy to conclude that only one of the five necessary conditions for considering Israel a democracy is present." In his view this situation mainly stems from "the basic nature of the Israeli state. Israel was founded as a frontier land of immigrant settlers...and its founders were mainly of a different ethnic, religious and cultural background to that of the broad local population." Israel, as a result, is "intrinsically unable, from an historic point of view, to separate religion from nationality and from the nationalism that is implicit in the 'Jewishness' of the state." "Democracy" and "Jewishness" Kimmerling stresses "are in some respects mutually exclusive."[10]

Prestate Zionist leaders, Kimmerling explains, saw Zionism as a secular movement and hoped to establish a liberal, democratic state; their nationalism was influenced by liberal, socialist and even communist ideologies. They rejected the ideas of Samuel Mohilever, one of the founders of Hovevei Zion and perhaps the first rabbi to address the needs and concerns of religious Jews in the early immigrant settlements – needs that would resurface in the restored Jewish homeland in Eretz Israel. In 1893 within the framework of this activity, Mohilever set up Hovevei Zion's "spiritual center" which he named Mizrachi (an acronym in Hebrew for "spiritual center"). Within nine years this center inspired the establishment of the Zionist religious party under the same name. Mohilever supported Herzl's initiative to convene the First Zionist Congress, and though health reasons prevented him from attending he sent Herzl a congratulatory letter that was read at the congress. In his letter, among other things, he wrote that "our Torah, the fountainhead of our lives, must be the foundation of our renaissance in the land of our forefathers." In time this was the spirit that animated the Mizrachi party's motto "Eretz Israel, for the nation of Israel, according to the Torah of Israel."

The party's program declared that its objective was to assemble "all those Zionists who seek to cleanse practical Zionism from any foreign element that is not consistent with political and practical Zionism." However, throughout the years Mizrachi was a minority faction within the Zionist movement and had to make do with very few achievements in the religious domain. This led some of the party's leaders to resign from the Zionist Organization at the beginning of the 1920s and join a number of Orthodox rabbis in a new political group that called itself Agudat Israel. The frontal clash between this party and the increasing influence of secular Zionism proved to be fertile ground for conflict between religious and secular Jews. The consequences of these clashes are with us to this very day. Like Aloni, Kimmerling points out that in the end, the Zionist leaders decided that the only way to avoid all-out confrontation was to appease the religious minority, even though that meant an erosion of democratic principles.[11]

Indeed, according to Kimmerling, the Western-oriented, secular Zionist movement, has morphed into an "essentially religion-based project, unable to disconnect itself from its original identity as a quasi-messianic movement. The essence of this society and state's right and reason to exist is embedded in religious symbols, ideas, and scriptures, even if there has been an attempt to give them a secular reinterpretation and context."[12] This has led to Israel being increasingly identified as both a democracy and a theocracy – concepts that are seemingly mutually exclusive but at the same time are complementary; "the one cannot exist without the other."[13]

Kimmerling catalogues the limitations on Israeli democracy currently built into the system: the secular Jewish majority is controlled by a parliamentary and judicial system manipulated by ultra-Orthodox interests that are essentially the interests of a minority; the civil and rabbinical judicial systems reflect varying degrees of "inequality" with respect to each others' needs so that neither group can be said to be wholly satisfied with the arrangement; religious laws imposed on the secular majority limit the equal rights of women enshrined in Israel's Basic Laws; the Arab minority and other minority groups enjoy a kind of "selective equality" that gives them individual but not collective rights; the state is the homeland by right of Jews everywhere in the world but Arabs enjoy no such right; finally, the state has raised the importance of national security to such a high level that it has become, in Kimmerling's words a "religion of security" that still further undermines civil equality and diminishes democratic values in Israeli society. All these, Kimmerling concludes, result in Israel only possessing "a veneer of democratic legitimacy."[14]

Ruth Gavison, an Israeli professor of law and a founding member of the Association for Civil Rights in Israel, believes that "Israel is a democracy with serious flaws and internal tensions that require urgent care and reform if it is to flourish." In her view these are issues that need to be addressed not merely on a theoretical but also on a normative level, while continually bearing in mind the pragmatic realities. Like Smooha, Gavison considers Israel to be essentially an ethnic democracy that has institutionalized the rule of the majority but nevertheless maintains a system of free elections, an independent judiciary, and freedom of speech and association. Like Smooha, Gavison points out that Israel is more of a democracy today than it was in the early years of independence.[15]

On the other hand, it is Gavison's view that choosing to describe
Israel's democracy solely as "ethnic" "obscures at least two fundamental
aspects that I think should be emphasized: the deep religious basis
of Judaism...and the difficulty in distinguishing between ethnicity
and nationhood. The same ethnic-national ambiguity is also true in
relation to the identity of Palestine and the Palestinians. It is clear that
a Palestinian state will have to contend with the tensions and links of
its citizenry to their religions, as is the case in many of the countries
of the region." This is the reason why Gavison prefers the description
"Jewish state" – a concept that has currently become controversial
in that it can be interpreted to mean one of three things: an absolute
theocracy; a state in which a clear majority are religiously observant
Jews; or simply a state in which the majority of the population are Jews.
It is evident, argues Gavison, that Israel is a Jewish state of the third
kind; 80 percent of its citizens are Jews, the country celebrates Jewish
holidays and festivals, has Hebrew as its official language and bases its
existence on the assumption that Judaism is not merely a religion but
also a nationality. That is the situation, she adds, despite the problematic
reality that "the Jewish religion is ever present in public life and that
matters of personal status are subject to Orthodox religious law."[16]

Gavison's demand that normative considerations should be part of the
debate is centered on the fundamental question of whether, in principle,
the existence of a Jewish state in Israel is justified. In her view the
answer is "yes," provided that the state is within the borders of June 4,
1967. "Clearly there can be no justification for a Jewish state extending
over the whole of Palestine," since such a state would be unstable and
undemocratic. Although Gavison concedes that Israel within the pre-
1967 border does not qualify as a liberal or consociational democracy,
its status within those borders as an ethnic democracy is legitimate.
"Where there is a minimum of political equality, a condition that is of
course essential to any democracy, democracy can exist despite the fact
that not all groups have an equal sense of 'belonging.'"[17]

Having said that, Gavison goes on to emphasize that important aspects
of Israel's current system cannot be justified and must be reformed. In
her view an end must be put to Orthodox control over personal status,

a written constitution must be adopted, the Law of Return reformed, Israeli Arabs must be placed in important governmental positions, land laws as they apply to Arabs must be reformed and the education system restructured so that in all matters relating to language and history there is equality between Jews and Arabs. Over and above all else, Gavison believes that there is a need to protect the system against it becoming a theocracy under the control of the rabbis and against disenfranchising the country's non-Jewish citizens. That said, Gavison favors the continued existence of a state with a Jewish majority seeking to maintain its Jewish identity and whose Arab citizens find ways of coming to terms with being a minority.[18]

The declaration establishing the State of Israel called for "the adoption of a constitution to be drawn up by the Constituent Assembly to be elected no later than October 1, 1948." Because of the pressures of the War of Independence the first assembly was not elected until January 25, 1949. On February 16 the assembly declared itself to be the first Knesset and decided not to draft a full constitution. Instead it was decided to draw up the constitution piecemeal, chapter by chapter, each to be a Basic Law. The Basic Laws so far enacted – in conjunction with the declaration of statehood – are considered an alternative to a constitution. Particularly important in this context is the statement in the Declaration of Independence that the State of Israel was to be "a Jewish state in Eretz Israel" that will "ensure complete equality of social and political rights to all its citizens irrespective of religion, race or gender." From this developed the widely used expression that Israel is a state that is both "Jewish and democratic." However, there is no shortage of critics who contend that this characterization is an oxymoron: if Israel, they say, is a Jewish state, it cannot be a state in which all citizens enjoy completely equal social and political rights. In the democratic world, citizenship and nationality are one and the same thing; in Israel there is a clear distinction between the two. Navigating the inconsistencies that stem from this is largely the task of the Supreme Court.

The Supreme Court's eighth president, Chief Justice Aharon Barak, played an active role in protecting the civil rights of citizens, taking into account the problematic constitutional structure of the state. In this context it is important to note a landmark decision by the Supreme Court in March 2000 brought to the court by an Arab married couple Adel and Iman Qu'adan. Adel, a male nurse at the Hillel Yaffe hospital in the town of Hedera and his wife, Iman, a teacher, decided to move home from the Israeli Arab village of Baka Al Gharbiyya to Katzir, a new communal development established by the Jewish Agency on state-owned land. But their application to become residents of Katzir was rejected on the grounds that the Jewish Agency's development was intended exclusively for Jews. After a number of unsuccessful attempts at compromise the court had no alternative but to rule on the appeal, and Chief Justice Aharon Barak determined that:

> From the values of Israel, as a state which is both Jewish and democratic, it does not follow at all that the state should discriminate between its citizens...the state – is a state of Jews. The regime is an enlightened one, bestowing rights upon all its citizens, Jews and non-Jews alike.... There is therefore no contradiction between the values of the State of Israel as a Jewish and democratic state and full equality between all of its citizens. On the contrary: equality of rights between all in Israel, irrespective of religion and irrespective of nationality, derives from the values of Israel as a Jewish and democratic state.

The Jewish Agency was therefore instructed to "reconcile" its policy with the principles of equality enshrined in Israel's Basic Law: Human Dignity and Liberty. Barak's cautious and scrupulous ruling was widely interpreted as siding with the "democratic" side of the question and immediately aroused the strong opposition of those demanding that Israel remain a "Jewish state." Rulings of this sort, in the view of Tom Segev, teach us that the Jewish state and the democratic state can successfully live together under one roof and that the two concepts are not necessarily mutually exclusive.[19]

The historian Alexander Yakobson has explained that since the policies of the Jewish state are not in any way unique, the uniqueness of Jewish democracy should not be viewed as being either exceptional or undemocratic. He compares Israel's democracy with a number of democracies where there is, to an extent at least, a link between identity and religion. Every such country, says Yakobson, adheres to its own model, one that does not correspond to the American example but is nonetheless widely viewed as democratic. He also compares Israel to countries that do not entirely conform to definitions of what constitutes democracy but are nevertheless regarded as such. One example of this is Greece, whose constitution grants the Orthodox Christian Church a special status and defines it as a component of Greek national identity. The constitution declares the objective of public education as being "the development of national and religious consciousness." It guarantees freedom of religion but at the same time states that the dominant religion is Eastern Orthodoxy. Apart from that the constitution also provides for specific benefits to those immigrating to Mount Athos: "ethnic Greeks from foreign countries immigrating to Greece are naturalized according to an expedited procedure."[20]

Ireland is another democratic country with close links to religion. The connection between Ireland and Catholicism was institutionalized in the 1920s after partition separated the Protestant north from the Catholic bulk of the island of Ireland. The 1937 constitution of the Irish Republic grants the Catholic Church a special position as the "guardian of the faith." In addition to that clause (revoked in a national referendum in 1971) the constitution's preamble clearly recognizes a link between religion (though not explicitly stated to be Catholicism) and Irish national consciousness. A preamble of this kind is plainly inconsistent with the American model; yet the Irish Republic is universally regarded as a democracy in every sense of the word.[21]

The similarly preferential status of the Lutheran church, Yakobson points out, was revoked in Sweden only in 2000, but Denmark, Iceland, Finland and Norway accord preferential treatment to their respective religions. In Denmark and Norway, the Evangelical Lutheran Church is considered by law to be the official church of both countries and receives official state support; moreover, all Danish and Norwegians royals must formally belong to the Evangelical Lutheran Church. Denmark and Norway are, nonetheless, considered to be legitimate democracies. [22]

It is up to every nation, says Yakobson, to create its own model of democracy based on its unique history, culture and circumstances. Since there isn't one particular formula that covers every case, Yakobson suggests that there is room for more flexibility when assessing the democratic norms in different countries that are considered democratic but do not necessarily fully conform to the axiomatic definitions of democracy.

It is right to emphasize that these debates are by no means merely academic. They have a significant impact on the continuing identification of contemporary Jews with Israel. Critics denying Israel's democratic character not only aid and abet the delegitimization of Israel internationally, but also act to erode the positive identification with Israel of Jews in the Diaspora. Inevitably, the very existence of these critics is likely to make their mark on both Jewish and Israeli identity.

CHAPTER 12

WHO IS A JEW?

A n answer to the question "Who is a Jew?" (or defining an individual's Jewishness) is an issue that has preoccupied Jewish religious and secular scholars alike for years. The answer remains elusive. The importance of this subject has grown since the establishment of the State of Israel. Israel's Declaration of Independence of May 1948 stipulated that the state was to be Jewish and the national homeland of the Jewish people. This was followed in 1950 by the enactment of the Law of Return which begins with the statement that "every Jew has the right to make aliyah [immigrate] to Israel," implying that "aliyah" bestows citizenship.[1] Initially the Law of Return did not specify who was entitled to be considered a Jew. Queries that arose in relation to this were referred either to officials in charge of the population registry or to the Minister of the Interior for them to make case-by-case decisions. In March 1958, the then Interior Minister Israel Bar-Yehuda, a member of the left-wing party Achdut Ha'avodah Poalei Zion, decreed that officials in charge of the population registry were not authorized to examine people who apply to them for registration and that "every person who in good faith declares himself to be a Jew is to be registered as a Jew and is not to be asked to supply any other proof."

These expansive criteria infuriated the National Religious Party (Mafdal), which demanded that the Prime Minister David Ben-Gurion rescind them and left the ruling coalition government when he did not immediately agree to their demand. Subsequently Ben-Gurion turned to fifty "sages of Israel" – prominent Jewish scholars in Israel and the Diaspora and asked for their opinion about the items of "religion" and "nationality" in Israeli identity cards. Thirty-seven of the forty-five recipients who responded to Ben-Gurion's inquiry stated that the Halachah (the body of Jewish religious law) was the only basis for deciding a person's Jewish identity. However, even before receiving replies from the sages of Israel the government decided to revoke Bar-Yehuda's directive.

In December 1959, following elections to the fourth Knesset, a new government was formed in which the Interior Ministry was handed back to the leader of the National Religious Party, Chaim Moshe Shapira. In January 1960 Shapira issued a new set of directives to officials in charge of the population registry without these having first been authorized by the government or the Knesset or officially published. The new directives ordered that "a Jew is a person born to a Jewish mother and has no other religion or one who has converted to Judaism according to Halachic law." In 1970 the Law of Return was amended. A clause was added (Clause 4A) stipulating that all the rights conferred by the law on Jews would also be vested in "the child and grandchild of a Jew, the spouse of a Jew, the spouse of a child of a Jew and the spouse of a grandchild of a Jew." Claus 4B, appended to the law at the same time, clarified that a Jew is "a person born to a Jewish mother or one who has converted to Judaism and has no other religion."[2]

Contrary to the demands of the religious parties, the law did not specify that a person's conversion to Judaism would have to be in accordance with "Halachic law." But in practice the Orthodox law became the sole criteria in Israel of who is and who is not a Jew. This outcome immediately sparked a protracted controversy in the Jewish world. The refusal of Orthodox rabbis to recognize religious conversions performed by rabbis of the Reform and Conservative movements generated a wave of protest in Israel and the Diaspora.[3]

One of the best-known disputes over the Law of Return erupted in 1962 in what became known as the "Brother Daniel" case. Samuel

Aharon Oswald Rufeisen (1922–1998) was born into a Jewish family in Poland. In his youth he was a member of Akiva, the religious Zionist youth movement. Following the Nazi invasion of Poland in the Second World War, he succeeded in getting forged identity papers that enabled him to pass himself off as a German and work as an interpreter at the German military police station in the town of Mir. With this identity and position as a cover, Rufeisen assisted the anti-Nazi underground by supplying it with arms and money and helped three hundred young Jews escape into the forests and be spared from death in a concentration camp. When his activities came to light, he himself escaped, joined the partisans and at a later stage found sanctuary in a Catholic monastery where he hid for more than a year. After the war, Rufeisen stayed in the monastery, converted to Christianity and became a monk in the Carmelite order. In 1958 Rufeisen moved to Israel, thereby fulfilling a long-cherished dream, and joined the Stella Maris Carmelite Monastery in Haifa under the name Brother Daniel. Four years later he applied for Israeli citizenship on the basis of the Law of Return. His application was rejected. He appealed to the Supreme Court, arguing that his nationality remained Jewish even after he had changed his religion and converted to Catholicism.

The Supreme Court denied his appeal by a majority vote of 4 to 3, ruling that Jewishness is determined by its definition in Jewish religious law and not by a subjective test of a person's declaration, albeit made in good faith. The majority ruling noted Brother Daniel's heroism during the Holocaust but found that this did not justify an amendment of the definition.[4]

Justice Haim Cohen, who sided with the minority, argued that throughout Jewish history in the Diaspora differing religious interpretations by various communities had been put forward on this matter even though the judicial interpretations in Israel had gained a special standing. In Cohen's view, anyone wanting to identify themselves with the "community" had to be considered a Jew – even if such a declaration could at times be made for improper reasons, such as to unlawfully gain a benefit. My Jewishness, Cohen declared, is based on three principles: All men are created in the image of God, we are all commanded to love one another and not to do unto others that which is hateful to us.[5]

Another controversy erupted in 1970 when Benjamin Shalit, a lieutenant commander in the navy, tried to register his children as Jews despite the fact that his non-Jewish wife had not converted to Judaism. The denial of his request led to an appeal to the Supreme Court. The appeal was granted by a majority of five to four and the court instructed that the children be registered as Jews, contrary to the Halachah. The Shalit ruling spurred an amendment of the Law of Return that same year. However, the confrontation between Shalit and the state did not end there. When his third child was born after 1970, Shalit demanded that he be registered as a Jew or as a "Hebrew." The demand was declined following the amendment of the law referred to earlier.[6]

It would seem that Shalit was opposed to the requirement that his children must convert in a religious ceremony which would, in any event, be an Orthodox one; Israeli law determined that only Orthodox religious courts were authorized to perform conversions within the borders of Israel, though it recognized non-Orthodox conversions abroad on the grounds that Israeli law did not apply beyond the country's boundaries. Moreover, in 1995 the Supreme Court ruled that the government could not contest or deny the validity of a document confirming a conversion performed abroad; the court ruled that every Jew able to produce evidence of having been converted in the Diaspora is entitled to be considered a Jew in so far as the Law of Return is concerned.[7]

In 1970, Ben-Gurion appeared before the Central Conference of American Rabbis – the principal organization of Reform Rabbis in the United States – and was asked who, in his view, was a Jew. "Any individual who comes to me and says, 'I am a Jew.' …I don't understand who raised the issue of who is a Jew, a Jew is a Jew – and that is it."[8] As mentioned above, twelve years earlier he himself had asked fifty "sages of Israel" to come up with definitions as to what defines Jewishness. More specifically, he asked: Are the children born in mixed marriages Jews? Does the state, when deciding the status of individual immigrants, need to adopt an entirely religious definition or can it use more subjective criteria? Do officials in charge of the population registry have to accept the declarations of new immigrants as to their status or must they demand biological proof of their Jewish extraction?

Ben-Gurion was particularly keen to get the opinion of the sages of Israel on the question of the registration of children born to a Jewish father and a non-Jewish mother when both parents wanted the children to be registered as Jews (as was in due course the situation in the Shalit case). Ben-Gurion explained to the sages why he himself believed in the following principles:

1. Israel guarantees freedom of conscience and religion as promised in its Declaration of Independence. All forms of religious or anti-religious coercion are banned and a Jew is entitled to be religious or non-religious.

2. Israel is today the center for the ingathering of the exiles. Immigrants come from East and West, from advanced countries and countries that are lagging behind. The merging of the exiles into a single national mold is one of the most vital and at the same time one of the hardest of Israel's tasks. An effort must be made to reinforce what is common and unifying and where possible push aside that which divides and alienates.

3. The Jewish community in Israel doesn't resemble the Jewish community in the Diaspora. Here we are not a minority subjected to the pressure of a foreign culture. Nor is there a fear here of the assimilation of Jews within a non-Jewish population such as there is in a number of free and prosperous states. On the contrary, non-Jews have the tendency and possibility to easily assimilate into the Jewish nation, particularly among families of mixed marriages who immigrate to Israel. Whereas intermarriage abroad is a disruptive factor leading to total assimilation and departure from the Jewish entity – mixed couples who come here, especially from the countries of Eastern Europe are, in effect, bringing about a total melding of the non-Jewish party into the Jewish nation.

Ben-Gurion added that the Jewish community in Israel had adopted an all-inclusive attitude vis-à-vis a variety of Jewish identities, accepting the fact that the Diaspora was inseparable from Jewish identity both historically and culturally.[9]

The 1966 Nobel Laureate for Literature, S. Y. Agnon, urged Ben-Gurion to "wash your hands of discussing religion so that you can turn your full attention to matters of state." At the time, Agnon's view was that "for now religion and state are like two neighbors uneasy at being close to one another." In any case he didn't give Ben-Gurion any clear answers to the questions he'd been asked, though he did declare that "I have nothing to add or subtract from what they [the ancient sages of Israel] have said."[10]

Another of the respondents, the well-known Israeli writer Haim Hazaz (1898–1973) took the view that "the Halachah has no role to play in the registration of the country's citizenry. The sole criteria for that must be the law of the country." He explained that "today there are hundreds of mixed-marriage couples here, survivors of the Holocaust. And if tomorrow the gates that are still locked were to open and thousands, perhaps tens of thousands of mixed-marriage couples were to come here.... What would we do with them? Force them to convert according to Halachic law? Or would we bar their entry into the country?"[11]

In his response to Ben-Gurion, the distinguished scholar Isaiah Berlin (1909–1997) wrote that if Israel was aspiring to be a liberal state and not a theocracy, it must not categorize its citizens on the basis of their religion or limit an individual's rights in personal matters. If the Israeli system was hoping to be thought of as modern and liberal, Berlin argued, its civil laws must reflect this aspiration and bestow religious freedom upon all its citizens. Every citizen, he opined, be he religious, atheist or agnostic, must be entitled to marry or divorce without the need to resort to religious procedure or ritual.

Berlin reminded Ben-Gurion that had it been up to the religious parties the State of Israel would never have been born. He also expressed his apprehension of a possible cultural war erupting among Jews due to disagreement between Israel and the Diaspora over the preference given to religious authority.[12] This view found an echo in the warnings voiced by the Jewish leadership in Britain, where Berlin lived, of a potential split between Israel and the Diaspora if Israel failed to end the stranglehold the Orthodox had on the definition of a Jew.

Such views have since become common among secular Israelis.

Yossi Beilin, the former leader of the small left-wing party Meretz, supports the idea of "civil conversion." In the twenty-first century, when the majority of the Jews in the world are not religious, it cannot be, Beilin argues, that Jewish Orthodoxy should be the sole arbiter of Jewish identity.[13]

Aliza Shenhar, a scholar of folklore (and the former rector of Haifa University) claims that the Halachic biological criteria for Jewishness contravenes the principles of humanism and is nowadays irrelevant. If a person wishes to belong to the Jewish people, she argues, no one nor any institution have the right to reject him. The purpose of the Zionist movement was to normalize the Jewish people and in seeking to achieve that objective Jewish identity was defined in terms of nationhood based on an individual's nationality and not religion. The only way, Shenhar suggests, is to adopt the declaration of Ruth the Moabite to her mother-in-law Naomi: "Thy people shall be my people and thy God my God."[14]

Shulamit Aloni, a champion of civil rights in Israel, thinks that the Supreme Court ruling in the Shalit case prompted world Jewry to reconsider the definition of a Jew. She quotes from Professor Samuel (Shmuel) Hugo Bergman's reaction to the amendment of the Law of Return in 1970: "I regard any link that is made between religion and race as an anachronism that nowadays contravenes an individual's spiritual development. No one denies that in the past such a link was justified, but today clashes with the spiritual level that man has achieved in his development.... Whoever in one way or another holds fast to the link between blood and religion must of necessity reach materialistic conclusions nullifying religious life altogether. In every link between religion and politics I see a great catastrophe both for the State of Israel and for the Jewish religion."[15]

The definitional question of "who is a Jew?" has become even more acute following the massive immigration of Jews in the wake of the collapse of the Soviet Union in the late 1980s and early 1990s. Reform Rabbi Gregory Kotler points to the huge impact that the 1970 amendment to the Law of Return had on the million immigrants from the former Soviet Union, among whom many were non-Jews married to Jews. The current definition of a Jew, Kotler argues, means that countless spouses are not recognized as Jews and suffer unjustifiable hardships. Laws written soon after the destruction of the Second Temple in 70 CE can barely be applicable to present conditions. This is also true of the situation beyond Israel's borders. Reform Jewry, the biggest branch of the Jewish religion in the United States, rejected the Orthodox definition of a Jew a long time ago. Since 1983 it has recognized that children born to either a Jewish mother or a Jewish father can be considered Jews. In doing so, says Kotler, the Reform movement has adopted a more inclusive definition that is better suited to contemporary conditions.

The purpose of the Reform movement's decision to accept the children born to a Jewish father as Jews, Kotler explains, was to lessen the extent of assimilation in the United States and keep mixed-marriage families within the fold. Orthodox Judaism's insistence on rigorous standards of conversion is contributing to the disintegration of the Jewish people, argues Kotler. Therefore, he concludes, their monopoly over these matters should be ended and Israeli and Diaspora Jewry as one should embrace a more modern, more liberal procedure for conversion.

Another Reform rabbi, David Ariel-Yoel, supports Kotler's argument. At the turn of the twenty-first century, Ariel-Yoel observes, the number of Jews in the United States is declining; the National Jewish Population Survey for the years 2000–2001 shows that the American Jewish population has declined from five and a half million, to five million two hundred thousand. Close to 47 percent of all Jews in the United States marry non-Jews and only the Reform movement is currently willing to accept such couples and their children as part of the Jewish community. Jewish identity, argues Ariel-Yoel, encourages the acceptance of the "other" – in this case the non-Jewish spouse. We therefore must disassociate ourselves from the ways of Orthodox and Conservative Jews that deny the Jewish identity of the non-Jewish spouse.[16]

In Reform synagogues in the United States, says Ariel-Yoel, the answer to the question "who is a Jew" is simple. A Jew is anyone who thinks he belongs in the Jewish community. Both the Halachah and the laws of the State of Israel are irrelevant. However, as Kotler points out, even the Reform movement flinches at the idea of accepting someone who hasn't gone through a conversion of one kind or another. Kotler insists that if Israel indeed wishes to continue to be the center of Jewish life, then it must alter its definition of Jewish identity.[17]

Realistically, given Israel's fragmented political map and the electoral power of the religious parties, such a radical change is not on the horizon. We can perhaps expect procedural and interpretative changes, but for reasons that go beyond the politics of the moment and have deep cultural roots, Israel is not yet ripe for substantive change on this issue.

CHAPTER 13

THE MIZRACHIM: THE JEWISH "OTHER" IN ISRAEL

T he encounter between the Zionist movement, the State of Israel and the Jews emigrating from Arab and Islamic countries (the Mizrachim) was, and continues to be, a troubling experience. It is a poignant example of the ways in which the "other" is treated within the context of Jewish identity. The Mizrachim (Oriental Jews), who account for about half of Israel's Jewish population,[1] have, for quite some time, been accusing the state of systematic discrimination and a persistent disregard of their demands. Over the past thirty years they have conducted a campaign to rectify the wrongs suffered by them. In the view of the Moroccan-born Israeli writer and academician Sami Shalom Chetrit this struggle achieved a change in the evolution of Israel's democracy.[2]

A key demand of Mizrachi activism is that the state acknowledges and apologizes for having turned the Mizrachi Jews into second-class citizens, and for its past ill-treatment of Mizrachi immigrants. The list of grievances includes the setting up of *ma'abarot* (camps of tents and tin huts) intended as very temporary accommodation, in which immigrants, mostly Mizrachim, were housed in many cases for shamefully long periods of time after their arrival in Israel;[3] the humiliating treatment of Moroccan and other Oriental immigrants as they landed in Israel, which included having their heads shaved and their bodies sprayed with DDT; the state-enforced secularization of Mizrachi Jews and the disintegration of their traditional family structures; and even instances in which agents of the state abducted Yemenite Jewish babies and placed them for adoption with Ashkenazi families who had lost their children in the Holocaust.[4] These abuses continue to rile the collective consciousness of the Mizrachi community.[5]

These feelings of injustice endure despite the widely held perception among Israelis that the social gap between the Ashkenazi (European) and Mizrachi (Oriental) communities was temporary and of no real consequence. Proponents of this view cite the substantial rate of inter-communal marriage (25 percent) and the high level of social interaction – both of which are often an outcome of universal military service, which has been an instrument of social integration and mobility. Also offered as evidence is the almost total rooting out of discrimination against, or shunning of, members of the Mizrachi community; the high level of representation of Mizrachim in governmental and military institutions; and the cultural revolution of the 1980s and 1990s in which Mizrachi music, culture and customs were embraced by the population as a whole, and which swept the Mizrachim to the summit of Israeli popular culture.[6]

Except that these genuine changes do not conceal the perpetuation of Ashkenazi cultural, political and class dominance in Israeli society. "The ethnic gap in the distribution of resources is significant," notes the sociologist Sammy Smooha. And the gap for younger, Israeli-born Mizrachim is as wide as it was in earlier generations for those born outside of Israel, and in some instances even wider. Most Mizrachim are still classified as manual labor and lower class, whereas most Ashkenazim are in the middle or upper classes of society. At the expense of the Mizrachim, Ashkenazim are overrepresented by a factor of 300–400 percent among university students and the more highly educated elite. Despite the prevalence of intermarriage "and fifty years of ethnic mixing," writes Chetrit, "only a minority of Jews have a next-door neighbor from the other ethnic group, only one-tenth of Jews are of mixed descent, and nearly 80 percent of the members of each ethnic group vote along ethnic lines."[7] As seen by the Ashkenazi establishment, adds Chetrit, the Mizrachim remain a backward, non-European element, the unwanted "others" of Israel's Jewish community.[8]

There are two different factions of Mizrachi activists in Israel. The dominant faction identifies with the state and seeks to become integrated within the continually evolving Ashkenazi establishment. Then, there is "an unorganized but expanding number" of young intellectuals and artists (the "New Mizrachim") who lend their support to the attacks leveled against the Jewish state by post-Zionists and "reject the process of Zionization experienced by their parents."[9]

Among the New Mizrachim – a group that does not attract a great deal of support from the Mizrachi community itself – are a number of Israeli academics such as Ella Shohat, Sami Shalom Chetrit, Eli Avraham, Yehouda Shenhav and Pnina Motzafi-Haller, all of them Mizrachim, and two Ashkenazi academics, Shlomo Swirski and Oren Yiftachel. Shohat and Swirski were the first to develop the movement's post-Zionist slant.[10] In their work, based on Edward Said's book *Orientalism*, they assert that Zionism and Israel resemble European "first-world" colonial and post-colonial models which suppress "third-world" Orientals – in which they include not only Arabs and Palestinians but also "Oriental Jews" or "Jewish Arabs" as they sometimes refer to themselves.[11]

Shohat rejects the "Zionist master narrative" that European Jews "saved" the Mizrachi Jews from the oppressive rule of their Arab "captors" and from the "primitive" conditions extant in the Arab and Muslim world. In her words "one of the hallmarks of colonialism is that it distorts and even denies the history of victims of colonization." The portrayal of Mizrachi Jews as coming from backward rural societies lacking all contact with technological civilization is at best a simplistic caricature and at worst utterly false. Shohat admits that Jewish life in Islamic countries was circumscribed by "fundamentally discriminatory Islamic precepts toward 'tolerated' and 'protected' religious minorities." However, basing herself on the views of Maxime Rodinson, Shohat insists that "this fact is easily explained by the sociological and historical conditions of that era, and is not the result of pathological anti-Semitism of the kind to be found among Europeans. The Mizrachi communities, while retaining a strong collective identity, were generally indigenous to and well rooted in their countries of origin, forming an inseparable part of their social and cultural lives."[12]

This view is also echoed in the writings of Sami Shalom Chetrit. Unlike Christianity, he points out, Islam always recognized Judaism as a legitimate, though inferior, religion, and Jews lived in the Islamic world in relative peace and coexistence. The falsely exaggerated historical account given by Chetrit gives the impression that Jews living in Muslim countries didn't suffer the kind of pogroms and violent anti-Semitism that the Jews of Europe experienced. He argues that it was the French, German and British colonialists who first introduced motifs of anti-Semitism to the Arab world and that the emigration of Jews from Arab and Islamic countries was solely the result of the Arab-Zionist conflict.[13]

In the view of the historian Norman Stillman, these claims stem from a "gross oversimplification."[14] It is undoubtedly true, writes Stillman, that the war in Eretz Israel was one of the reasons behind the emigration of Mizrachi Jews from Muslim countries. But the history of these Jews in the Arab and Muslim world informs us of other more important factors for this emigration. Above all else it was the "modernization" that the area underwent that contributed to this phenomenon.[15] At the same time as the Ottoman Empire was progressively declining, so the tolerance of the majority toward the Christian and Jewish minorities also faded. This compelled the minorities to turn to Europe.

Most of the Jews in Islamic countries were poor, uneducated and lagged behind Europe's Jews. However, the nineteenth century saw a growth in the number of those who "regarded a Western education (which at first meant primarily a basic knowledge of Western languages) as an essential prerequisite for their entry into the modern world."[16] They achieved this goal thanks to the Alliance Israelite Universelle and the network of schools that this organization established in the region. "In a period during which the world was inexorably being driven into adopting a modern economic system," explains Stillman, "this network, that also included vocational schools, produced small cadres of Westernized Jews who enjoyed a clear advantage over the mostly uneducated Muslim population. Together with the rapidly progressing indigenous Christian population that benefited from missionary schools, a significant number of Jews gained an unprecedented degree of upward economic mobility. They achieved a position in the Muslim world that was wholly disproportionate to their numbers or their social status within the general population."[17]

More and more Jews sought to benefit from the spread of European influences. They supported European economic and cultural interests and welcomed the growing role of the European colonial powers in their countries of residence. Having acquired foreign languages, these Jews were particularly well qualified to manage the trade with the West and to provide various services to Western diplomats. "Throughout the Maghreb," Stillman writes, "local consular agents, vice consuls, and honorary consuls were all Jews."[18]

Thus it can be said that the unequal treatment of Jews and Christians in the Muslim world led these minorities to identify with Colonial Europe and seek its protection, which resulted in their further alienation from the anti-colonial Muslim majority. This dynamic process of vulnerable minorities seeking to defend themselves in ways that only increased their vulnerability led to the progressive dimming of prospects of Jews in the Muslim world. Indeed, when the inevitable backlash against pro-European minorities came, Muslims focused their anger on the Jew rather than the Christian because the latter were far better protected by the European powers.[19]

Stillman notes the Zionist tendencies among Mizrachi Jews in the area and stresses that this form of Jewish nationalism coincided with the eruption of anti-Western nationalism on the part of a Muslim majority that had become far less tolerant of its minorities than it had been in the past. Pogroms that led to the deaths of between two and four hundred Jews in Baghdad in 1941, and one hundred and forty Jews in Tripoli in 1945, kindled an understanding among Jews "of the kind of violent treatment that they might suffer at the hands of a native Muslim regime."[20] More than any other factor, it was this realization that led to the exodus of Mizrachim from the Arab and Muslim world.

And yet, despite the fact that eventually the Mizrachi Jews would need a safe haven, initially the leaders of the Zionist movement gave no thought to the fate of these communities. As Chetrit points out, Zionism was influenced by European national movements, and the solution of the Jewish problem offered by Zionism was targeted at European not Mizrachi Jewry. The change in this attitude came after World War II and the establishment of the State of Israel. When it became apparent that as a result of the Holocaust and the Iron Curtain that had descended across the continent between the Soviet bloc and the West, the expected immigration of European Jewry would be far smaller than assumed, only then did the Zionist establishment begin to consider the situation of the Mizrachi Jews. "If the truth be told," admitted Baruch Duvdevani, the Jewish Agency's official in charge of immigration in the 1950s and 1960s, "as long as millions of European Jews were alive, no one paid any heed to the mere half million Jews in North Africa and Asia."[21]

Between 1948 and 1958, about half of the one million immigrants to Israel were Mizrachim. Those who didn't find work in urban centers idled away their time in poverty-stricken transit camps or were dispatched to develop agricultural settlements in unsafe areas of the country along borders that were rife with Palestinian infiltrators. During that same period 80 percent of Mizrachi children attended separate schools in which the curriculum often differed from that of the usual state school. According to one study, the small number of high schools in centers of Mizrachi immigrants reflected the establishment's desire to bring about a Mizrachi industrial and agricultural workforce. Chetrit maintains that this belies the longstanding claim of the government and Zionist establishment that the discrimination against Mizrachim was never intentional.[22]

Moreover, anti-Mizrachi sentiments among Israel's leaders and intelligentsia were common. Ben-Gurion is said to have commented that Mizrachi immigrants lacked even the most elementary knowledge because they hadn't had either a general or a Jewish education.[23] He is also credited with saying that he didn't want Israelis to become Arabs and that it was therefore necessary to fight against the Levantinism that corrupts individuals and society.[24] It is claimed that Ben-Gurion's fear that the state could lose its Jewish-European identity led to attempts

to either slow down the immigration from North Africa or limit its
size.[25] The policy that was put into place by the government aimed at
detaching the immigrants from the "Orient" and imposing on them a
new Israeli identity. This policy, combined with the sharp decline in
their standard of living, caused the Mizrachi community a "severe
shock." Becoming integrated into this new Israeli identity was for them
a painful and traumatic process which at limes led to criminality, drug
abuse and emotional difficulties.[26]

The first eruption of Mizrachi violence against the Ashkenazi
establishment was the rioting in the Wadi Salib neighborhood of Haifa
in 1959. Most of the Arab residents had abandoned the district in 1948
and were replaced by poor North African Jews, many of whom were
unemployed. The angry and violent riots in this neighborhood and the
surrounding areas raged for several weeks. They were accompanied by
acts of arson and vandalism in other Mizrachi communities in the country.
These events took place on the eve of elections to the fourth Knesset,
and the government succeeded in calming the situation by sympathizing
with the demonstrators and promising to improve their living conditions.
But Mizrachi discontent continued, leading, in 1971, to the emergence
of the Black Panther movement as the clearest expression to date of the
community's grievances. This movement's membership consisted in the
main of second-generation North African immigrants who insisted that
they no longer be described as "recently arrived immigrants" but rather
as belonging to an indigenous "second Israel." This "other Israel" they
declared, was being subjected to economic deprivation in poor urban
neighborhoods and in remote and neglected development towns. The
Black Panthers staged large demonstrations together with extreme left-
wing and anti-Zionist organizations, which often ended in unprecedented
clashes with the police. But the demonstrations continued and reached
their peak with the setting up of a Marxist party modeled on the political
movements of the Afro-American community in the United States.[27]
These events were to serve as a basis for the emergence in due course of
the post-Zionist New Mizrachim.

The Israeli historian Amnon Raz-Krakotzkin argues that the
subordination of the Mizrachim in Israel was a direct consequence

of the Zionist mainstream's ideology of negating the Diaspora. The Mizrachim, he argues, did not uproot themselves and move to Israel in order to be rid of their cultural heritage and embrace the Zionist ideal of the "new Jew" who was to replace the despised Diaspora Jew; instead they wanted to preserve their unique cultures in a sovereign and free Jewish state. But the Mizrachim quickly learned the bitter price of integrating into Israeli society: they were compelled to shed their much loved cultural practices that had always been the fount of their Jewish identity.[28]

Baruch Kimmerling, on the other hand, justifies Israel's need during its first years of statehood to mold a new Israeli identity encompassing all the new immigrant communities. This identity, as Kimmerling sees it, would become the "new Israeli nationalism" reinforcing the identity of the country's prestate Jewish population. "The creation of this new identity," according to Kimmerling, became a necessity for two reasons. First in order to preserve "the stability and continuity of the initial social order of the immigrant settler Jewish community of colonial Palestine." And secondly in order to maintain "the balance of political, economic, and cultural power already existing within the community since 1933." Moreover, Kimmerling stresses, the second and third generations of post-statehood immigrants have successfully assimilated into this new Israeli identity while at the same time preserving their own space within Israeli culture through Mizrachi music, food, unique celebration of Jewish holidays and special manner of speaking.[29]

A major turning point in the process of Mizrachi integration was the Likud's victory in the 1977 general election in which Mizrachi voters enthusiastically endorsed the winning party. Though the number of Mizrachi Members of Knesset was no greater than in the elections of 1974 and did not reach 25 percent, the defeat of the *anciens regime* and its replacement by a new political establishment was interpreted as a repudiation of the anti-Mizrachi approach that had supposedly prevailed until then. These political developments did not, however, make it any easier for the mass of Mizrachi Jews to be accepted by the secular culture of the Israeli mainstream. An odd trend, pointed to by Kimmerling, is the way in which young Mizrachim began joining

Orthodox Jewish learning centers (yeshivas) led by Ashkenazi Orthodox rabbis. This trend led eventually to the establishment of Shas, an Orthodox Mizrachi political party that successfully recruited Orthodox Mizrachim as members and acquired significant political influence in the furtherance of the interests of its supporters.[30]

The turn toward Orthodoxy in religion and a strengthened Jewish identity is not consistent with the paradigm enunciated by the New Mizrachim, the essence of which is an "Oriental" identity that merges Mizrachim (Jews) and Palestinians (Arabs). The historian Hanna Yablonka, on the other hand, contends that the supposition that Mizrachi Jews cling to a separate Israeli identity is profoundly mistaken. In her research she found that the first generation of Mizrachim (1933–1960) who came before and after the establishment of the state displayed a sense of solidarity with the tragedy that had befallen European Jewry, which they themselves witnessed as it unfolded. The second generation (1960–1980) had a far more complex and more bluntly stated approach. This was mainly because they felt that the Ashkenazim had excluded them and appropriated the Holocaust to themselves as a tragic event that they could not share with the Mizrachim who had not experienced it. "For the second generation of Jews from Muslim countries," Yablonka writes, "the Holocaust is a blend of a painful sense of exclusion and an oppressive need to be part of its remembrance, something that has become an essential and inseparable part of Israeli identity. They yearned to belong to this collective memorialization because to be detached from the narrative of the Holocaust would have left them feeling that they were no more than second fiddle in the Israeli consciousness."

The third generation of Mizrachim (1981–2003), however, has no such ambivalence about the Holocaust. They demonstrate a profound identification with it, to the point that the Holocaust is now part and parcel of Mizrachi identity. "Being part of the Holocaust," Yablonka concludes, "is no longer dependent on personal or family ties."[31] In her view, despite persistent social frictions and a residual sense of anger, this is a clear expression of the unequivocal Mizrachi identification with Jewish society in Israel and of their complete integration into the mainstream of Israeli life.

CHAPTER 14

JEWISH IDENTITY IN TODAY'S
DIASPORA

S ince the last decade of the twentieth century, an empathic embrace of the Diaspora as an element of Jewish life has become an increasingly important strand of Jewish identity. The historians Deborah Dash Moore and S. Ilan Troen have argued that Jews throughout the world are distancing themselves from Zionism's ideal of the ingathering of the exiles in favor of a diversity and multiplicity of identities.[1] The idea that there is not just one Jewish people or culture is the theme of a new history of the Jews, *Cultures of the Jews*, in which the editor, David Biale, and other researchers try to show that throughout Jewish history there always was a dynamic tension between unity and diversity.[2]

In this spirit, more and more Jews in the Diaspora are seeking to develop a Jewish culture that is not linked to the Jewish state and that could be an alternative to Zionism and Israel as the focus of Jewish secular identity. Increasingly, there is a renewed interest in European Yiddish culture, particularly in traditional Yiddish folk music known as *Klezmer*. As well, a great deal of energy is being invested in a revival of Sephardic and Mizrachi culture. An expression of this is the setting up of Ivri-Nasawi, an association of Sephardic/Mizrachi writers and artists in the United States. The term *ivri* is derived from the Hebrew *avar* (crossed over) and is a reference to Abraham having crossed over

into Eretz Israel from the east bank of the Jordan River. *Nasawi* is
the acronym for a new international association of Sephardi/Mizrachi
artists and writers in the United States.[3]

At the same time, there are academics who make a point of stressing
the importance of the Diaspora in Jewish life. After a long interval a
number of scholars have begun to directly challenge the Zionist thesis
that Jewish history would have reached its zenith with the establishment
of Israel. They have done so by focusing their attention on various
Jewish communities and cultures in remote areas that have until now
been ignored; they are once again researching such manifestations of
Jewish nationalism in the Diaspora as Volkism and Bundism and are
again paying homage to the ghost of Jewish rootlessness.[4] The historian
Howard Wettstein has claimed that "exile" and "Diaspora," terms that
have long been considered synonymous, are in fact very different in
Jewish history and culture. Exile, according to Wettstein,

> is to be in the wrong place; it is to be dislocated, like a limb out
> of socket.... [It] suggests anguish, forced homelessness, and the
> sense of things being not as they should be. *Diaspora*, on the
> other hand, although it suggests absence from some center –
> political or religious or cultural – does not connote anything so
> hauntingly negative. Indeed, it is possible to view Diaspora in a
> positive light.[5]

Similarly, there are those who, influenced by the important work of the
post-colonialist scholar Homi Bhabha,[6] have began to use the concept
of hybrid and fragmented Jewish identities in ways that are similar to
those employed by post-colonial theoreticians studying nations under
colonial rule.[7] "The post-colonial adaptations of the concept 'Diaspora,'"
writes Michael Galchinsky, "stress the transnational, hybrid and fluid
communities created by both the forced and voluntary migratory flows
and lead us to understand that in the era of de-colonization the diasporic
communities can subvert the ideologies and practices of nations and
empires founded on the brutal homogenization of the controlled people.
These adaptations show that the increasing number of Diasporas whose
members transfer information, funds and affection back and forth

across national frontiers, undermine the continuing attempts of various nations to 'imagine communities' that are autonomous and not open to replenishment from the outside."[8]

The vision of the hybrid and transnational character of cultural identities was embraced by Paul Gilroy in his classic study, *The Black Atlantic: Modernity and Double Consciousness*. Gilroy writes that the ability of blacks to live in their own Diaspora is dependent on them possessing a "double consciousness." According to Gilroy, racial and ethnic identities are never "pure" but are rather the outcome of continuous mixing. Cultures change and stay alive in the context of persistent contact with other cultures. This reality, Gilroy argues, is clearly demonstrated by the Jewish experience, on which he based his study of the black Diaspora. The similarities between the two Diasporas, he explains, are striking. Both peoples were forcibly driven out of their homelands and had no option but to negotiate with "host" societies in which they were destined to be the ultimate "other." Both peoples embraced nationalist ideologies of "returning" to the lost homelands. Gilroy opposed the pan-African nationalism espoused by Marcus Garvey and Martin Delany – the black equivalent of Zionism – and instead adopted W. E. B. Du Bois' concept of a "double consciousness" in his support of a kind of ethnic particularism that is not based on the possession of a country but is, instead, a "nation" in an eternal Diaspora.[9]

It is along such lines that a number of popular Jewish writers have begun to explore the Diaspora as a reflection of the Jewish people's enduring diversity rather than of its rootlessness.[10] Similarly, a number of Jewish intellectuals have called for the revival of Jewish culture in the Diaspora. Richard Marienstras, for example, has promoted the idea of reviving secular Hebrew and Yiddish culture, which in his view represent "the cultural politics of the Diaspora."[11] The literary scholar Leah Garrett has suggested that the "Jewish condition" is traditionally viewed in one of two ways: "Critics often see Jews as having 'legs' rather than 'roots.' If they merely walk across the land without striking roots, then their attachment will always and necessarily be to the lands they have travelled through ('their' lands). The second option is Zionist nationalism that enables 'us' to be at home in our homeland." Garrett offers a third alternative: Yiddish literature. "The third possibility is what we experience in travel literature. The use of literature to refashion the world and to imagine the 'here and now' of Eastern Europe as our here and now. In this way, Jewish writers recreate the Jewish map and re-establish the link between 'here' and 'there' as a process of modernization." For them "Zion" can be anywhere in the world – that is to say, anywhere that Jews happen to live at any given moment.[12]

Daniel and Jonathan Boyarin are possibly the two most ardent advocates of the notion of the Jewish Diaspora. In their view, "the solution of Zionism – that is to say, Jewish state hegemony, except insofar as it represented an emergency and temporary rescue operation – seems to us the subversion of Jewish culture and not its culmination.... Capturing Judaism in a state transforms entirely the meanings of its social practices."[13] The Jewish ideal, they insist, is the Diaspora. "We propose Diaspora as a theoretical and historical model to replace national self-determination."[14] The link to Eretz Israel, argue Daniel and Jonathan Boyarin, had traditionally served to sublimate violent impulses inherent in any nationalist ideology seeking political power. At the time that link ensured the preservation of Jewish identity, Jewish culture and Jewish continuity. Today this model needs to be revamped so that there is both religious and cultural identification with "Zion" without the quest for political power or political sovereignty. The Boyarins visualize a future of permanent and illustrious Diasporas, not just for Jews but for all peoples. Jewish history over a period of two thousand years during which Jews lived apart from but also as part of the society of other nations is, in their view, a model for the future interaction of various groups. This concept enables the Boyarin brothers a "formulation of Jewish identity not as a proud resting place (hence not as a form of integrism or nativism) but as a perpetual, creative diasporic tension."[15]

This "pro-Diaspora" trend, says the historian Todd M. Endelman, has become common in Jewish studies almost overnight. "The classic Zionist analysis with its pessimistic view of the survivability of Diaspora communities is more or less dead in academic circles. Even in Israel itself, it is supported by only a handful of elderly scholars whose worldview was shaped many years ago."[16] The rise of these "pro-

Diaspora" views results from the weakening of nationalism and the rapid globalization of society – the mass migration of peoples almost all of whom regard themselves as living in a "Diaspora"; the expansion of global communication and transportation; the mounting crisis of nation-states flooded with immigrants; and the crisis of traditional identities in an ever growing multicultural world.[17]

However, Endelman warns, "it does not mean that this historiographical viewpoint has taken over the field. There are scholars such as myself, who remain skeptical about the claim that Western Jews have successfully coped with the challenge that emancipation and assimilation posed to their survival as a group. These scholars try to offer a more balanced assessment of the condition of Judaism and Jewishness in open societies over the past two hundred years. Those who take this approach are far from being an endangered species."[18] The sweeping critique of Zionism made by the Boyarin brothers and other "pro-diasporists," adds Bernardo Sorji, "is weakened by the omission of the historical context which led the Jews to identify with that movement, signifying something more than just an 'epistemological detour.' ...Their idealized view of diasporic Rabbinic Judaism fails to take into consideration that it is grounded in a power structure, that up until modern times Jews in the Diaspora have always lived with stigma and profound insecurity...."[19] Or as Michael Galchinsky succinctly put it: "Although recent post-colonial theories have much to recommend them by, they need to be criticized for unduly minimizing the suffering that was a frequent component of Diaspora...."[20]

A feature of the "pro-Diaspora" trend of thought is its repudiation of Zionism's long-held notions of masculinity. This rejectionist view has become a major component of the outlook of a number of Jewish exponents of "Queer Theory." Queer Theory emerged in the 1990s and deals with issues of "identities," including feminine identity and homosexual and lesbian identity. A new school of thought driven by a group of courageous scholars claims that there are links between Jewishness and queerness, between homophobia and anti-Semitism, and between Queer Theory and the development of theories about Jewishness. These scholars have found a "complex of social arrangements and processes through which modern Jewish and homosexual identities emerged as traces of each other."[21] Possibly the first to point to similarities between the two was the homosexual historian John Boswell, who offered a thesis of parallel persecution:

> The fate of Jews and homosexuals has been almost identical throughout European history, from early Christian hostility and all the way to extermination in concentration camps. The same laws that oppressed Jews, oppressed homosexuals; the same groups determined to exterminate Jews tried to wipe out homosexuality; the same periods of European history that refused to make room for Jewish distinctiveness, responded violently to sexual non-conformity; the same countries that insisted on religious uniformity imposed the standards of the majority when it came to sexual conduct; and even the same methods of propaganda were used against Jews and homosexuals – portraying them as animals bent on the destruction of children and the majority.[22]

Thereafter, a number of scholars have broadened Boswell's analysis. Sander L. Gilman and Jay Geller document prejudicial ascription of "softness" to Jewish men prior to the modern era.[23] George Mosse has scrupulously analyzed how debates on nationalism and citizenship in post-Enlightenment Europe (especially in Germany) were closely linked to discussions of "masculinity." He also demonstrates how such debates explicitly linked Jews (particularly but not exclusively Jewish men) with homosexuality.[24]

The emergence of new scientific disciplines in the nineteenth century strongly contributed to pinpointing clear social and moral differences between various ethnic groups by identifying the main "innate" characteristics of each group.[25] Daniel Boyarin, Daniel Itzkovitz and Ann Pellegrini point out that "this biologization of difference can be seen in the invention or, perhaps more accurately, *re*invention of Jewish difference as a matter of race. It was as if Jewish gender and sexual life, both real and imagined, provided the key to unlocking Jewish racial difference. Long-standing stereotypes of Jewish gender difference were thus translated into signs of racial difference...."[26] European society ceased to judge the Jew through the prism of religious categories and instead saw the various characteristics differentiating Jews from others as enduring and natural racial features that included sexual deviancy. "Thus claims abound in both popular and scientific literature in Europe and America insinuating the Jewish male's sexual difference from other men."[27]

Some such differences were "the traditional long gown (Shylock's 'Jewish gaberdine') and uncut hair, the lively gesticulation (and wild, ecstatic dancing) of the Hasidic sect," all of whom looked strange and un-masculine. Another difference noted was the way in which Jewish men supposedly spoke "with a breaking, monotonous, undulating voice" that linked them to effeminate, homosexual or castrated men and to women.[28] A common charge leveled against Jews in the early years of the twentieth century was that they were especially feminine, "no more than degenerate, masturbating women."[29] One of many who claimed this was the Austrian Jew Otto Weininger, whose widely read *Sex and Character* was published after he committed suicide in 1903 at the age of twenty-three.[30]

But the allegation regarding Jewish men's femininity was not merely a stereotypic anti-Semitic perception; at least two Jewish scholars have expressed similar views. Aviva Cantor has argued that the Jewish community in the Diaspora became one extended family, a family that was steeped in female values such as cooperation and nonviolence. In response to the destruction of the Second Temple, the rabbis of that time concluded that this national disaster had resulted from the "tendency on the part of Jewish men to resist tyranny militarily no matter what the cost, to engage in wildcat revolts, and to fight last-ditch battles." If violence had proved futile in the homeland, the rabbis thought, then such tactics would surely be all the more ruinous in the Diaspora. Therefore, says Cantor, the rabbis ruled that violence should only be used as a last resort when all other options had been exhausted and that instead, opposition should be expressed spiritually.[31]

The first steps taken by the rabbis, according to Cantor, was to ban violence within the community, to prevent class conflicts, condemn violence against women and extol the virtues of stoicism and self-control. The consumption of alcohol was frowned upon and the use of "violence as a safety valve," even against animals, was forbidden. Putting an end to violence ensured that even the most heated arguments and the bitterest disputes would pass without the risk of their deteriorating into intracommunal fighting. Furthermore, an end to violence against women also ended blood feuds to preserve a family's honor that could undermine Jewish solidarity. Cantor adds that there were two further reasons for the banning of violence against Jewish women: the desire to make women feel free to leave the house in order to make a living and the fact that Jewish women were the prime targets of Christian hostility.[32]

Jewish women, Cantor emphasizes, were the lightning rods of non-Jewish hostility and were constantly under the threat of rape by non-Jews. What distinguished them from equally vulnerable non-Jewish women was their inability to rely on their menfolk to defend them – a fact that was apparent to non-Jewish men who knew that the Jewish community would not risk its existence to defend a woman or avenge the violation of her honor. Thus Jewish women were fair game, easy targets to be attacked without the risk of possible retaliation.[33]

The shame felt by Jewish men because of their inability to protect their womenfolk, says Cantor, led to self-doubt and demoralization that endangered the survival of the community. To prevent this, Jewish men had to be given more power within the community. Yet this was not consistent with the ban on violence. However dominant men may have been within the community their powerlessness vis-à-vis the outside world and the banning of violence continued to shame and demoralize them.[34] Cantor claims that the rabbis resolved this

> by changing the concept of what constituted male power and, even more fundamentally (since power is part of the definition of manhood), what constituted masculinity. They stripped male power of the glorification and practice of violence, of rugged individualism, rapacious exploitation, machismo, rampant cruelty, conquest, military prowess, physical heroism, and the abuse of women. They redefined power as knowledge, learning, and studying. They defined manhood itself in terms of commitment to

and achievement in learning Torah. Thus they replaced the classic patriarchal definition of masculinity, man-as-macho fighter, with the alternative definition of man-as-scholar.[35]

Studying Torah became an existential imperative, work that was essential to Jewish survival. In order that every male Jew could potentially participate in this study it had to be democratized, and given that the function of such study was to restore the male ego, it had to exclude women. The net result, Cantor concludes, was a Jewish community based on male dominance but imbued with feminine values.[36]

Daniel Boyarin concurs with this view and places an even greater emphasis on it than does Cantor. For the Jews who lived under Roman rule, Boyarin claims, the softness of rabbinic masculinity – with its focus on study and its image of "the gentle, humble, compassionate, 'maternal' male" – did more than merely protect the Jews. It was also a way for them to express their own self-worth by rising above the "harshness" of Roman militarism and by consciously opposing its "phallic, aggressive machismo as a definition of manliness."[37] The "passive, pale, gentle, and physically weak" Jewish masculinity was one of resistance and not merely of nurturing. This was because the most effective way of resisting Roman imperial power was precisely by practicing the "passive" and "weak" art of evasion, circumvention and pretence.[38] "Jewish society," Boyarin asserts, "needed an image against which to define itself and produced the 'goy' – the hypermale – as its countertype, as a reverse of its social norm.... Premodern Jewish culture...frequently represented ideal Jewish men as femminized [spelling intentional] through various discursive means. This is not, moreover, a representation that carries with it any hint of internalized contempt or self-hatred. Quite the opposite; it was through this mode of conscious alternative gendering that Jewish culture frequently asserted its identity over-against its surroundings."[39]

Moreover, Judaism's ideal of feminine Jewish men was, Boyarin suggests, an explicitly erotic model of masculinity, thought of as desiring and desirable. He points out that scholars were often described as feminine and beautiful (recalling as an example the story of Rabbi

Yochanan bar Nafcha and Resh Lakish) and were thought to be sexy
not because of their physical prowess but because of their commitment
to learning. Christianity, Boyarin observes, also offered an alternative
to the Roman notion of manliness. However, because Christianity
sexualized the idea of self-sacrifice and equated the penis with the
phallus it required its martyrs or holy men to be either celibate or
castrated. Jews, on the other hand, rejected the phallus as a symbol of
virility and created a sexualized type of feminine masculinity.[40]

Unfortunately for them, however, Jews lived in a European cultural
environment that was often contemptuous of learning and saw it as
a "female occupation." In the modern period these societies labeled
Jewish men as cowardly, submissive "nebbishes"; Jewish women as
powerful oversexed seductresses; and Jews as a whole as obsessive
sexual perverts.[41] The degenerate modern Jew appeared in the
consciousness of nineteenth-century Europe at exactly the same time as
did the modern homosexual. "This is more than historical coincidence,"
Boyarin writes, "...The very notion that humans can be distinguished
and categorized – as if they belong to separate sexual species – on the
basis of whom and how they characteristically desire is a fundamentally
novel and culture-bound historical development... [and] is by and large
a product of the nineteenth century."[42]

The modern homosexual and the modern Jew were both seen as
perverted, diseased, hypersexual and dangerous to children. Medical
thinking in the nineteenth century assumed that

> Jews were riddled by diseases, including madness, because of
> their marriage practices...their refusal to marry outside their inner
> group. These marriages were regarded as criminal, even when
> such "inbreeding" was not consanguineous.... The Jews were
> described not only as permitting sibling incest... in the course of
> history, but also actually practicing it even after they claimed to
> have outlawed it. It was thought that the pathological result of
> such practices was premature sexual maturity.[43]

Jewish hairiness was considered a sign of Jewish hypersexuality;
and Jewish "insanity" was seen as being reflected in "child abuse"

and even in the murder of children for ritual purposes. "Child abuse cases in late nineteenth century literature usually had a female child victim (Christian) and a Jewish male abuser who re-enacted the sexual fantasy of the Jewish rapist/murderer and his victims, like those that that featured so prominently in the debates about Jack the Ripper during this period. Child murder and sibling incest came to be linked in the forensic science of the period as the twin signs of the madness of the Jews."[44]

Interestingly enough, until the modern period Jews were remarkably indifferent to the scandalously scornful Christian view of them. When emancipation was finally on offer, more and more Jews wanted to integrate into European society. That was the first time they became fully exposed to the stinging impact of the universal contempt with which they were viewed by the broader society. Jewish "self-hatred," largely a nonexistent phenomenon during the time when Jews sought a separate existence in premodern Europe, apparently became rife with the dawn of the modern era.[45] In the face of the constant Christian assault on "Jewish manliness," European Jews who had acquired a general education – the *maskilim* who laid the foundations of such a large segment of contemporary Jewish knowledge, the Zionists and others – now rebelled against their "alternative gendering," despite the fact that this gendering was validated by Jewish culture itself.[46] Max Nordau, the hugely popular writer and Herzl's number two in the Zionist movement, thought that Zionism would revolutionize the image of the Jew by creating the "new Jew" and by a return to what he called "muscular Judaism" (*Muskeljudentum*). "Zionism," he declared, "regenerates the Jewish body through the physical education of the young generation, which will regenerate the long-lost muscular Judaism" of the Bar Kochba revolt against the Romans. His vision was embraced by the entire Jewish national movement, which established the first Jewish sporting association in Germany in 1898 and named it, not surprisingly, Bar Kochba. This was followed by the establishment in Europe of similar associations of the same name.[47]

Ironically, a similar process took place during the twentieth century in gay urban "gym culture," which rejected the image of the homosexual

"sissy" in favor of the exaggeratedly macho muscleman.[48] Recently, a
"post-gay" movement has emerged that questions the necessity of an
autonomous "gay culture" in separate urban "gay ghettos" and calls for a
form of gay assimilation.[49] Moreover, homosexual theoreticians are also
critical of traditional homosexual identity by adopting postmodernism's
rejection of "essentialism" and denying that homosexuality has any
innate quality about it. Identity, they insist, is fluid and transient, and
sexual "orientation" is a social construct that is subject to change.[50]

CHAPTER 15

FORCE AND JEWISH IDENTITY

S ince the beginning of the twentieth century, Jewish attitudes to the
use of force – a crucial element in the evolution of Jewish identity
– have fundamentally changed. Following the failure of the uprisings
in Judea in the first and second centuries CE resulting in the Roman
destruction of Jewish autonomy, Jews developed an aversion to the use
of physical force. This negativity, and a general reluctance to employ
any form of force, was a consistent feature throughout the history of
Jewish exile. The main reason for this was the Jews' dependence on the
goodwill of those who ruled them, combined with their minority status.
This pragmatic attitude often evolved into an ideology.

In the early days of Zionism, two of the most prominent Jewish
thinkers, Ahad Ha'am and Micha Josef Berdichevsky, offered opposing
viewpoints on the usage of force. Ahad Ha'am justified the traditional
Jewish dislike of physical force by arguing that Jewish singularity
was anchored in the moral and the spiritual power of its people. He
attributed Jewish survival to these twin values and to an avoidance of
the embrace of force by other nations that eventually disappeared. Ahad
Ha'am's view reflected the extent to which Jewish powerlessness had
become grounded in ideology. This in turn perpetuated powerlessness
as the distinguishing characteristic of Jewish identity in the Diaspora.[1]

This view riled the writer Micha Josef Berdichevsky (1865–1921),
who was influenced by Friedrich Nietzsche and the vitalism movement

of the early twentieth century. Berdichevsky believed in the revitalization of Jewish nationality and in a form of government modeled on that adopted by the newly established nation-states of Europe. He called for the revival of a Jewish nation that would resemble all other nations by discarding the mantle of morality as the essence of its existence. Berdichevsky pressed for the creation of a secular Jewish identity molded by historical events that preceded the Diaspora, such as the period of the Maccabees (164 BCE to 63 BCE).

Berdichevsky described the dispute over Jewish identity as a clash between "the book and the sword," two opposing forces that constantly collided throughout the course of Jewish history. This clash was personified by Moses, who received the ethical law on Mount Sinai, and Joshua, the conqueror, who followed him. During the period of the First Temple, these ethical precepts and the preaching of the prophets continued to clash with the activities of the kings of Judah and Israel. This conflict was clearly evident during the period immediately before and after the destruction of the Second Temple, in the confrontation between the Zealots and other Jewish militants, and the rabbinic sage Yochanan ben Zakkai. From then on, "the book" was the prevailing element in the life of Diaspora Jewry even though, according to Berdichevsky, "the sword" never really disappeared.[2]

The rise during the modern period of an increasingly violent form of anti-Semitism finally convinced the Jews of the Diaspora that the adoption of force was, in fact, their only option. In particular, it was the Kishinev pogrom of 1903, and the hundreds of pogroms that followed the Russian Revolution of 1905 in which thousands of Jews were killed, that led to this conclusion.[3] The poem, *The City of Slaughter*, was penned by the Jewish national poet and early Zionist, Haim Nahman Bialik, following a visit to Kishinev shortly after the deadly pogrom. The poem had a profound impact, leading many Jews to become secular and more receptive to new ideas.

Among Jews, modernity legitimized the use of force and began the slow erosion of powerlessness as a Jewish ideal.[4] This became evident early on in the history of Zionism. Max Nordau, Theodor Herzl's close associate, made an impassioned plea for what he termed "muscular Jewry," while the prominent Zionist leader Ze'ev Jabotinsky condemned Diaspora Jewry's aversion to physical manliness.[5] Earlier still, Leon Pinsker, a leader of the Hovevei Zion movement, argued that Diaspora Jewry had remained powerless primarily because it possessed no territory of its own. This, according to Pinsker, was the main source of Jewry's negative attitude to force. From that he drew the conclusion that it was the Jews themselves and their Diasporic mentality that were responsible for the spread of anti-Semitism.

Bialik called for an end to the disgrace and degradation that had been the Jewish people's lot for so long and urged Jews to defend themselves. The poet Shaul Tchernichovsky and the writer Yosef Haim Brenner, both prominent in the Zionist movement, first in Russia and then in Palestine, echoed Bialik's appeal. Their call to Jews to defend themselves also contributed to the gradual erosion of the established Diasporic refusal to come to terms with the need for self-defense instead of expecting foreign rulers to defend them against the rioting mob.[6]

This dynamic can also be plainly seen in the development of the Zionist movement. Initially, Zionists tacitly assumed that Palestine could be settled by the Jews without aggressiveness and use of force; they did not foresee an active resistance to such settlement by the country's Arab inhabitants.[7] On the contrary, the first Jewish settlers were convinced that the "Semitic people" had mutual interests and believed that Arabs and Jews could coexist without becoming embroiled in conflict. However, from time to time there were voices within the Zionist camp that disagreed with this assumption. For example, the thinker Hillel Zeitlin rejected the rosy scenarios of the Zionist mainstream explaining that "What all the [Zionists] forget, mistakenly or maliciously, is that Palestine belongs to others, and it is totally settled." Zeitlin argued that it was therefore impossible to realize Zionism's objectives without resorting to force.[8] Yet before the 1920s, voices such as Zeitlin's were generally dismissed out of hand; the consensus within the Zionist movement was that Jewish settlement of Palestine could be achieved through peaceful means.[9]

Though the Zionist belief in the possibility of reconciling Jewish and Arab claims remained intact, the periodic eruptions of Arab hostility did lead to the creation of an organization known as Hashomer

(The Watchman) to protect vulnerable Jewish settlements. Members of this group quickly became the prototype for a different breed of Jews, signaling the idea that Jews must stand up in defense of their settlements. A member of Hashomer was a Jew who had acquired a new identity, a precursor of the "Sabra"; a free actor, a "cowboy" of sorts, proud of his strength and ready to use it.[10]

In line with this thinking, Ze'ev Jabotinsky and Joseph Trumpeldor began, in 1915, to organize a Jewish legion, hoping that it would become a component in the British Army during the First World War. The British turned down this particular initiative though they did eventually agree to the formation of an auxiliary unit known as the Zion Mule Corps. This force played a part in the Gallipoli Campaign and became the first Jewish military unit in the British army. In Palestine, at approximately the same time, Aharon Ahronson set up the underground network known as Nili, a Jewish paramilitary group designed to engage in espionage and help the British defeat the Ottoman army.

At the end of the First World War in 1918, Palestine underwent a fundamental change. After ruling the area for four hundred years, the Ottoman Empire collapsed and its rule over Palestine was replaced by the British Empire. Its Egyptian Expeditionary Force, under the command of General Allenby, overran Palestine and after a period of time the League of Nations awarded Great Britain a mandate over significant areas of the Middle East, including Palestine. The terms of the Palestine mandate were based, inter alia, on the Balfour Declaration of 1917. Thus the Zionist settlers gained a new status and new opportunities. Those Zionists who supported an enhancement of force and favored its use – the most prominent of these being Jabotinsky – came to be known as "activists," while those who were opposed – most notably Ahad Ha'am – were labeled as "guardians" of the status quo.[11] In 1920, Zionist activists founded the Haganah, a prestate military organization that rapidly came under the authority of the Zionist leadership in Palestine and whose ideological agenda was defensive; its initial purpose was to protect the lives and property of the Jewish community. However, the Haganah's military orientation gradually changed and over time its activist identity expanded.

The heroism of the Zionist activist Joseph Trumpeldor, killed in an Arab attack on the northern Jewish outpost Tel Hai in March 1920, was a seminal event in the evolution of an Israeli ethos of Jewish force. Trumpeldor's last words – as paraphrased by Haim Brenner – "It is good to die for our country" – became an emblem of Zionist history. His death was to be a model for Jewish force in the service of Zionism, the defense of the homeland and the renewal of pride in Jewish honor through the use of force.[12] But at the time of Trumpeldor's death the majority of Jewish settlers in Palestine continued to believe in a strategy of defense and to hope that their objective would ultimately be achieved without resorting to force.

The Zionist movement only placed the use of force at the heart of its strategy after a slow and gradual process. During the early years of the British mandate, the Zionist leadership's philosophy was one of "evolutionary, lukewarm defensive ethos," with a preference for "day-to-day development" rather than embarking on an active confrontation with Arab belligerence.[13] Ze'ev Jabotinsky, who in 1923 founded Betar and in 1925 established the Union of Revisionist Zionism, fiercely opposed this strategy and called for a more pragmatic and activist approach like that of other European national movements.

Toward the end of the First World War Jabotinsky began to campaign for the establishment of a Jewish legion as part of Allenby's Egyptian Expeditionary Force. His persistence led to the formation of the 38th Battalion of the Royal Fusiliers, which came to be known as the first "Hebrew legion." Most of the battalion's recruits were Jews of Russian nationality living in Britain. The regiment, in which Jabotinsky was himself an officer, set off for training in Egypt in February 1918, and after a few months played an active role in military operations in the Jordan Valley. A short time later, two more battalions of Jewish soldiers (the 39th and 40th Battalions of the Royal Fusiliers) were added. The 39th Battalion was set up in the United States; among those who enlisted were David Ben-Gurion and Yitzhak Ben-Zvi. The 40th Battalion, named the First Battalion of Judah, recruited its members in the first part of 1918 in those areas of Palestine already under British control.

Jabotinsky hoped that these battalions would become the nucleus

of a Jewish military force in Palestine. The British, however, wanted
to prevent such a development and disbanded them at the beginning of
the 1920s. Jabotinsky continued to insist that the Zionist leadership take
pragmatic and energetic steps to hasten the development of a national
homeland supported by the British government; he firmly believed
that Britain's vital political interests in the Middle East were entirely
consistent with such steps and all that needed to be done was to ensure
that the British were made aware of this. Jabotinsky had no doubt that
a future Jewish-Arab conflict was unavoidable and therefore persisted
in his campaign for the creation of an organized and disciplined Jewish
military force. Though he had participated in the first initiatives that led
to the establishment of the Haganah, he thought of it as being no more
than a civilian militia rather than the structured and disciplined force
that he believed the Zionist movement required. But the leadership
of the Yishuv rejected Jabotinsky's approach. Its assumption – which
within a few years proved to be wrong – was that the armed forces of
the mandatory power would protect the Yishuv's security.[14]

Jabotinsky visualized the creation of a new Jewish identity forged
by ideals that differed from those of mainstream Zionism. In his book
Samson (1930), he portrayed the biblical hero Samson before his death,
blind and powerless, ready to destroy the Philistine temple in Gaza
and die beneath its ruins. Before doing so, Jabotinsky has Samson
instruct the Israelites to take three steps: Anoint a king and accept his
rule over them; gather iron – i.e., weaponry; and learn to laugh. Thus,
in Jabotinsky's interpretation, Samson's legacy contained no moral or
spiritual commandment. Its sole message was that Israel be a nation like
all other nations: arm itself and be prepared to use its military might.[15]

Jabotinsky resolved to inculcate young Jews with his own
worldview. To that end he established the youth movement Betar,
which was to be the foundation of his revisionist movement. Betar's
primary purpose was to train its membership for military confrontation.
Jabotinsky envisioned Betar's cadets developing a wholly new Jewish
identity whose motto would be "proud, generous, and cruel." There was
an irreconcilable clash between Jabotinsky and the members of Brit
Shalom, who advocated a compromise between Jews and Arabs. And

yet, Jabotinsky was able to picture an idyllic scenario in a distant future in which "there (in Palestine on both sides of the river Jordan) the son of Arabia, the son of Nazareth and my son will live a life of plenty and happiness." In the same vein he even spoke of the possibility that the president of the hoped-for state would be a Jew, and that an Arab prime minister would serve under him. However, Jabotinsky noted that "it is impossible to dream of an agreement between us and the Arabs of Palestine being accepted willingly. Not now, nor in the foreseeable future." A military confrontation between Jews and Arabs appeared to Jabotinsky to be an inevitability.[16]

The riots of 1929 in Hebron and Safed which culminated in the murder of dozens of Jews – though not necessarily Zionist settlers – convinced the Zionist leaders that war was inevitable and that self-defense was a primary need of the community. At first, the leadership tried to blame the British for their inability to control the Arab militants and impose a peace. But it quickly became apparent that such finger pointing was futile and that other solutions had to be found to resolve the Yishuv's security problems. The notion of an "evolutionary, lukewarm defensive ethos" had to be modified to a more pragmatic one. The Zionists began to understand that a peaceful solution was not within reach and therefore started to change their position about the use of force.

Time and again the revisionists called for an "iron wall" – an expression coined by Jabotinsky – of military might, which would ensure the Yishuv's future.[17] Youngsters who responded to these appeals joined Irgun Bet (Organization B), a paramilitary group that had broken away from the Haganah in protest against the strategy of defense and operated under the aegis of the revisionist movement. Their fervent hope was to be part of a new, awakening Jewish identity. In 1930, the revisionist activist Abba Ahimeir established the underground movement Brit Habiryonim (The Ruffians Alliance), which declared its opposition to what Ahimeir termed "the foreign occupation" – i.e., the British. He called on the country's Jewish youth to join Brit Habiryonim and Betar in fulfilling the ideal of protecting the national interest of the Yishuv which, in Ahimeir's view, was the most significant moral obligation of the settlers. He saw it as his duty to educate and train the country's youth for a future war of independence.[18]

For Ahimeir, Joseph Trumpeldor was the iconic symbol of militarism and a clear illustration of the necessity of going on the offensive. Ahimeir considered the willingness to use force as the ultimate test of every revolutionary leader and longed to bring the Zionist movement into line with other European independence movements. In furtherance of this, he adopted national displays and symbols of independence such as the blowing of the shofar at the Western Wall at the end of the Day of Atonement, an act the British authorities had banned. In articles which he published in the revisionist weekly journal the *People's Front* – of which he was the editor – Ahimeir strongly denounced the Zionist leadership. He was especially disparaging of Chaim Arlozorov, a leader of Mapai (the then Labor Party) and the head of the Jewish Agency's political department. In the wake of Arlozorov's murder in June 1933, Ahimeir was arrested on suspicion of incitement to murder. But about a year later the mandatory court acquitted him of that charge. He remained in prison for a further year for having organized Brit Habiryonim, which by then had been outlawed by the mandatory authorities. After this episode Ahimeir's political activity waned, though many of his views continued to inspire the revisionist movement.[19]

Chaim Arlozorov himself came into Mapai as one of the leaders of Hapoel Hatzair, a workers' party opposed to Jewish military activism. And yet Arlozorov, too, reached the conclusion that as far as the conflict with the Arabs of Palestine was concerned, the Yishuv would not be able to remain pacific. Toward the end of his short life he even talked of the possibility of an armed Jewish uprising to gain control of Palestine. David Ben-Gurion, who following Arlozorov's murder shifted the focus of his activities from the Histadrut (the Labor Federation) to the Palestine Zionist Executive (the Jewish Agency) and was elected as its head two years later, agreed with Arlozorov's latter-day thinking but tried nonetheless to maintain a dialogue with the Arabs.[20]

Hitler's rise to power in Germany finally put an end to the Zionist ethos of defense. From then on, according to Shapira, a new, more aggressive strategy was adopted which involved changes in Jewish identity as it related to the use of force. The Arab revolt that erupted in Palestine in 1936 and the inability or unwillingness of the British authorities to stop acts of hostility against Jews proved, yet again, that Jewish self-defense was the only effective response to murder and destruction of property. The extent of the violence displayed in the 1936 revolt, and the help which the Arabs received from the Nazi regime in Germany and the Fascists in Italy, led to calls from the Jewish street for revenge, though the Zionist leadership went to great lengths to limit acts of vengeance. The Jews of Palestine, Shapira concludes, became increasingly convinced that the "new Jewish identity" in Palestine required political independence and the use of force as a way of protecting Jewish life and honor, in contrast to what had repeatedly taken place in the Diaspora.[21]

Members of the Haganah began to expand the clandestine training programs they conducted in the use of weaponry. At the same time Irgun Bet transformed itself into a highly militant revisionist underground movement known as Etzel (an acronym for Irgun Tzva'i Leumi, the National Military Organization). It called on its members to sacrifice their lives for the community as a whole and to identify with Jewish heroic fighters such as Judah the Maccabee and Bar Kochba.[22] Failure to respond to the call was branded as shameful cowardice.

At the end of the 1930s, the socialist Zionist Yitzhak Sadeh initiated an offensive strategy known as "exiting the fence." Despite wide opposition within the Yishuv, this marked a new chapter in the employment of available Jewish force. The new strategy involved small units under Sadeh's command sallying forth from Jewish settlements at night to attack areas from which Arabs attacked. There was an increasingly clear perception within the ranks of the Haganah that a strategy of defense was not sufficient and that they shouldn't flinch from taking the initiative in launching military operations. These ideas were reenforced with the arrival in Palestine of Orde Charles Wingate, a British officer of Scottish descent who, though not a Jew, was a Zionist at heart. He instilled a new understanding of military power within the Haganah.

The story of the settlement of Hanita epitomized the mythology of

Jewish force during that period. On March 21, 1938, at the very height of violent Arab attacks on Jewish settlements, four hundred men and women, including one hundred members of the Haganah under the command of Yitzhak Sadeh, set out to establish a new settlement in western Galilee, an Arab heartland. As they were taking control of the area, an announcement made it abundantly clear that any attempt to attack the new settlement would be driven back with maximum force. Even though the establishment of Hanita cost the lives of ten settlers, its imprint was unmistakable. The Palestinian Jew had shed his old persona and discovered a new identity. Over time one of the expressions of this new identity was to be found in symbolic patriotic songs lauding the combination of the scythe and the sword.

Thus a new consensus began to evolve on the need for future independence based on military power. The older generation realized that their offspring had assumed a new identity, were strong and self-confident, and exhibited none of the fears and complexes associated with the Diaspora.[23] This new generation was strongly patriotic, devotees of a secular Zionist ideology and yet students of the Bible as the historical narrative of the Jewish nation.

It is evident that Jewish ambivalence toward Arabs living in Palestine increased during the period of British rule. The Arab presence was increasingly seen as a dangerous threat. The question of whether Jews and Arabs could one day coexist in Palestine was constantly on peoples' minds. Throughout that period the need for Jewish force was seen as the issue that transcended all others.[24]

In 1937 the Peel Commission, a British commission of enquiry into the violence that had erupted during the previous year, recommended the establishment in Palestine of two separate states: a Jewish state whose territory would include the Galilee, the Jezreel valley and the coastal plain down to Beer Tuvia – 17 percent of the country; and an Arab state consisting of the rest of Palestine west of the Jordan River. The Zionist leaders reluctantly accepted the plan while the Arabs turned it down flat. Given the circumstances, the British quickly shelved the plan and two years later came up with an alternative scheme. In May 1939, with a Second World War looming on the horizon, the British published a "White Paper" strictly limiting Jewish immigration into Palestine with the aim of eventually establishing one independent state with an Arab majority. Ben-Gurion condemned the document as a betrayal and launched an intense campaign to foil its implementation. With the outbreak of war in September 1939, Ben-Gurion famously called on the Yishuv to fight the war as if there were no White Paper and fight the White Paper as if there were no war.[25] After the White Paper the majority of Jews in Palestine became convinced, one way or another, that they would have to force the British out of the country.

In 1942, while acknowledging the 1937 Peel Commission plan to partition the country, American Zionists adopted the Biltmore Program which called for unrestricted Jewish immigration into Palestine after the war and for the establishment of a Jewish Commonwealth in the whole of the territory.[26] This was at a time when the full extent of the Holocaust in Europe was as yet unknown. The Biltmore Program was approved on the assumption that after the war millions of Jewish refugees would leave Europe and migrate to Palestine.

The historian David Biale has noted that the transition of European Jewry from a state of powerlessness to the possession of power grounded in an independent state in Palestine amounted to a complete transformation within the course of one generation – a very short period for such a complete change in a people's identity. It was Biale's assumption that this rapid metamorphosis led to a "crisis of Jewish ideology."[27] Political powerlessness, spanning the whole period from the great rebellion in 70 CE and the failure of the Bar Kochba revolt sixty-five years later, ended with the Zionist mutiny against the British and the establishment of the State of Israel.[28] The Jews suddenly began to abandon what, in Michael Selzer's view, had long been their unique contribution to the world: the hope of changing it through "powerlessness and suffering."[29]

According to Biale, the modern Jewish national identity and the use of Jewish political power emerged more or less at the same time. In the middle of the nineteenth century, Jews began to apply minimal levels of political power. In 1840, at the time of the infamous Damascus blood libel, Jewish leaders tried to use their influence to help their brethren living in that city. Similarly, the highly influential businessman Sir Moses Montefiore tried, at approximately the same time, to intervene on behalf of Russian Jewry. In 1860, the Alliance Israelite Universelle was established in France with the aim of defending Jewish rights, improving their social and political status and promoting Western culture in their midst. In 1893, the Central Association of German Citizens of Jewish Faith was founded in Berlin to protect Jews against eruptions of anti-Semitism. In Russia, self-defense became a central plank in the political platforms of both the Bund and Poalei Zion.

And yet, when compared to what was to happen in the wake of the Holocaust, these early changes seem negligible. As Biale points out, the Holocaust, which resulted in the disappearance of the Jewish "nation" in Europe because of Jewish powerlessness, entirely altered the course of Jewish history. Moreover, the scale of this catastrophe was such that the Jewish response to it differed significantly from other historical responses to national tragedy.[30] And the main component of the response was the elevation of force as a fundamental element of Jewish identity.

These changes were most evident in Palestine itself. There, Jewish identity became inextricably linked to the Holocaust. As Ben-Gurion said in a speech in 1947, "We should not be optimistic and take things lightly and we should not say that what happened in Europe to six million cannot happen to the 650,000 Jews in Eretz Israel."[31] The employment of force by the Yishuv signaled the end of such Jewish powerlessness, an impotence that had reached its nadir during the Holocaust. An existential fear directly linked to the Holocaust became a basic feature of Israeli identity and has remained so to this day.

Attainment of sovereignty and a policy of using force became an idée fixe in the consciousness of the Jewish community in Palestine after the Holocaust. Many Palestinian Jews regarded the use of force – including acts of terrorism – as the only way of accelerating the withdrawal of the British. In the course of the War of Independence of 1947–1949 the ethos of a defensive strategy made a comeback and collided with the increasingly dominant view within the Yishuv of the need for an offensive military strategy. These fault lines in relation to force and its usage were revealed to be important elements of Jewish identity.[32]

This dynamic intensified still further during the Six-day War of 1967. The war ended in a massive Arab defeat, in which the Israel Defense Forces (IDF) gained control of the Sinai Peninsula, the entire area of Palestine west of the Jordan and the Golan Heights. Many Israelis believed that Israel had become a major military power. But the war generated new questions concerning the issue of Israeli and Jewish identity, questions that remain unresolved to this very day. How did the persecuted become the conqueror, and in what way did this upheaval alter Jewish identity? How has an expansionist and annexationist form of Zionism that endangers the democratic character of the state affected the Jewish identity of that state?

Some of those who are critical of Israel's military action in 1967 reject the descriptions of a widespread fear among Israelis in the period immediately prior to the Six-day War that they were facing another holocaust. Tom Segev, who has written a comprehensive account of the war, adamantly insists that such fears were entirely genuine.[33] In an interview with the author, he confirmed that a powerful feeling of an impending holocaust gripped the country. In various archives, says Segev, he found letters sent in 1967 by American Jewish children and their parents to US president Lyndon Johnson pleading with him to save Israel. These children based their information on letters they had received from family and friends in Israel expressing an existential fear of a second Jewish holocaust.[34]

Moreover, at a personal and political level it is impossible to understand the issue of Jewish power without taking on board the fact that the Holocaust and the "never again" commitment it spawned is a core element of Israeli identity. Iconoclasts such as Avraham Burg may wish to argue that "the Holocaust is over" and that Israelis should therefore no longer be compelled to live in its shadow with the mentality of a people under siege or in a ghetto.[35] But many prominent Israelis disagree with this line of thinking.[36] In talking to the author, Tom Segev emphasized that the Holocaust continues to be an essential invigorating force in Israeli life. He points out that Jews from surrounding countries in the Middle East who did not experience the Holocaust firsthand nonetheless now have a personal, intuitive identification with it. Even some Israeli Arabs, according to Segev, have internalized the Jewish Holocaust as can be seen from the Holocaust museum in Nazareth, an Arab initiative wholly managed by Arabs.[37]

As Jabotinsky foresaw, Samson's persona and the Masada revolt supplied symbols to an evolving Israeli identification with force. However, in Biale's view, this transformation has not resolved the age-old Jewish question; contempt for the persecuted has turned into a disdain for the persecutor and anti-Semitism has simply evolved into anti-Zionism.[38]

The unending conflict with the Arab world only served to reinforce the Zionist strategy of an "iron wall" – a strategy that calls for the use of overwhelming force.[39] This dynamic process possibly reached its peak during the Lebanon war of 1982. In Biale's view, that was when the use of force finally became an integral component of Jewish identity.[40] The Israeli invasion of Lebanon – seen by many Israelis as the first war of choice in the country's history – demonstrated that the use of force by the Jewish state was no longer limited to defensive operations. For Biale, that war symbolized a delayed reaction to the Holocaust. It completed the total transformation of Jewish identity from the powerlessness of European Jewry to the powerful State of Israel. Many in Israel saw the war as an abuse of the state's might. It reignited the old question on the role of moral considerations in the employment of military power.[41]

As has been stated, the Holocaust consciousness significantly influenced Israeli/Jewish thinking on defense. This is proven by the fact that resorting to preemptive strikes is regarded as self-evident – that is how Israelis viewed both the 1981 attack on the Iraqi nuclear reactor and the 2007 attack on the Syrian nuclear reactor before they became operational. This notion of a first strike is reflected in the ongoing debate about an attack on the Iranian nuclear facilities before they turn from being a potential threat to an actuality, threatening the survival of the Jewish state. It is noteworthy that many foreign governments apparently accept the primacy of the existential decree that "it never happen again." This is evident from the muted protests, if indeed there were any such protests, against past preemptive Israeli strikes.

Professor Ruth Wisse, an acknowledged authority on Yiddish literature, points to what she sees as the profound "contradiction of Jewish power" in that Israel's military might has not resulted in its acceptance or enhanced the state's admissibility within the international community. This stands in contrast to what the military prowess of other nations has achieved in terms of international recognition and acceptance.[42]

Nonetheless, Professor Wisse unreservedly supports Israel's continuation of an "iron wall" strategy and insists that the unwavering Arab rejection of the Jewish state fully justifies such an approach. At the same time, she strongly objects to the glorification of powerlessness in Jewish history and claims that from the perspective of Jewish thought it is, in fact, unethical.[43] Wisse bases herself on Plato who, in an early version of *The Republic*, ranked the importance of the republic's soldiers as second only to that of the rulers themselves. Wisse also cites the Constitution of the United States which recognizes the need for a "common defense." What then, asks Wisse rhetorically, leads Jews to be so apologetic when it comes to their use of force? Her answer is that the Jews suffer from a clear "political deficiency." Throughout history, the Jewish preoccupation was with the arts and religion rather than the political sciences. That, according to Wisse, accounts for their undistinguished performance in the art of politics and above all their tragically late recognition of the value of political power.[44]

Wisse's theory explains the strong link between contemporary Jewish identity and the burning issue of the use of force by Jews. Stated succinctly, the issue opposes the immutable commitment to never again be powerless against the avoidance of the usage of force and a stubborn identification with the victims of the powerful. In today's world, identifying oneself as a Jew involves deciding which side of the coin to go for, and which Jewish tradition to espouse: Should it be the Jew of early times, militarily heroic and brave, or the Diaspora Jew, the quintessential embodiment of the oppressed "other" in both the medieval as well as in the modern world.

It seems that parallels to all of this can be found in contemporary debates about Jewish identity.

CHAPTER 16

RELIGIOUS JEWISH IDENTITY

A cross the generations religion was unquestionably the single most important factor in the survival of Jewish identity. Ahad Ha'am's adage "more than Jews kept the Sabbath, the Sabbath kept the Jews," is a clear pointer to the role that religion played in securing the persistent existence of the Jewish people. Moreover, Judaism is the only religion that is linked to a particular geographic area, and the complex tension between land and people has been a continuous motif in religious Jewish identity.

Traditional Judaism encompasses the observance of all the wide-ranging ritual laws which touch on every aspect of a Jew's life. It is a life of distinct customs, a separate dialect; until modern times, Jewish life even included a recognized legal autonomy. From a theological perspective, it is a life sanctioned by God, Whose authority is transmitted through the Oral Law, received on Mount Sinai by Moses together with the Written Torah. The Oral Law was, indeed, passed on orally from one generation to another until the second century CE when it became a written text knows as the Mishnah. Over time, the Mishnah was expanded and interpreted, whereupon the interpretations together with the Mishnah formed the Gemara, or Talmud. The accepted laws and values of Jewish life, originally derived from the Mishnah and Gemara, are known as the Halachah. From a sociological point of view the Halachah ensured the Jews a "unique ethnic identity and, indeed, a singular national identity"[1] and thus also secured the continued survival of Jews as Jews in the Diaspora.

ORTHODOX JUDAISM

This traditional Jewish identity is today known as "Orthodox Judaism," though this term did not appear until 1795. During the nineteenth century the term was commonly used to describe all those Jews who rejected any of the changes that stemmed from the Enlightenment, Jewish assimilation or secularization, and insisted on maintaining the national/ethnic identity molded by the Halachah.[2] However, in the absence of any ultimate authoritative hierarchy, or any other body that could be said to represent the Orthodox movement as a whole at all levels of the community and in every country, Orthodox Judaism was, from the outset, riven by fierce factionalism and divisions that were difficult to bridge.[3]

Making sense of the huge diversity within religious Orthodox Judaism is a difficult task. Generally speaking it is possible to divide Orthodox Judaism (which represents 10 percent of American Jewry[4]) into three groups: the Charedim or ultra-Orthodox (a term regarded by some as derogatory); the Centrist Orthodox; and the Modern Orthodox. However, these blocs are by no means monolithic.[5] The Charedim, who account for roughly a quarter of Orthodox Jewry in the United States, and between 250,000 and 300,000 in Israel, are split between two camps. First there are the Chasidim; each Chasidic sect is loyal to a particular dynasty, led by a charismatic and highly venerated Chasidic *admo"r* (a Hebrew acronym of an honorific title given to certain rabbis that stands for "Our Master, Our Teacher, and Our Rabbi"). Then there are the Lithuanians (Litvaks) who strictly follow the teachings of the head of their yeshiva. (The term "Litvak" is used, especially in Israel, to describe rabbis and yeshiva students adhering to certain lifestyles and ways of study originating in eastern Europe). Built into these two subgroups are additional factions, their number being dependent on how many *admo"r*s or heads of yeshivas there are who have the standing to attract a group of Chasidim or yeshiva students around them. One isn't simply a Chasid or member of a yeshiva; one is either a follower of a certain *admo"r* or of a certain head of a yeshiva.[6]

On matters of substance, Orthodox Jewry is split on a wide range of theological and sociological issues. Thus, for example, on the issue of God's revelation to Moses on Mount Sinai there are those who unequivocally believe that the Almighty literally dictated every word of the Torah to Moses. Others are less adamant and say that the precise way in which the Torah was handed down by the Creator is a matter open to interpretation, but that the event itself undoubtedly took place.[7] As for the Halachah, the vast majority of Orthodox Jews are firm in their view that it is eternal and unchangeable, though there is a minority whose position is less rigid, pointing out that the Oral Law did, in fact, downplay the severity of some of the biblical laws.[8] The debate about the compatibility of Jewish nationalism and Orthodoxy has been raging for more than a century, first in Europe and then in the United States. Divisions of opinion about Zionism among Orthodox Jews are quite fierce. Unlike most Charedim, Orthodox Centrists and the Modern Orthodox accept Zionism. Chabad's Chasidim are to a certain extent an exception within the Charedi community on this issue. They enthusiastically support the State of Israel but completely avoid identifying themselves with any aspect of Zionism.[9]

As regards adaptation to the surrounding culture, there were Orthodox Jews who feared any hint of such adaptation, even to the point of rejecting political emancipation. Others welcomed the emancipation, but were adamant about complete social and cultural segregation from non-Jews. There were also those who accepted social and economic adaptation, but clung to a Judaism that was impervious to change and thus kept them shielded from the influences of the outside world. This group adopts secular education not only as a way of improving their socioeconomic situation, but also because of its contribution to the appreciation of the transcendental nature of Judaism. This is, of course, a reference to Modern Orthodox Jews, who were, and still are, the subject of scathing attacks by those Orthodox Jews who oppose any penetration of secular culture into Judaism.[10]

Disputes over cooperation with non-Orthodox rabbis have erupted ever since the Jews first used the term "Orthodoxy." The abhorrence of those who tried to bring about reforms in the Jewish religion caused certain nineteenth-century Orthodox leaders to support organizational separation from the Jewish community as a whole; others had reservations about this idea as they wanted to preserve Jewish unity. Agudat Israel, which was founded in 1912, was nearly torn asunder by the debate over withdrawal, but in the end those who supported such separation gained the upper hand. Meanwhile, the Mizrachi community adopted a more liberal view and sanctioned cooperation with non-Orthodox and even secular Jews.

The whole subject is still the source of bitter and passionate controversy within the Orthodox camp, where there is a very wide range of views: from hatred of non-Orthodox Jews to the point of being willing to use violence against them, through support for total separation without enmity, up to tacit acceptance of a pluralistic Jewish world, while still rejecting its views; from outward acceptance of all Jews, but maintaining, in practice, an intolerance toward the non-Orthodox streams, up to a genuine interest in cooperation with all Jews – at least in the United States. Ironically, even some segments of the most inflexible camp in the United States do not appear to be sufficiently Orthodox from the perspective of their Israeli counterparts. As far as the Israeli ultra-Orthodox are concerned, American Charedim are not what they claim to be. They are simply Americans who have been tainted by contact with US culture no matter how hard they try to isolate themselves from it.[11]

American Orthodoxy's apparently inevitable adaptation to its surroundings, says Jeffrey S. Gurock, has a basis in history. Life in America has always led to an "inescapable reality" of adapting religious practices and compromising on adherence to Halachah – even among the most extreme Orthodox.[12] Economic distress caused Orthodox Jews, who were a significant part of the Jewish migration from eastern Europe to the United States at the turn of the twentieth century, to begin to be less faithful to the Halachah even before they had departed Europe. Observance slackened in Russia, Poland and Rumania, countries in which many Orthodox Jews were obliged to work on the Sabbath. Various documents also testify to the fact that many did not scrupulously adhere to religious practices during the voyage to America (such as washing their hands as prescribed or praying at specific times). Many men shaved off their beards immediately after disembarking, and there were similarly many women who uncovered their hair as soon as they were on dry land. Though their tefillin (phylacteries) and candlesticks were carefully stowed away in their tattered suitcases, their usage increasingly diminished.

Even those who were determined to resist acculturation were forced in the end to bow to economic considerations and social pressure. In light of laws that enforced the closure of business on Sundays there were very few Orthodox Jews who could afford the luxury of an additional day off – the Sabbath – from their working week, a phenomenon that was even more conspicuous in smaller American towns. Maintaining a traditional Jewish identity based on the Halachah became more and more difficult for Orthodox Jews and was even more difficult for succeeding generations educated in America's public schools. Many second- and third-generation immigrants continued to identify themselves as Orthodox but their adherence to the Halachah during the 1920s and 1930s became increasingly superficial.[13]

The immigration of Chasidic Charedim to the United States after World War II added another element to the mix. Since the 1970s, as their numbers grew and their Orthodoxy intensified, the influence of the Charedim on the American Jewish community has significantly increased. The pattern set by earlier generations has been turned on its head. The Charedi children are more traditionalist than their parents were and their intolerance of diversity is greater than that of the previous generation. The unavoidable outcome is an increasing polarization between the traditionalists and the modernists as well as growing friction within the two camps.[14] This continuing polarization within Orthodoxy, one scholar concluded, "seriously threatens to split the whole movement."[15]

And yet, even the most die-hard Charedim in Israel are taking their first tentative steps toward modernization. During Israel's first two decades as an independent state the government gave financial assistance and an exemption from military service to a limited number of yeshiva students for whom "learning [the Torah] was their profession," in order to revive within the Jewish state the world of yeshiva learning that the Nazis had destroyed in eastern Europe. In 1968 the number of such yeshiva students was 400 and in that same year the number doubled to 800.

In the wake of the political upheaval in Israel in 1977 (which brought the Likud to power) the new prime minister, Menahem Begin, abolished the "quota" and allowed this exemption from military service to be granted to any Charedi Jew who was willing to devote himself full time to learning in a yeshiva. By the early years of the twenty-first century, the numbers involved had already grown to some eighty thousand men, about half of them married and raising a family. A finding in 2010 suggested that 65 percent of all Charedi men between the ages of thirty-five and fifty-four were unemployed as a matter of their own choice, three times more than had been the case thirty years earlier. That said, the sharp rise in the cost of living during those three decades meant that the benefits paid by the state to Charedi families became woefully inadequate.

From the mid-1990s and onward, Charedi rabbis began to permit some members of their flocks to take vocational training courses so as to ease their dire economic distress. Undoubtedly this trend will be accelerated as a result of the Supreme Court's ruling in 2010 that the discrimination between yeshiva students and secular students had to be ended. With the anticipated doubling of the Charedi population in Israel to more than one million by 2022, there will be intensifying pressure from both the secular population as well as from within the Orthodox community itself to increase the effort to integrate the Charedim into modern Israeli society.[16]

The political power and influence of Israel's religious parties is disproportionate to their numbers in the country, a situation that is greatly resented by the secular population. The power of these parties stems from the lack of separation of religion and state, and the need of secular parties to placate their religious counterparts so as to induce them to join the governing coalition. This situation has led to a deepening rift between the secular and religious populations of Israel and has had a negative impact on the shaping of a unified Jewish identity.

REFORM JUDAISM

Traditional Judaism's ethnic/national identity proved to be highly problematic in all matters related to the acculturation of Jews during the period of the Enlightenment and thereafter. Those who supported acculturation began to distance themselves from the Halachah not only because of its burdensome ritual imperatives but also because of the separate ethnic/national identity that it denoted. For early reformers of Judaism – beginning with Moses Mendelssohn in the eighteenth century – the aim of the reforms was to remove the Halachic obstacles to their full integration, as Jews, into non-Jewish society. Reforming Judaism by a transition to a non-ethnic/non-national religious existence was seen by the reformers as a necessary step toward securing the continued survival of Judaism in modern Europe.[17]

The reformers are commonly thought to have all been German Jews, despite the fact that among them there were Jews from numerous European countries. Their aim was to find a "third way" between traditional Judaism and assimilation into the non-Jewish society (ending in their total disappearance). They hoped that by introducing modern aesthetics into the synagogue they could win back the large number of Jews in central Europe who had detached themselves from Judaism but had not yet converted to Christianity.[18] At the same time they hoped that by presenting Judaism as an absolutely acceptable and modern religious denomination they would succeed in improving the image of Jews among enlightened Christians.[19]

In traditional Ashkenazi synagogues the acts of worship were highly individualistic. Prayers were only said in Hebrew and sung to ancient melodies, while the use of musical instruments on the Sabbath and during High Holidays was strictly banned. "This religious atmosphere," says Robert Seltzer, "spontaneous and informal, looked disrespectful, undignified, Oriental, to those acculturated Jews who had instigated the reforms."[20] In response to these shortcomings the early Reformists made the following innovations: they turned the synagogue into a more dignified place of worship and had the prayers chanted in greater harmony by introducing a mixed male and female choir into the service; they shortened the liturgy and modernized it in both Hebrew and German; they emphasized the significance of Sabbath prayer over the daily morning, midday and evening prayers; they abolished the accents and musical motifs that characterized "Oriental" readings of the Bible as well as the traditional "national" prayers that spoke of a return to Zion and the imminent coming of the Messiah; most importantly of all, they introduced a weekly sermon that underscored the rational and ethical aspects of Judaism.[21]

The significance of these changes can be better understood if seen against the background of the reformers' primary belief in the legitimacy of religious innovation which, they insisted, had been a feature of Jewish life for generations. "The guiding principle of the contemporary Reform movement," suggests Dana Evan Kaplan, "is its ability to adapt Jewish religious beliefs and practices to the needs of the Jewish people from generation to generation." If Jewish sages were able to create various laws in response to specific historic circumstances, then the rigid adherence to Halachah by contemporary Jews, irrespective of current historical circumstances (which is to say, modern science) is hard to justify.[22] In the words of Rabbi Samuel Holdheim (1806–1860) one of the first members of the Reform movement:

> All the talk about Talmudic Judaism is tantamount to an illusion. Science has determined that the Talmud has no dogmatic or practical authority. Even those who do not acknowledge this, bypass the Talmud. The question is, who gives us the right to change the liturgy? This question requires a clear-cut answer. The rabbis who determined the traditional order of prayer during the period of the Second Temple had the authority to do so for their day only; their dictates were fine for that time, with limited validity. Today we possess the very same authority in relation to our generation. However, even if the Talmud does not bind us, we do not want to erase the importance of an intellectual activity that spanned two thousand years. All we are saying is this: anything that, following a careful, unbiased critical examination, contradicts the sensibilities of our time is unacceptable to us.[23]

This issue was widely discussed among Jews who had undergone modernization. The person who put it into classic textual form was Solomon Maimon (1753–1800). He was considered so brilliantly well versed in the Talmud that he was ordained before the age of twenty, but he quickly abandoned the rabbinate for the modern world. In his autobiography, Maimon questioned the value of the Talmud:

> Take the subjects of the Talmud…in which the oddest rabbinical conceits are elaborated through many volumes with the finest dialectic, and the most absurd questions are discussed with the highest efforts of intellectual power; for example, how many white hairs may a red cow have, and yet remain a *red* cow; what sorts of scabs require this or that sort of purification; whether a louse or a flea may be killed on the Sabbath – the first being allowed, while the second is a deadly sin; whether the slaughter of an animal ought to be executed at the neck or the tail; whether the high priest put on his shirt or his hose first; whether the *Jabam*, that is, the brother of a man who died childless, being required by law to marry the widow, is relieved from his obligation if he falls off a roof [on top of the widow] and sticks in [her] mire. *Ohe jam satis est!* (Enough already!)[24]

Although Maimon was not a Reform Jew, his position represented the period well: Halachah had clearly lost its significance for many Jews who had chosen modernization and acculturation.

The response of the Reform movement that began to emerge in the nineteenth century (what has been labeled "Classical Reform") was to downplay the role of Halachah and instead emphasize the universalist ethics that Judaism represented. Reform's version of Judaism as a modern, rational religion was based on what was considered to be the paramount message of the prophets: the struggle for social justice. While recognizing the universalist teachings of the prophets, the reformers persisted in pointing to the uniqueness of Judaism and its mission to disseminate ethical monotheism. This approach combined the Jewish belief in one God with rational thought and scientific progress. Emphasizing the nation of Israel's mission "justified the continued existence of the Jewish people by arguing that their survival as a religious group was essential if the Jews were to bring to the world their universal message of ethical monotheism."[25]

Since individual and congregational autonomy were considered a guiding factor of the Reform movement, the precise way in which Classical Reform was expressed varied from one synagogue to another.[26] Nonetheless, historians have tended to portray the Reform movement as having clearly discarded Judaism's ethnic/national identity.[27] This is evident in the movement's early attitude to Zionism. Reform Jews in America thought that acculturation (or Americanization) did not allow for any degree of double loyalty. Loyalty to Zionism, or Eretz Israel, necessarily precluded loyalty to the United States ("our Zion"). Thus Reform ideology declared its commitment to full integration save for holding onto Judaism's most fundamental religious beliefs. In that respect, "Judaism" would parallel "Christianity" as a purely religious sect. Like their non-Jewish neighbors, Reform Jews were patriotic Americans. The only difference between the two would be their religion. Jews consequently had to distance themselves from the merest hint of tribal exclusiveness.[28]

However, in Professor Yaakov Ariel's opinion, this accepted view of Classical Reform is a myth, because it fails to take into account "the astonishing gap between the declared ideals of the Reform movement...and the attitudes of its rank and file members.... The Reform movement's character was almost diametrically opposed to its proclaimed universalist aspirations. As a parochial, tribal, ethnocentric group, Reform Jews were concerned with 'Jewish' issues at the local, national and international level, and were involved in the lives of their non-Reform Jewish brethren."[29] This dichotomy was inevitable in light of the mass migration of Jews from eastern Europe to America in the last two decades of the nineteenth century. The new immigrants felt alienated from the "non-Kosher" Judaism of Classical Reform. At that stage the Reform establishment realized that it would have to adjust itself to a new demographic cohort of American Jews – one that adhered to traditionalist practices that the Reform movement had long ago discarded, such as the use of Yiddish and a messianic belief in a return to Zion. Nor could they ignore the fact that the immigrants and their children were sympathetic to Zionism and vehemently rejected the idea that their Zionism was in some way anti-American.[30]

Increasing anti-Semitism in the course of the twentieth century served to intensify this dynamic. The evolving political situation compelled the Reform movement to resign itself to, and ultimately to embrace, a more particularistic concept of Jewish identity and define Judaism in terms that focused on Jewish peoplehood. In the mid 1920s, the movement's attitude toward Zionism also began to change when leaders such as Judah Magnes, Abba Hillel Silver, Louis Newman and Stephen S. Wise broke away from the majority's anti-Zionist stance. After the Holocaust, support for Zionism spread throughout the movement (with the exception of small groups such as the American Council for Judaism). From then on, it has been wholeheartedly committed to the establishment of the State of Israel and the promotion of its interests.[31]

Similar progress has been made in the observance of Jewish rituals. Reform Judaism was never able to reach a consensus on the issue of ritual compliance and by the middle of the nineteenth century it covered an extensive array of views on the subject. In general it can be said that the Reform movement tended to shed religious commandments (such as kashrut) that kept Jews isolated from non-Jews and that maintained a distinct Jewish way of life that hampered the process of social integration. But this, too, ultimately changed. Later on in the twentieth century there was a better understanding among Reform Jews of the central role played by ritual observance in Jewish life as they readopted ceremonies and traditions that Classical Reform had abandoned. They did and do this, so they insist, not because they have come to accept the Orthodox view that these are God's commandments but out of a realization that these ceremonies and traditions give every individual Jew an added sense of spirituality. As Kaplan put it, "the traditional belief that religious laws had to be obeyed because they were God-given has been re-interpreted and is now understood as an acknowledgment of God's indirect inspiration in what is essentially a process of human spiritual expression."[32]

The innovations introduced by Reform Judaism in the last decades of the twentieth century include: the recognition, in 1983, of patrilineal Jewish descent – whereas the Halachah recognizes only matrilineal descent – so as to unambiguously welcome the many offspring of mixed marriages; the appointment of women as rabbis and cantors as well as to various other religious posts (the first woman was ordained in 1972 and female rabbis are now so integrated that it is barely worthy of noting); having gender-sensitive prayers included in the service (such as praising "our foremothers" as well as "forefathers"); and supporting gays and lesbians (including, since 1980, their ordination as rabbis). These milestones have been accompanied by "a new Reform revolution" aimed at revitalizing and restructuring the movement by emphasizing music and introducing emotive elements in Reform synagogue services. Since most Reform Jews do not understand the Hebrew words of the daily prayers and are unable to read these words in the prayer book, the Reform movement has initiated a program in Hebrew reading skills so as to "open the gates of prayer" to all ordinary Jews.[33]

In addition, the Reform movement has committed a significant proportion of its resources to developing its sister movement in Israel, the Israel Movement for Progressive Judaism (IMPJ), which was officially launched in 1971. In cooperation with the Conservative movement, IMPJ embarked on a far-reaching campaign to encourage Israelis to take part in the synagogue services of both movements and encourage non-Orthodox marriage ceremonies. However, thus far they have been unable to end the Orthodox monopoly over religious affairs in Israel.[34]

CONSERVATIVE JUDAISM

In 1845, at the second conference of Reform rabbis in Frankfurt, a stormy debate erupted on the use of Hebrew in Reform services, prompting Rabbi Zacharias Frankel to walk out of the conference hall in protest. Frankel (1801–1875) would go on to exemplify the "historical school" that promoted positive-historical Judaism, accepting the Reform view of an evolving dynamic Jewish tradition but demanding that the "positive" aspects of the Jewish tradition be preserved.[35] Frankel argued that the basis for maintaining traditions – and in particular the laws that merited being kept – was not merely a homage to their past utility but also the sentimental attachment that ordinary Jews continued to feel for them. In Frankel's view, the ultimate judgment about the preservation of Jewish traditions would be made in accordance with the religious feelings of the majority of the Jewish people rather than by the historical judgment of intellectual elites.[36]

The name Conservative Judaism was first coined by Solomon Schechter (1847–1915) who in due course became the president of the Jewish Theological Seminary of America (JTS).[37] Conservative Judaism, the single largest Jewish denomination in the United States in the decades following World War II, represented the centrist perspective that embraced both tradition and change and kept past traditions that were still regarded as relevant to today's world.[38] How precisely this was implemented varied from one synagogue to another since the movement as such had no accepted, binding policy. Conservative Judaism never annunciated an official set of principles in the way that Reform Judaism had done. There was thus always a vagueness about its goals and beliefs, an outlook that was "amorphous and incoherent" which in Mordechai Kaplan's words was *"nicht milchig undt nicht fleischig"* – "neither dairy nor meat."[39] And yet, the written works of the Jewish Theological Seminary's faculty and its graduates clearly reveal the Conservative movement's fundamental premises as they have evolved in the course of the twentieth century: Judaism had to be adapted to the modern age, but in so doing the traditional laws, rituals and beliefs (as well as the Hebrew language) had to be preserved as much as possible.[40]

In the view of many, such an approach makes Conservative Judaism nothing more than a carbon copy of Orthodox Judaism. This conclusion was reinforced by the fact that rabbis who were trained and ordained by Orthodox institutions, who also continued to identify themselves as Orthodox, regularly officiated in Conservative synagogues.[41] But Conservative Judaism differs in a number of important ways from Orthodox Judaism. Firstly, the Conservative movement regards Judaism as an evolving religion; in the view of Conservative Jews, Judaism's strength lies precisely in its ability to adapt to changing circumstances. Secondly, within the Conservative movement the emphasis is on a plurality of views and diverse voices that seek to balance tradition and modernity. Unlike Orthodox Judaism, the Conservative movement never compelled its members to adhere to a particular set of ideological principles. Thirdly, Conservative Judaism is distinguished by a consistent effort to establish an appropriate legislative mechanism to help adapt traditional Judaism to modern conditions. Fourthly, Conservative Judaism had, and has, a strong commitment to hold on to the innovations first introduced by the movement's early reformers so as to continue to attract new members. These innovations included allowing families to sit together in synagogue (without there being separate areas for men and women), sermons in English, modern religious schools, and a rabbinical leadership trained "scientifically." And fifthly, since its foundation, the Conservative movement has emphasized the notion of Jewish peoplehood, the importance of which was downplayed by Orthodox Judaism (not to mention Classical Reform).[42]

Among Jewish theologians of the Conservative movement there always were those who held supernatural concepts of God. The essays, lectures and sermons of Conservative thinkers, with few exceptions, spoke of "a creating, choosing, revealing, active, omnipotent, omniscient, benevolent, personal God."[43] Jewish Conservative thinkers also generally take a middle position between Orthodox and Reform in relation to the question of whether the Torah was directly revealed to Moses on Mount Sinai by God. Unlike the Orthodox, Conservatives do not claim that God revealed himself to Moses and dictated every word (verbal revelation). Nor do they accept the Reformists' belief that the Torah is a human creation (progressive revelation). The Conservative centrist view is that the Torah was written by human hand with inspiration from God (continuous revelation).[44]

A similar "mid-way" view applies to the Conservative movement's approach to the Halachah. The movement stresses the importance of conserving the laws and rituals of traditional Judaism but recognizes the need to change them so that they are relevant to the needs of the present. For example, the prohibition on traveling on the Sabbath remains in force with one exception: travel to a synagogue to facilitate prayer. Similarly, the laws relating to Kashrut remain, but with a waiver:

a person is required to maintain strict adherence to these laws at home, while in public places compliance is less rigid. A third example can be seen in the Conservative stance on divorce. During the Talmudic period Jewish law (based on the rabbinic interpretation of the first verses of Deuteronomy 24) gave the husband the sole right to divorce his wife. The Halachah qualified this seemingly arbitrary right by giving wives a lien on their husbands' property, thus creating a built-in financial settlement for any divorce. The amendment, however, could not be enforced in a modern state in which the rabbis have no jurisdiction in civil matters. The Reformist responded to this with a total annulment of the need for a religious divorce. The Orthodox, on the other hand, stood firm on adherence to religious law. By adding a paragraph to the *ketubah* (Jewish marriage contract), the Conservative movement found a middle way between these two opposing positions. This additional clause stated that in the event of a divorce both husband and wife would have to appear before a rabbinic court and abide by its ruling. Thus, instead of husbands deciding the matter, the authority to grant a divorce was handed over to the rabbinate. As always, the Conservative movement found a way to both maintain and change the Jewish tradition.[45]

During the 1960s, Conservative Judaism began to lose its dominance among American Jews. Increasing assimilation and intermarriage, together with a growing attraction of progressive social movements and countercultures, widened the gap between observant rabbis and their far less observant flock. Many of the more fastidious congregants joined Orthodox synagogues, while others abandoned the Conservative movement in favor of Reconstructionist Judaism. The debate over the desired response to these developments polarized the movement between those who favored more reforms and those who demanded less change.

The primary bone of contention during the 1970s and 1980s was the role of women in the movement. In 1972 only 7 percent of Conservative synagogues allowed women to read from the Torah during the service; just four years later that number rose to 50 percent. And yet, in 1974, the movement's Committee on Laws and Standards found it difficult to reach a clear decision on the issue of women being counted as part of the quorum of ten required by religious law for the conduct of a religious service. In the years between 1977 and 1983, the issue of the ordination of women led to stormy debates in the rabbinical assembly and among members of the Jewish Theological Seminary's faculty. In 1979, the traditionalists succeeded in blocking this move but were then forced to come to terms with it in 1983 and with the follow-up decision in 1987 to allow women to serve as cantors. The question of gender equality led some traditionalists to leave the movement and in 1979 to found the Union for Traditional Conservative Judaism, a move that still further weakened the movement. In the year 2000 only 26 percent of American Jews who were members of a synagogue and only 33 percent of families within this segment of the population identified themselves as Conservatives.[46]

RECONSTRUCTIONIST JUDAISM

Reconstructionism is the only religious branch of Judaism to have evolved entirely in the United States. It is also the only branch of the religion to have been inspired by just one man, Rabbi Mordecai M. Kaplan (1881–1983), and to have been developed by a small band of believers.[47] Kaplan, who arrived in America from Lithuania at the age of eight, grew up in an Orthodox community and served as an associate rabbi in an Orthodox synagogue in New York before joining the faculty of the Conservative movement's Jewish Theological Seminary in 1909. However, in Kaplan's view none of the three established branches of Judaism had succeeded in solving the problems that stemmed from the increasing acculturation and modernization of the American Jewish community. In 1920, he formulated a bold vision that challenged conventional thinking (published in its final form in his book *Judaism as a Civilization: Toward a Reconstruction of American-Jewish Life*).[48]

Kaplan believed that Judaism was an evolving "Jewish civilization" that encompassed all Jews and all things Jewish including land (the Jewish homeland, Eretz Israel), language, history, culture, literature, art, faith and a religion, the essential purpose of which was to serve the ever-changing needs of the Jewish people. Judaism, Kaplan claimed, was not God's revelation nor even a human creation inspired by God, but was rather the outcome of the Jewish people's historical experience. The Torah, Kaplan stated, was not God-given. It was a historical human creation that documented the Jewish people's search for God; the Halachah and the commandments were not divinely ordained but were rather constantly evolving "customs" created by the Jewish people themselves.[49] Controversially, Kaplan also rejected God's supernatural nature. In his view, God was the process, or the "power that leads to salvation" which, Kaplan thought, meant the attainment of personal and social fulfillment. In other words, God was the power that enabled humans to attain personal and social fulfillment in this world by creating a free, just and cooperative society.[50]

Kaplan denied that he was attempting to create a new religious branch and insisted that Reconstructionism was nothing other than a "state of mind." But increasing attacks on his views by the rabbinate perhaps made the emergence of Reconstructionism as a fourth religious branch inevitable.[51] The Reconstructionist Rabbinical College (RCC), which opened in 1968, became the most liberal theological seminary in the United States and paved the way for the adoption of a long line of progressive positions on social and religious issues. As early as 1968, Reconstructionism became the first denomination to recognize a person as Jewish based on patrilineal descent, and in 1984 was the first to ordain gay and lesbian rabbis.[52]

Until the founding of the RCC, the shaping and definition of Reconstructionism had been in the hands of Kaplan himself and a small band of his pupils and followers. But from the moment that Reconstructionism emerged as an autonomous movement with its own rabbinate and its own synagogues, it began to evolve in ways that Kaplan, ever the rationalist and naturalist, had perhaps never at first imagined. Particularly easy to discern, after the RCC's founding, is Reconstructionism's greater spirituality, including its integration of practices and ideas from Hassidic, kabbalistic and meditative sources, together with its greater willingness to incorporate the Halachah.[53]

And yet, "the emphasis Kaplan placed on belonging over believing or behaving remains central to Reconstructionism."[54] Belonging had long been defined by Kaplan at the macro level as an expression of common peoplehood. From this stemmed his consistent and enthusiastic support for Zionism. Later on, the movement broadened this concept to encompass the micro level. Belonging to a community or a group was as important as belonging to the Jewish people.[55] Reconstructionism advanced the concept of the synagogue as a community center (that came to be known as the "shul with a pool"). The synagogue was transformed so that it was not simply a house of worship but a broad, multipurpose social hub, a social center that was designed to include within it all aspects of secular and religious Jewish life.[56]

Over the past two decades, Reconstructionism has witnessed a significant growth in the United States, though it still only represents a small fraction of American Jewry. Despite a doubling in its size in recent years, it comprises no more than two percent of the American Jewish community.[57]

In conclusion, premodern traditional Judaism entailed all-embracing rituals and customs that assured Jews of an ethnic/national identity that clearly separated them from their surroundings. Orthodox Jewry continued along this path even when this engendered an acrimonious split over its approach to modern Jewish nationalism as expressed by Zionism and the State of Israel. Early, or Classical Reform Judaism, through its rebellion against traditional Judaism, adopted a Jewish identity that was neither ethnic nor national. However, today the decisive majority of members of Reform congregations continue to express their Jewishness in tribal and ethnic ways. Moreover, the political turn of events in the twentieth century forced the Reform movement to return to a more particularistic notion of Jewish identity and to embrace the idea of Jewish peoplehood. As a result, the Reform movement moved closer to Conservative Judaism, which had rebelled against Classical Reform – without rejoining Orthodox Judaism – and had, from the outset, stressed the idea of Jewish peoplehood. Another branch of Judaism, the Reconstructionist movement, still further expanded on the ethnic/national identity of Conservative Judaism. In the view of Reconstructionists, Judaism was in fact "Jewish civilization" engaged in an evolution that covered all aspects of Jewish life, religion being only one of them. It can therefore be said that all four streams of contemporary Jewry support the notion of Jewish peoplehood. If there is a non-ethnic Jewish identity it would seem that its definition is relevant for those who are not members of these four branches or, alternatively, those who deny the existence of a Jewish national identity.

The position of religion as a central component of Jewish identity has undergone significant change as a result of the increasing secularization of Jews throughout the world, and as a consequence of the establishment of the State of Israel. The Jewish state has a clear secular majority. Yet, despite this fact, Israel does not separate religion from state and grants the Orthodox enormous political power, none of which it possesses in the largest Jewish Diaspora – the Jewish community of the United States. As is known, in the United States religion is a purely personal matter. The intense confrontation between the religious and secular communities in Israel will undoubtedly have a profound influence on the role that religion plays in the shaping of Israeli Jewish identity in years to come.

CHAPTER 17

MODERN JEWISH

FUNDAMENTALISM

M odern Jewish fundamentalism surfaced in the wake of Israel's victory in the June 1967 war (the "Six-day War"). The war left Israel in control of the Sinai desert, the Golan Heights, and other parts of Eretz Israel (Judea and Samaria, the Gaza strip and East Jerusalem) which had remained beyond the Jewish state's borders after the 1948 War of Independence.[1] More than two thousand years earlier, Judea and Samaria had been the heart of the ancient Jewish homeland. The restoration of Jewish control over these lands has been seen, since 1967, as their divine liberation and has become a cornerstone of the religious belief of very many Jews.

Indeed, God's redemption of His chosen people has been at the core of Jewish faith since biblical times. This salvation has always been interpreted to mean the return of the Jewish people to the ancient homeland and the restoration of their sovereignty over that land.

The idea of redemption has echoed throughout Jewish history. For example, in the year 165 BCE, during the Hasmonean period, Jews reestablished an independent kingdom in Eretz Israel.[2] The call for redemption resurfaced during the Great Revolt against the Romans in the years 66–67 CE and the Bar Kochba revolt of 132–135 CE. Rabbi Yochanan ben Zakkai, the Jewish spiritual leader in the last part of the first century CE, opposed the revolt against the Romans. When it became apparent to him that the revolt was doomed to failure he moved to Yavneh, a small town some distance from Jerusalem, and there set up his own seminary, "Kerem Yavneh." He also reestablished a functioning Sanhedrin (supreme judicial council) to serve the surviving Jewish community of Judea. He firmly believed that Judaism could survive solely through the study of the Torah and the observance of religious law without resorting to political activity that appeared to be beyond its reach. Ben Zakkai's disciple, two generations removed, Rabbi Akiva, rejected this political defeatism and backed the Bar Kochba rebellion in the belief that Bar Kochba was the messiah.[3] Rabbi Akiva would become an inspirational symbol for Gush Emunim, the Jewish fundamentalist movement that championed the idea of the resettlement of Judea and Samaria after the Six-day War – a program that began in earnest after the Yom Kippur War of 1973.

Even though mainstream religious leaders shunned messianic movements during the entire period of Jewish exile, the messianic dream, a return to Zion, stayed alive in Jewish consciousness, ready to emerge at times of crisis. As Maimonides, the preeminent Jewish philosopher of the Middle Ages ruled, redemption and the return from exile were and remained two of the central tenets of Jewish identity.[4]

From time to time throughout the history of Jewish exile, false messiahs appeared, most often in the midst of a period of harsh repression. The most famous of these was Shabtai Zvi (1626–1676), who convinced a large number of Jews that he had the power to bring redemption. He rapidly captivated Jewish communities all over the Diaspora, amended laws and abolished certain religious customs. But then in 1666, he was jailed by the Ottoman authorities and the spell he had woven was replaced by a grim crisis; when he was given the choice in jail between converting to Islam and execution, he chose the former. His decision to convert shocked the entire Jewish world (except for a small number of his own disciples who followed in his footsteps and converted to Islam).[5]

The shadow of the Shabtai Zvi episode contributed to the strong opposition of eastern Europe's rabbis to messianic ideologies. For them, this included secular political Zionism and its promise to improve the situation of Jews by human rather than divine action. These rabbis considered Zionists to be hypocritical fraudsters who were endangering Jews by distancing them from traditional Judaism. The few rabbis who supported Zionism did so because they saw the movement as trying to save Jews from pogroms and persecution rather than because of its messianic message of redemption.[6]

The 1967 Six-day War radically altered the views of mainstream religious Jewry. The unification of Jerusalem and Israel's seizure of Judea, Samaria, and the many ancient holy places in those areas reawakened the dormant messianic aspirations of many religious Israelis, aspirations now clothed as Israeli patriotism. The fusion of Zionist pioneering and religious revivalism produced a new brand of Jewish fundamentalism.

The clearest expression of this new phenomenon was Gush Emunim, a messianic religious movement that was formed in the wake of the trauma that followed the Yom Kippur War (1973). It was a movement that included secular Israelis, and aimed at advancing Jewish settlement of the West Bank (Judea and Samaria) and its annexation by Israel.[7]

Gush Emunim based its ideology on the teachings of Rabbi Avraham Kook, Eretz Israel's first chief rabbi appointed in 1921 at the beginning of the British mandate, and his son Zvi Yehuda Kook. Rabbi Kook the father was tolerant toward the country's secular Jews because, he argued, their scorn for the religion did not negate their role in the realization of the pragmatic objective of building a Jewish state. Kook believed that secular Jews played an important part in the process of redemption by working the land, building roads and housing, thus paving the way for future redemption. Rabbi Kook the son followed in his father's footsteps by calling on his followers to settle in Eretz Israel and take control of it by secular means.[8]

This philosophy, embraced in its entirety by Gush Emunim, enabled the movement's members to form stable coalitions with secular Israelis who believed in imposing Israeli sovereignty over the whole of Eretz Israel. Revisionist political Zionism, which over the years had coalesced into the Likud Party, became the driving force behind modern Jewish fundamentalism and the adoption of a new messianic Jewish identity. Between 1977 and the end of 1984, Likud governments invested more than one billion dollars in the construction of Jewish settlements in the West Bank.[9]

To some Israelis the West Bank settlers were heroes, whereas others regarded them as scoundrels. This was certainly the verdict passed on Rabbi Moshe Levinger, a disciple of Rabbi Kook and one of the founders of Gush Emunim, who began his settlement activities a few years before the founding of the movement. During Passover of 1968, he arrived in Hebron as the leader of a group whose declared objective was to celebrate the holiday in the city of their forefathers. Having done so they then announced their intention to stay in Hebron as the nucleus of a Jewish settlement. Those who objected to such a plan in the heart of an Arab city were reminded of Hebron's place in Jewish history. This dated back to the time when Abraham bought the Cave of Machpela, where the forefathers and foremothers of the Jews are buried (Genesis 3:9), through to Hebron having been King David's first capital, to the 1929 Arab massacre of its Jewish community. Israel at the time was ruled by a National Unity government and none of its members wanted the government dissolved. Levinger and his followers were therefore allowed to remain in Hebron. After a period of time the Jewish presence in the city's center was transferred to a new settlement outside the city which was named Kiryat Arba. Levinger personified the defiant and over-confident Jewish settler – the fundamentalist zealot determined to settle Judea and Samaria.

Gush Emunim was supported by an earlier movement established immediately after the Six-day War at the initiative of, among others, the poet Nathan Alterman and known as the Movement for Greater Israel. The movement included intellectuals, senior military officers and important politicians, secular as well as religious people. In its first few years, the movement also included members of the Labor Party, mainly those in the Kibbutz Hameuchad (United Kibbutz Movement) and the Moshav Movement.[10]

The ambivalence of the Israeli public toward Jewish settlement in the occupied territories undoubtedly heightened after the traumatic Yom

Kippur War and was the background to the formation of Gush Emunim and the main motivation for its activity. One of the high points of this was the establishment of Elon Moreh in a densely Palestinian-populated area of the West Bank. The building of this settlement began in 1975 and brought the settlers into serious friction with the government. This provocative act, says the historian Ian Lustick, marked the beginning of the settlers' struggle to resist the government's intention to return the territories to Arab control following peace negotiations.[11]

After Likud's victory in the elections to the ninth Knesset in 1977, the settlers found a crucial ally in Ariel Sharon. Sharon was appointed as Minister of Agriculture and chairman of the Ministerial Committee on Settlement Affairs in the new government and became the settler movement's strongest supporter. He pressed for the setting up of more and more settlements and undertook to see to it that there would be over a million settlers in Judea and Samaria by the end of the twentieth century. His words and deeds lifted the settlers' self-confidence and gave an enormous boost to the Movement for Greater Israel.[12]

Gush Emunim saw the resettlement of Judea and Samaria as nothing less than the beginning of the Jewish people's redemption. Its members made it clear that they were willing to sacrifice their lives to prevent an Israeli withdrawal and the handing over of these areas to a sovereign Palestinian authority. As alumni of the religious youth movement, Bnei Akiva, whose maxim was "Torah and Labor," they recruited members of the movement to ensure the continued Jewish control of the whole of Eretz Israel. Bnei Akiva members did, indeed, embrace Gush Emunim's redemptive messianism, reinforcing the settler movement with their idealism, their patriotism, the military training they had received as volunteers to combat units and their pioneering spirit.[13]

In 1980, Israel's Supreme Court ruled that the Elon Moreh settlers were on land that had been illegally confiscated and ordered that they be evicted. The leaders of Gush Emunim vehemently objected to the ruling and threatened violent resistance to any attempt by the government to enforce the court's decision. The Likud government of the day, denounced by Gush Emunim for betraying Jewish interests, settled the matter by moving Elon Moreh to a different location. Prime

Minister Menahem Begin tried to avoid a violent confrontation with the fundamentalists without undermining the recently signed Camp David peace agreement between Israel and Egypt. Begin was clearly supportive of Gush Emunim and its agenda – building settlements in Judea and Samaria – a plan that was consistent with his view of the settlement project as a natural extension of the pragmatic Zionist policy of creating "facts on the ground."

The story of Elon Moreh, Lustick claims, strengthened Gush Emunim and proved that its political activism had paid off. The Jewish fundamentalists blamed themselves for not preventing the peace agreement between Israel and Egypt and the traumatic forced evacuation of the town of Yamit in northern Sinai. They vowed to never permit any further withdrawal from the territories that had come under Israeli control in 1967. Such a commitment followed the most extreme elements within the movement who claimed the right to use force to oppose any governmental decision that, in their view, went against God's will and the process of redemption.[14]

In due course, Jewish fundamentalism embraced even more extreme views. A dramatic escalation of its activities occurred with the appearance on the scene of Meir Kahane. In the 1970s, Kahane had founded the Kach movement, calling for the "immediate transfer of the Arabs from Israel to their own countries" and demanded that terror be responded to with terror. It can be said that a reflection of Kahane's views is to be found in the actions of the "Jewish underground" in the West Bank between 1980 and 1984, and its use of violent brutality against the Palestinians. The most spectacular of all its plots was the plan to blow up the Al-Aqsa Mosque in Jerusalem, the third holiest site in Islam. The plot was discovered in time and thwarted.[15]

Ian Lustick concedes that while there are no Jewish fundamentalists who call for a genocide of the Palestinian population, there are those who, like Kahane, advocate the "transfer" of Palestinians. There are also some who believe that coexistence with Arabs is possible only if it doesn't in any way pose a danger to the Jewish agenda.[16]

The emergence of Gush Emunim proved to be a considerable challenge to Jewish identity in a Jewish state by defying the authority of the Israeli government and insisting on its adherence to a higher authority. Its members took pride in their scorn for contemporary Western ideals of democracy. According to a leading fundamentalist, Moshe Ben-Yosef, "There is no Western culture – neither American, Russian, German, nor French – that is not foreign to the culture and history of Israel." Any Israeli government that is prepared to return territories loses its legitimacy and will be resisted with force, was the somber warning of another extremist, Eliyakim Haetzni. Some fundamentalists simply define as traitors anyone who opposes their ideology. The assassination of Prime Minister Yitzhak Rabin in 1995 aroused the fear that the polarized internal conflict over withdrawal from the territories was escalating dangerously.[17]

Though it is contemptuous of Israel's democratic system and denies the legitimacy of any consensus that opposes it, the Jewish fundamentalist movement, like other extremist movements before it, is a beneficiary of that very system. A consensus for peace and compromise has existed among Israelis for a very long time. The fundamentalist response to this is clear and unequivocal: Peace in exchange for an Israeli withdrawal is unacceptable. The Arab-Israeli conflict, insist the fundamentalists, is analogous to the Hundred Years' War in Europe. Arab Jihadist ideology and deep-rooted anti-Semitism, they add, preclude the possibility of any peace agreement. Islamic racism and the religion's core belief that Jews are inferior to Muslims mean that any Israeli concession or withdrawal is bound to be imprudent and dangerous.

CHAPTER 18

ANTI-SEMITISM AND JEWISH
IDENTITY

I n the words of the historian Robert S. Wistrich, "There has been no hatred in Western Christian civilization more persistent and enduring than that directed against the Jews."[1] The ways in which this hatred was expressed through the ages varied a great deal but the pattern remained remarkably similar. This applies first and foremost to this hatred's manifest irrationality. Indeed, one of the leading scholars in the field has suggested that anti-Semitism could be defined as an irrational hatred entirely unconnected to religious beliefs and which ascribes powers to Jews that they do not possess.[2] Thus, during the Middle Ages, along with the charge of deicide (the murder of Jesus Christ), Christians developed a host of irrational fantasies about Jews: that to demonstrate their contempt for Christ they murdered Christian children for ritual purposes, usually at Easter and usually by crucifixion; that they procured Christian blood (usually, but not always, the blood of murdered Christians) to make matzot or for other Passover rituals; that they desecrated the wafers used in holy communion by stabbing them and making them bleed; that they practiced witchcraft and black magic, and, together with the Antichrist were involved in secret plots to destroy Christendom; that they poisoned wells during the Black Death (the bubonic plague that swept across Europe in the middle of the fourteenth century). In modern times these were supplemented by new irrational Manichean myths of Judeo-Masonic, Judeo-Bolshevik and, most recently, Judeo-American conspiracies to control the world. There were constant warnings of the "Jewish menace" – world domination by Jews either through their gaining control of the international financial system or by their promotion of a worldwide social revolution.[3] The common denominator between the various charges made against them in modern times is that every one of them held Jews to be "responsible for all that is wrong with the world."[4]

For some time now, scholars have been trying to understand the reasons for this unyielding hatred – a subject that is widely debated. It would seem that a growing consensus is emerging around the notion that anti-Semitism is deeply embedded in Christian and Islamic cultures (particularly Christian culture) and that these religious-cultural prejudices are passed on from one generation to another as a sort of cultural code that is continually transmitted and spread within the society and its culture.[5] As one historian put it, "the firm base of visceral antisemitism in the West was laid down by this long-persistent conditioning that made suspicion and condemnation of Jews integral parts of prejudices and aversions that could be evoked almost at will."[6] Against the background of it "having become entrenched in European consciousness," it is hardly surprising that hatred of Jews manifested itself in the course of every religious and social upheaval in Europe during the Middle Ages and the early years of the modern era.[7]

In the view of the historian Esther Benbassa, this relentless enmity and the consequent suffering have shaped the history and the religion of the Jewish people in a very predictable way. "It is the case with every persecuted people that continual suffering is the ultimate unifier. The slavery of one's ancestors, the colonization of the previous generation or the one before it, the genocides and the constant revival of their memory, all serve in their own way to consolidate, solidify identities and forge clearly distinct groups." In effect, this shared suffering led to the "fusing of groups of people under external attack and facing the recurring temptation to abandon the group for a less dangerous existence." This shared suffering was a major element in the "foundation of Jewish identity for hundreds of years, from one generation to another, such suffering was ritualized by the same prayers recited on the same days of the year in various places by all Jewish populations."[8]

In addition to prayer, from the Middle Ages and on Jews also engaged in a "discourse of suffering" – a discourse that became the "common denominator" of Jewish life in the Diaspora.[9] A number of notable medieval Jewish narratives focus on the theme of Jewish suffering. Thus, for example, three accounts of the First Crusade (1096– 1099), and a fourth of the Second Crusade (1146–1147), describe in minute detail Christian massacres of Jews and Jewish resistance and martyrdom. Another narrative describes the persecution in 1007 of the Jews of Rouen, France, and the attempts to force them to convert. Such are the writings of the Jewish poet and biblical commentator Rabbi Ephraim ben Jacob, known also as Ephraim of Bonn. His *Book of Remembrance* begins with a terrifying account of Jewish suffering during the Second Crusade. The book goes on to describe seven other episodes of Jewish persecution during the twelfth century in France, Germany and England, starting with the accusations of ritual murder leveled against Jews in 1171 in the town of Blois, France. Another writer described the hardships endured by Jews between the mid-fourteenth century and the end of the fifteenth century, including Jewish suffering during the Black Death of the mid-fourteenth century. In the view of the historian Mark Cohen, these narratives served to "recount (and often sacrilize) the suffering of European Jewry.… Viewed alongside a much larger harvest of liturgical poetry – elegies and dirges – they form the basis for a collective memory of suffering inflicted by Christians. This, in turn, is linked with the older, biblical-rabbinical historical perception of persecution in exile (*galut*), usually viewed as punishment for past sins, eventually to be relieved by the Redemption."[10]

This led to the creation of an additional strata of Ashkenazi liturgy in which the ancient liturgy of suffering was both echoed and augmented – all to guarantee the cohesion of the Jewish people and to prevent apostasy.

Thus Judaism has "molded a long term collective identity by creating equations of punishment/redemption and destruction/redemption."[11]

This became more important after the Chmielnicki pogroms in Poland and Ukraine (1648–49), which engendered tales of Jewish martyrdom and reinforced the recurrent theme of Jewish suffering and the anticipated ultimate redemption. Liturgical lamentations and sorrowful elegies had a powerful impact on Yiddish literature, which passed on the recurring theme from one generation to another. The attachment of such importance to suffering was undoubtedly behind the pronouncement by the Vilna Gaon (the "Genius of Vilna" – Rabbi Eliyahu ben Shlomo Zalman Kramer [1720–1797], the preeminent figure in Lithuanian yeshivot in the eighteenth century) that "the Torah is acquired only through suffering." This idea, Benbassa claims, was painfully clear. "To be a Jew meant to suffer."[12]

In the wake of their expulsion from Spain, Navarre, Provence and the kingdom of Naples and the forced conversion in Portugal, Sephardi Jews created their own distinctive liturgy of suffering and redemption. The Portuguese experience was a catastrophe that "precipitated a massive trauma which, from a subjective point of view, was comparable to that of the Holocaust." Ashkenazim had sought to use the story of suffering to assist Jews internalize their tragedy, lessen their despair and strengthen the stability to endure as a unified community. Sephardim, on the other hand, embraced suffering as a necessary prelude to the Messianic age: the profounder the despair, they believed, the stronger the expectation of Messianic redemption. "Creation follows destruction, as light follows darkness.... The Judeo-Spanish language...preserves... this vision in the proverb, *"tanto eskurese es para amaneser"* – "the night is never blacker than just before dawn."[13]

Benbassa is convinced that the liturgical and narrative descriptions of Jewish history as "nothing but suffering," are not accurate (or at least incomplete). In so claiming she reflects the trend among contemporary Jewish historians following in the footsteps of Shalom Baron and Cecil Roth, both of whom avoided "maudlin" depictions of Jewish history. Baron pointed out that it was not accurate to say that Jews were the most persecuted or oppressed group in medieval times. Throughout most of that period, Baron claimed, their position was preferable to that of Christian serfs. Moreover, Jews were able to form relatively privileged and mobile communities in the areas where they were tolerated and protected. In truth, the ambivalence of the Christian world toward Jews, involving both abuse and tolerance, was far better than the treatment by that very same world of numerous heretical groups that were simply annihilated.[14]

Nonetheless, a review of Jewish history invariably arouses a reaction similar to that of the historian Martin Gilbert when working on his *Jewish History Atlas*. "My main concern," explains Gilbert in a preface to this atlas, "was to avoid undue emphasis on the many horrific aspects of Jewish history.... But as my research into that history progressed, I was surprised, depressed, and, to some extent, overwhelmed, by the perpetual and irrational violence which pursued Jews of every generation and in almost every corner of the globe."[15]

Such a visceral reaction was undoubtedly an important reason for the tearful way Jewish history was presented when it became a subject of scholarly discourse the nineteenth century. Undoubtedly, this approach also reflected the enormous antagonism that Jews faced when they tried to integrate into the European society of that era. However, in Benbassa's view, there were also utilitarian reasons for depicting Jewish history as nothing but suffering: this served as "a shield against fears that Jewish identity would disintegrate" as a result of Jewish emancipation. There were those who hoped that by continuing to equate Jewish identity with the modern Jewish historiography of suffering would, in effect, lead to "uniting secularized Jews or Jews who were in the process of secularization with those Jewish communities enduring trials and tribulations."[16] This, after all, is an approach that has been adopted by many groups in today's secular and increasingly global world. "Memories of suffering compensate for our alienation from religion, our solitude and our lack of solidarity. They have led to identities based on victimhood – another way of being and existing that has the power to bind us to an imaginary community of sufferers, present or past."[17]

As could be expected, this dynamic was bound to intensify after the Holocaust. Many Jews believe that the Nazi genocide was the inevitable culmination of hundreds of years of Christian persecution. Suffering and victimhood had become major elements of Jewish identity.[18] The world's disregard of the Jews during the Holocaust made past ideas of Jewish universalism perverse and outdated. The Jews' total isolation during the Holocaust necessitated the continuation of that isolation after it. If the Holocaust shattered Jewish life in Europe, says the literary scholar Harold Fisch, "then it also shattered the dream of emancipation...the great liberal hope first enunciated at the time of the French revolution has come to an end. For a century and more, Europe had seemed a continent that held hopes of liberty, fraternity and equality, a secular messianism in which the differences between men, be they black or white, Jew or Gentile, would melt away. The Holocaust changed all of this."[19] It may be that today's postmodernism and multiculturalism make such disillusionment appear outdated or misplaced. However, for the six million Jews who perished in the Holocaust both postmodernism and multiculturalism appeared far too late. Consequently, it seems too late to reverse the way in which entire generations of Jews have interpreted that catastrophe.

Jews recognized that political impotence was no longer an option after the Holocaust and became far more willing to use political power to advance their interests. Jews all along the political spectrum embraced the attainment of political sovereignty in Eretz Israel as well as the bold use of political pressure and lobbying in the Diaspora.[20]

At the same time Jews were frequently gripped by persistent fears of vague threats and undefined dangers. Polls taken among American Jews showed them believing that anti-Semitism was a serious problem in the United States, even though the facts suggested otherwise, and that they ranked the Holocaust first and American anti-Semitism third in the elements of Jewish identity.[21] Many believed in a "shared Jewish destiny" that would ultimately end badly. "Those whose current fate is good are waiting for it to go bad, as this is the true Jewish destiny."[22] Many also continued to hold fast to their instinctive lack of trust in the non-Jewish world. This deeply sensed fatalism was perfectly illustrated in a confrontation in the early 1970s between two American Jews of different generations:

> Do you have any non-Jewish friends? The question was thrust at me quite unexpectedly by a middle-aged Jewish doctor during

an informal evening's discussion about the Middle East. A man of forcefully liberal persuasions, the doctor...revealed that he had been a conscientious objector before Pearl Harbor, after which he enlisted without qualms.... The setting – Berkeley's liberal hills – was also disarming, so that taken together the combination of circumstance and speaker left me unprepared for the "moment of truth" (what else could one call it?) that followed. For when I responded affirmatively to his inquiry, that several close friends were indeed "Christian" (though they were no more religious than I), he paused dramatically and asked: Would you trust them with your life?

Yes, I would trust my life with Christian friends (for that is what one means by friends)... [H]e looked at me regretfully and said: You are naïve.[23]

These gloomy conclusions reached by many Diaspora Jews were echoed by an incalculably greater number of Jews in Israel. Before World War II, Zionists tended to interpret the rise of Nazism as vindication of Zionist ideology. After the war, the only possible response was one of despair. In the blink of an eye, the Nazis exterminated the Jews of eastern and central Europe, the world's most cohesive Jewish community (even nation) and considered to be the single most important reservoir of potential immigration to the Jewish state. As seen, with sadness, by the Israeli historian Jacob Talmon, the Zionist national liberation movement achieved its goal at the very moment that it lost its standard bearers. The winds of Auschwitz and Treblinka swept away the ashes of two million potential citizens of the State of Israel, Jews imbued with a strong and genuine feel for Zionism and with the firmest of Jewish roots. The Jewish people will never be able to replace them.[24]

These were, of course, the same communities that produced Zionism's early pioneers and those who perished were the very families they had left behind. One can well imagine the self-recrimination that must have taken root among Zionists after the war. Could they have prevented the catastrophe by accepting the British offer in 1903 of a part of Uganda as a temporary refuge? Should they have made a greater effort to persuade Europe's Jews to immigrate to Eretz Israel when its gates were still open? Tom Segev concludes that ultimately "though the Yishuv leaders certainly could have displayed greater compassion for and identification with the Jews of Europe, they could not have done more to save them; the Yishuv was helpless when faced with the Nazi extermination program."[25] This feeling of impotence and isolation was then dramatically repeated in 1948. In the face of the Arab states' war against the Yishuv immediately after the UN decision of November 1947 to partition Eretz Israel, and despite the widespread view that another genocide of the Jews was about to happen, the Western powers failed to intervene. They left the Yishuv to fend for itself in the same way that they had treated European Jewry only a few years earlier.[26]

During the 1950s Israelis said little about the Holocaust, perhaps because of the feelings of shame and remorse that many of them had. They once more cloaked themselves in their identity of the "new Jew" that ennobled the strength and self-reliance that characterized Israeli life: they disassociated themselves from the "mentality of exile" and the feebleness and passivity of Diaspora Jewry. Many distanced themselves from the Holocaust survivors who had made it to Israel, looked down upon them and made them feel ashamed that they had survived, and guilty for having allowed their communities to be destroyed.[27] As Amos Elon wrote in 1971:

> The Holocaust remains a fundamental trauma of Israeli society. One cannot possibly exaggerate its effect on the process of nation building.... There is a latent hysteria in Israeli life that stems directly from this source.
>
> It accounts for the prevailing sense that they are isolated from the world, a salient characteristic of the Israeli temperament since independence. It explains the nagging suspicions, the ever stronger impulse to rely only on themselves in a world that allowed the Holocaust to happen. It explains the fears and prejudices, the passions, pains, and pretentiousness that are the fabric of Israel's public life and will in all likelihood affect the nation for a long time to come. The sustained memory of the Holocaust lends

plausibility to Arab threats of annihilation. In this way memory strongly supports a national policy of stubbornness and resolve. But even if there were no Arabs or by some miracle their enmity was to disappear overnight, the influence of the traumatic memory would continue and be no less marked than it is today.[28]

The Eichmann trial in 1961 was a turning point in Israeli attitudes. From that point on, Israelis became increasingly preoccupied with the Holocaust, and it became a main factor in shaping Israeli identity. In Segev's view, this change was probably unavoidable given that Israel, unlike virtually any other country, constantly had to justify its existence to the world (as well as to itself). What better reason could there be for the need for Jewish political power than the calamitous helplessness they experienced during their most terrible crisis?[29] The Holocaust was also a justification for Israel's clandestine nuclear project by clearly demonstrating that the worst could always happen and when that moment comes it is impossible to rely on the world to act on behalf of the Jews.[30] The nuclear issue also touched the still-exposed raw nerves of the Yishuv's remorse vis-à-vis the lot of European Jewry and highlighted the painful paradox that the United States had to a large extent obtained the atom bomb thanks to Jewish brainpower. As one Israeli – presently retired and living in one of the established settlements but still well informed and well known in some circles for a number of hair-raising escapades – told Amos Oz in an anonymous interview, "Listen, friend, if that celebrated Jewish mind had spent less time saving the world, reforming humanity – Marx, Freud, Kafka, and all those geniuses, and Einstein, too – and instead had hurried up a bit, only ten years, and set up a tiny, Lilliputian Jewish state, sort of an independent bridgehead just from Haderah down to Gedera, and invented in time a teeny-weeny atom bomb for this state – if they'd only done those two things – there never would have been a Hitler. Or a Holocaust. And nobody in the whole world would have dared to lay a finger on the Jews."[31]

Israel's Holocaust trauma was significantly reenforced in the period that preceded the Six-day War of 1967. Arab radio broadcasts, widely quoted in the Israeli press, threatened the massacre of all Israelis not evacuated by the American Sixth Fleet; the media frequently reported the use made by the Egyptian army of chemical weapons in its intervention in the civil war in Yemen; public parks and parking lots were readied as cemeteries for the tens of thousands of Israelis who were expected to be killed in the coming war; and, in the face of the Western powers' hesitancy to respond to the closure of the Straits of Tiran by the Egyptian dictator Gamal Abdul Nasser, Israelis felt isolated and abandoned. All of these factors combined to rekindle the fear of an impending second Holocaust.[32] This is how Yariv Ben-Aharon, a kibbutz member and commander of a reserve unit, remembered those days:

> People believed that if we didn't succeed in the war we would be annihilated. They believed there would be a massacre if we were not victorious. They were fearful. It was the Holocaust that had inculcated this demand, this tangible idea, in the mind of everyone who had grown up in Israel even if he personally had not experienced the Holocaust, but had only heard or read about…"genocide." The concept was a reality. It could be done. This was the lesson of the Holocaust.[33]

Fears of a Holocaust also contributed to the Israeli army's fighting spirit and its courage during the fighting. As one of the officers involved recalled, "Two days before the war, when we felt that we were at a decisive moment and I was in uniform, armed and grimy from a night patrol, I came to the Ghetto Fighters Museum at Kibbutz Lohamei Hagetaot. I wanted to bid farewell to the memories of the fighters, both those who had – and those who had not – reached this day when the Jewish nation was rising up to the challenge of defending its existence. I had a clear feeling that our war began there, in the crematoria, in the camps, in the ghettos, in the forests."[34] As Knesset member Arieh Ben-Eliezer put it, "At our sides fought the six million, who whispered the eleventh commandment in our ear, Thou shalt not be killed."[35]

These fears weighed even more heavily during the Yom Kippur War of 1973.The devastating shock to Israel of the surprise Egyptian and Syrian attack led many Israelis to understand the plight of Jews during the Holocaust in an entirely new way.[36] "Without the Americans," recalled Colonel Ehud Prayer, then deputy chief education officer of the Israeli army, "we wouldn't have been able to hold out. We felt totally isolated: the country was about to be destroyed and no one came to our aid.... Until then we had believed in the pairing of the words *Holocaust* and *heroism* and identified ourselves with heroism. The war made us understand the meaning of the Holocaust and the limitations of heroism."[37]

The wave of Palestinian terror attacks during the 1970s and 1980s deepened Israel's sense of vulnerability. A poll taken in 1993 revealed that no less than 85 percent of Israelis were at the time personally afraid of being attacked by an Arab in the course of their daily lives.[38] The Iraqi missile attacks during the first Gulf War of 1991, necessitating the distribution of gas masks to everyone and an order that there be a sealed room in every residence, heightened still further the existential terror and turned the evident fear of annihilation into a personal reality for every Israeli.[39] "The psychological blow to the country was immense. Specifically there was the fear of chemical weapons and their association with the gas chambers of the Holocaust which evoked a level of public anxiety far out of proportion to the probability of such weapons being used or to their real destructive potential."[40]

The recurring crises made it painfully clear that the Jewish state which had been established to solve the problem of Jewish vulnerability in the Diaspora had, ironically, duplicated it. As were the Jews of the Diaspora over the ages, so now the Israelis were isolated, constantly insecure and apart from their neighbors both in terms of culture and religion. More and more Israelis have come to see their existential predicament as an extension of the age-old Jewish existential plight, and regard hostility toward Israel as just the most recent expression of the eternal hatred of non-Jews, the clearest expression of which had been the Holocaust. They have developed a dual identity of being both Jewish and Israeli, and their unrelieved Holocaust anxieties have made them more Jewish and less Israeli.[41]

Similarly, as Jewish and Israeli identities have become increasingly intertwined, so Israel's existential struggles have had a profound impact on Diaspora Jewry. Some Diaspora Jews were very impressed by Israel's military prowess. Natan Sharansky has noted that Israeli militarism not only gave Soviet Jews the strength that anti-Semitism had robbed them of, but also clearly enhanced their image in the Soviet Union.

> The brilliant victory of the Israeli military (in 1967) enabled us to stand tall. People suddenly began to treat Jews differently. Even the anti-Semitic jokes changed. They were no longer about the mendacious, cowardly, Jew. Now their focus was on the brave and victorious Jew, the upstart who had risen to great heights.[42]

Others were gripped by a deep fear of Israel's destruction and were unshakably sympathetic to Israel's adversity. The French Jewess, Annette Wieviorka, remembers that "during the waiting period preceding the Israeli victory [in 1967] the dread that seized the Israeli population" was equally felt by French Jews as if they too were facing genocide.[43] This, as revealed in the below interview, was also the feeling of Daniel Cohn-Bendit, the well-known radical Jewish-French student who meanwhile had become a member of the European parliament:

> What was the turning point in your life?
> It was the war.
> The Second World War?
> No.
> The Algerian war?
> No. *The* war: the Six-day War of 1967.... Until then I was a Jew without any major problems.... Then came the Six-day War and *bam*! Problem! I remember that I had an exam at the time. Once an hour I forgot about the exam so I could listen to the news. I didn't say anything to anyone, but I was worried.... It was unconscious. I didn't try to theorize about it but, in fact, I was split in two.[44]

The Arab calls to drive the Israelis into the sea had greatly riled Cohn-Bendit, as would the anti-Semitic jibes hurled at him while in police custody a year later at the height of the 1968 student protest strikes.[45] Both greatly intensified the existential fears of many Jewish-French intellectuals and radicals of Cohn-Bendit's generation. Pierre Goldman, the son of Polish resistance fighters in Poland during World War II and author of *Dim Memories of a Polish Jew Born in France*, expressed this clearly:

> To be a Jew is…my condition, it's a space that I fill in the existential sense.… And why is it so important? Because of anti-Semitism. Because of the hatred. The only answer to the question of what it means to be a Jew is Auschwitz.[46]

The Jewish preoccupation with anti-Semitism and the Holocaust and the celebration of military strength clearly increased both in Israel and the Diaspora in reaction to the intensification of anti-Semitism in the Muslim world and its reappearance in the West. The extent of this reemergence is the subject of an ongoing debate as to whether it is legitimate to equate anti-Zionism with anti-Semitism. Natan Sharansky has suggested a useful barometer for this equation: anti-Zionism or anti-Israeli rhetoric, he argues, becomes anti-Semitic when it meets the 3D test: the demonization of the Jewish state, the application of a double standard when criticizing Israel, and the delegitimization of the Jewish state.[47]

The demonization is revealed when critics liken Israel to Nazi Germany or engage in what Sharansky calls "Holocaust inversion" – the depiction of the Jewish victims of the Holocaust as criminals plotting a new Holocaust of the Palestinians.[48] The French philosopher Pierre André Taguieff argues that this is a function of what he describes as "the Zionism of the fantasy world" in which the Jews are now seen as bloodthirsty imperialists secretly conspiring to conquer the world.[49] A glaring example of a double standard is the vehement denial of the right of the Jewish people to self-determination in their own nation-state while supporting the existence of other such nation-states in the Third World and heaping praise on the national movements that lead them. Another example is the protest against Israel's policy toward the Palestinians while ignoring far harsher policies elsewhere – such as the maltreatment of more than one hundred million "untouchables" in India.[50] Delegitimization includes the rapidly growing movement to boycott Israel in western countries.[51] The impact of the "3Ds" on ordinary

Europeans was demonstrated in a dreadful way in a poll conducted by the European Commission in 2003. The poll, in which seventy-five hundred Europeans took part, revealed that 59 percent of them regarded Israel as the greatest threat to world peace (ahead of Iran, North Korea and Afghanistan).[52]

More distressing still is the extent of extreme anti-Semitism that has surfaced in the Muslim world since the 1970s. One cannot attribute this, writes Robert S. Wistrich, solely to the Arab-Israel conflict because the focus of this anti-Semitism is not on Israel or on the national or territorial conflict with Jews, which in theory is open to compromise. Instead, the Muslim world's body politic has become steeped in a Nazi-like anti-Semitic worldview: the belief that the "collective Jew," embodied in the image of the State of Israel, is a satanic force that seeks world domination. All the old medieval Christian fantasies have returned in a Muslim guise, including accusations of ritual murder, blood libel, and the poisoning of wells. "In this paranoid universe there are no limits to the Jewish global conspiracies against Arabs, Islam, and humanity as a whole," says Wistrich pessimistically. "Israel is the 'little Satan' controlling America and the West – the source of all corruption.... The demonic images of Jews now prevalent in significant parts of the Muslim world are sufficiently radical in both tone and content to create a new justification for genocide."[53]

As far as it relates to Jewish identity, Diaspora Jewry reacts in three different ways to this renewed outburst of anti-Semitism. The first and most common response, suggests Danny Ben-Moshe, is to identify even more closely with Israel. Sometimes this culminates with actually immigrating to Israel but in general the increased identification is limited to the gnawing conviction that enduring anti-Semitism requires that Israel remain a refuge for Diaspora Jews in case it is needed. "The just-in-case syndrome" is for many Diaspora Jews the basic way in which Israel features in their identity; because of anti-Semitism and as a response to it – "this includes even the most personally successful Jews in the most successful Diasporas, such as America." Ben-Moshe points out that this syndrome appears frequently even among Jews not known for their affinity to Israel. One example is that of Ian Katz, a senior editor of the British daily *The Guardian* which is regularly critical of Israel. Though Katz sticks by his opposition to Israeli policy he admits that "somewhere inside me there is always a small persistent voice that can be heard saying: these people are putting their necks on the line, making sacrifices, doing ugly things, so that there will be a safe refuge for you if you ever need it. Who are you to criticize them?"[54]

The second response of Diaspora Jews, according to Ben-Moshe, is to work toward strengthening the principles of democracy and multiculturalism in the countries in which they live. This often is combined with moving closer to Israel since the two responses are not mutually exclusive. The same cannot, however, be said about the third response: distancing themselves from Israel and regarding Israeli policy as a cause of anti-Semitism.[55] Indeed, this position often entails a denial that there is such a phenomenon as resurgent anti-Semitism. An example of this is provided by Michael Neumann, a professor of philosophy at Trent University in Toronto. In Neumann's view, the renewed attacks against Jews stem solely from Israel's "crimes" and from Diaspora Jewry's support for these "crimes." If anti-Semitism is defined, as Neumann thinks it should be, as "clearly unjustified and serious hostility" to Jews, "not because of anything they could avoid doing, but because they are what they are," then, he insists, the recent attacks against Israel and Jews cannot be defined as anti-Semitism.[56] But even if they could be,

> the real scandal today is not anti-Semitism but the importance it is given. Israel has committed war crimes. It has implicated Jews generally in these crimes, and Jews generally have hastened to implicate themselves. This has provoked hatred against Jews. Why not? Some of this hatred is racist, some isn't, but who cares? Why should we pay any attention to this issue at all? Is the fact that Israel's race war has provoked bitter anger of any importance besides the war itself? Is the remote possibility that somewhere, sometime, somehow, this hatred may in theory, possibly kill some Jews of any importance besides the brutal, actual, physical persecution of Palestinians, and the hundreds of thousands of

votes for Arabs to be herded into transit camps? Oh, but I forgot. Drop everything. Someone spray-painted anti-Semitic slogans on a synagogue.[57]

The response in Israel to resurgent anti-Semitism in the West and the nightmarish attitudes now evident in the Islamic world could have been predicted: the indubitable strengthening and reinforcement of the legacy of the Holocaust as a major component of Jewish/Israeli identity. Research conducted in the 1990s found that consciousness of the Holocaust was increasing in the country. A survey of five hundred students at a teacher's training college found that approximately 80 percent identified with the statement "we are all Holocaust survivors."[58] It would seem, therefore, that in the wake of the failure of the Oslo peace process, the eruption of the second Intifada in 2000 and the accompanying campaign to delegitimize Israel in the West, identification with the Holocaust will only grow. For Israelis, identifying with the Holocaust leads directly to the "decisive principle: the vital need for a strong, self-confident, sovereign state for all Jews...; the need for solidarity among Jews; the importance of self-defense; and the obligation of Jews to rely solely on their own strength and remain alert to any manifestation of anti-Semitism, so as to be ready to fight it as soon as the first signs appear."[59] Does this not (alas) symbolize the way in which victims of oppression would be expected to react? "Memory of suffering," Zygmunt Bauman teaches us,

> does not guarantee a lifelong commitment to the fight against inhumanity, cruelty, and the infliction of pain wherever it happens and regardless of who the sufferers may be. At least an equally probable outcome of martyrdom is the tendency to draw an opposite lesson; that humankind is divided into victims and victimizers, and so if you are (or expect to be) a victim, your task is to turn the tables ("the strongest survives").... Life is about surviving, to succeed in life is to outlive the other. Whoever survives – wins. The victimized ancestors are pitied, but also blamed for letting themselves be led, like sheep to the slaughter; how can one blame their descendants for setting themselves

against a future slaughterhouse in every suspicious looking street or building and – more importantly still – for taking preventative measures and trying to disarm the potential slaughterers.[60]

As the anonymous Israeli interviewed by Amos Oz bluntly declared, "A people that allowed its children to be made into soap and its women's skin into lampshades, is a worse criminal than its murderers. Worse than the Nazis. To live in a world of wolves without fists, without teeth and claws, is a crime worse than murder."[61] In this natural gut response to the Holocaust, in their understandable mistrust of the world and their suspicion of mere onlookers, today's Jews, Bauman suggests, have, ironically, handed "the greatest posthumous triumph" to the architects of the Final Solution. "What they failed to achieve when alive they may hope to achieve in death. They did not succeed in turning the world against the Jews, but in their graves they can still dream of turning the Jews against the world, and thus – one way or another – to make the Jewish reconciliation with the world, their peaceful cohabitation together with the world, all that more difficult, if not completely impossible."[62]

For this reason, one Holocaust survivor, the distinguished Israeli historian Yehuda Elkana, wrote a controversial article entitled "*Bizechut Hashichechah*" (In defense of forgetfulness), arguing that remembering the Holocaust was harmful if Israelis learned the wrong lessons from it.

> I see no greater threat to the future of the State of Israel than the fact that the Holocaust has been systematically and forcefully instilled in the consciousness of the Israeli public, even in that large segment that did not experience the Holocaust as well as the generation that was born and grew up here. For the first time, I understand the gravity of what we were doing when, decade after decade, we sent every Israeli child to repeatedly visit Yad Vashem, our national Holocaust memorial. What did we expect these young children to do with this experience? We declaimed with closed minds and even closed hearts and without explanation – "remember!" For what? What is the child supposed to do with these memories? For many the images of atrocities are likely to

be interpreted as a call to hatred. "Remember" can be understood as a summons to continued and blind hatred.

Conceivably the larger world should remember. I am not even sure about this. But in any case that is not our concern. Every nation, mostly the Germans, will decide in their own way and according to their own considerations whether they want to remember. We, on the other hand, must forget. I don't today see either a political or educational role more important for the leaders of this nation than to stand up for life, to commit themselves to the building of our future and not be preoccupied night and day with symbols, ceremonies and lessons of the Holocaust. They must uproot the dominion of historical "remembrance" over our lives.[63]

In response to Elkana, Tom Segev wrote that "Israelis cannot and should not forget the Holocaust. They need, rather, to draw different conclusions. The Holocaust summons all to preserve democracy, to fight racism, and to defend human rights.... Instilling the humanist lessons of the Holocaust will be difficult as long as the country is fighting to defend itself and justify its very existence; but it is essential."[64] Professor Avi Sagi also argues that the Holocaust must remain an important component of the Jewish/Israeli identity but strongly emphasizes that it must not become the cornerstone of this identity.[65] Esther Benbassa wholeheartedly agrees with both these views. Jewishness that solely exists on anti-Semitism and suffering, she argues, will be an "anemic Jewishness and will be futureless.... Is there not room for a different kind of Jewishness? So long as the only alternative to a Jewishness based on faith and observance is one founded on victimhood and suffering, we have every reason to think that this alternative will very soon die away because it has no viable future."[66]

CHAPTER 19

THE A. B. YEHOSHUA POLEMIC

T he issue of modern Jewish identity became a topic of heated debate
in the American Jewish community following remarks made in
May 2006 by the well-known Israeli author A. B. Yehoshua, at an event
marking the one hundredth anniversary of the founding of the American
Jewish Committee (AJC). On a panel discussing "The Future of the
Past: What Will Become of the Jewish People?" Yehoshua darkened
the festive mood with the gloomy thought that Jews had little reason
to celebrate the events of the previous hundred years. The twentieth
century, he argued, had witnessed the tragic failure of European Jewry
to save themselves from the Holocaust by leaving for Eretz Israel while
there was still time. Restating a long-held Zionist belief, Yehoshua
noted sadly that only a trickle of Jews had reached Eretz Israel during
the 1920s, going on to say that "the Zionist solution, which was proven
to be the best solution to the Jewish problem before the Holocaust, was
tragically missed by the Jewish people." (According to the English
version of his remarks he also reminded his listeners that this was the
time when the Communist revolution in Russia cut off Soviet Jewry,
the gates of America were closed because of the Great Depression, and
fascism and Nazism were destroying the democracies of Europe.) "If,
during the 1920s, when Eretz Israel's gates were wide open, a mere half
million Jews had come (less than 5 percent of the Jewish people at that
time), instead of the tiny number that actually came, it would definitely

have been possible to establish a Jewish state before the Holocaust in part of Eretz Israel. Not only would this state have resolved the Israeli-Arab conflict at an earlier stage and with less loss of life, it would also have been able to provide a safe haven for the hundreds of thousands of east European Jews who sensed the impending storm. Thus it would have been possible to significantly reduce the number of victims of the Holocaust."[1]

The second profound failure of twentieth-century Jewry, Yehoshua continued, was the inability or refusal of Diaspora Jewry to learn the lessons of the Holocaust or to fathom the "qualitative change that has occurred in Jewish identity with the return to complete sovereignty" following the establishment of the State of Israel.[2] Jewish sovereignty in a Jewish state, said Yehoshua, created a type of Jewishness that was "immeasurably fuller and broader and more meaningful than the Jewishness of an American Jew."[3] Later on, Yehoshua was also quoted as saying in the course of the discussion that "Judaism cannot exist outside Israel."[4] However, no such comment appears in the transcript of the debates[5] and Yehoshua himself vehemently denied saying any such thing, even noting that to have said so would have been "utterly absurd."[6] On the other hand, Yehoshua did argue that Jewish existence and Jewish identity could only be complete in a Jewish state, whereas in the Diaspora they could be nothing other than partial. This was a theme that he had returned to frequently over the years, for example in a debate with David Grossman and Anton Shammas fifteen years prior to the debate at the AJC. In his opinion, Yehoshua had said, "Israeli" was the most authentic, perfect, complete and proper word for describing the concept "Jewish." Israeliness, claimed Yehoshua, was the total, perfect and original Jewishness, complete with answers for every aspect of life.[7] What precisely he had meant by this earlier statement was explained more fully at the AJC conference.

> Identity is something that you belong to, first of all to country, to territory, to framework, and things like that.... We live also and all the time [with] the idea...[that] we have peoplehood, and we are responsible to each other....

Jewishness like Americanism is what Americans are doing for good and for…bad…and the decisions we are doing every day. And these are the Jewish decisions.… Are we going to torture a Hamas member in order to get information about another terrorist, about another terror attack that is coming? …This is a decision that…religious Jews…[have never] done in Diaspora.…

You are not doing any Jewish decisions.… All of the decisions that you are doing are done in the American framework. You are not deciding about the Iraq war through [a] Jewish aspect. You are deciding it according to…American interests.… You are playing with Jewishness – plug and play. You're playing [in] a certain way with Judaism.[8]

Jewish identity, Yehoshua stressed, was a national matter, not a religious one[9] – and only in Israel can Jews fully express their national identity and ultimately survive as a nation. He would consider it "normal" if, in a hundred years' time, there would no longer be Jews living in the Diaspora – "because it's very natural that every one of you will…extend his identification with the country in which he's living."[10]

Another member of the panel, Leon Wieseltier, the literary editor of the journal *New Republic*, was quick to respond to Yehoshua's thesis. "It wasn't territory that kept Jews alive.… The decisive issue is whether Jews were involved in their Jewishness in an active manner." When Yehoshua asked him to give an example of "an act of Jewishness," Wieseltier offered the teaching of Hebrew and learning Jewish history as good examples. "These are not worthless activities," Wieseltier insisted, because without them "Jews will not survive even if the State of Israel does."[11]

But Yehoshua stuck to his guns. Living in the Diaspora, he argued in 2003, had been a "neurotic decision" made by Jews throughout their history even in times when moving to Eretz Israel and settling there had been a viable option. He didn't deny that living in the Diaspora had become "an integral part of Jewish identity," but added that "Jewishness in the Diaspora is like masturbation. Here, in Israel, it is the real thing."[12]

Many of those attending the AJC conference were deeply offended by Yehoshua's comments and pressed him to apologize immediately.[13] This reaction, said Yehoshua, surprised him, since all that he had done was to repeat things he had said many times previously. He not only regarded his thesis as unquestionably valid but also later quipped that "if they were *goyim* [non-Jews], they would understand it right away."[14]

One of the voices agreeing with Yehoshua was that of Hillel Halkin (1939–), an American-born author and critic who migrated to Israel in 1970 and was published in Israel, the United States and England. "Israel," he said, "*is* the only place in the world in which one can live a Jewish life that is total – in which, that is, there is no compartmentalization between the inner and the outer, between what is Jewish and what is not. It is the only place in the world in which Jews are totally responsible for the society they live in, for the environment that surrounds them, for the government that rules them. It is the only place in the world where Jewish culture is not a subculture in a greater culture but is rather that greater culture itself."[15] Tzvia Greenfeld, an ultra-Orthodox woman who had been a member of Knesset (from the left-wing party Meretz), agreed with Yehoshua and wrote that the debate he had initiated was essentially one between two utterly distinct groups: "Those who believe that Israel offers the sons and daughters of the Jewish people an opportunity to reenter history not merely as individuals, but rather as a meaningful collective with a common cultural vision; and those who...are content with the continuation of a passive Jewish existence outside of history." Jews who continue to live in the Diaspora, Greenfeld concluded, were "relinquishing a Jewish existence that is truly meaningful: the opportunity and the responsibility of shaping and engaging in a comprehensive moral reality in the spirit of the prophets of Israel."[16]

Leonard Fein credits Zionism for having "delivered on its main promise. It became the sought-for haven; it created a nation-state that is strong, productive, resilient, ever so lively." Zionism accurately foresaw the dangers of both assimilation and persecution that threatened European Jewry: "We would either be seduced or be raped;

either way, we were doomed." Zionism, however, failed to anticipate the emergence of a vital and dynamic American Jewish community. That failure led it to make an erroneous assumption about a critically important issue – that "if you build it, they will come."[17] Tony Karon concurs that this assumption was a mistake: "The idea that the modern state of Israel expresses some ageless desire among Jews across the Diaspora to live in a Jewish nation state is wishful thinking. Before the Holocaust, Zionism had been a minority tendency among Western Jews, and scarcely existed among those living in the Muslim world. And a half century after Israel's emergence, most of us choose freely to live, as Jews have for centuries, among the nations. That choice is becoming increasingly popular among Israeli Jews, too: 750,000 at last count [who departed Israel to live in the Diaspora.]"[18]

In light of this reality – a reality Yehoshua angrily contested at the AJC conference – Yehoshua found himself, claims Fein, deviating from the Zionism that he so fervently preaches.

> The question that A. B. Yehoshua raised at the Washington symposium is, essentially, a post-Zionist question: What is the relationship between the state of Israel and the Jewish people? Yehoshua's answer to that question is, as I understand it: Nothing.... People who live in Israel are Israelis. Their Jewishness...is in the language they speak, in the air they breathe, in the vital (as also the mundane) ways they choose to exercise the power and the responsibilities that come with statehood. He evidently believes that...the Jews outside the Land...live in an illusory world, that the old Zionist analysis (seduction or rape) remains correct, that the professed (but waning) affection of the Jews for Israel ("Next year in Jerusalem") is an empty gesture, that there is no substance to "Judaism" beyond Israeliness.... He is not all that different from...[the] Canaanites.[19]

Natan Sharansky took this argument a step further. Yehoshua, he explains, is not only wrong to separate Israeli Jews from Diaspora Jews, he is wrong to separate Zionism from Judaism.

Yehoshua's remarks about the relations between Israel and the Diaspora, infuriating as they may be, are less disturbing than the way in which he described his own identity: My identity is Israeli, said Yehoshua, the Jewish religion does not play a role in my life, it is the territory and the language that form my identity.... But there is no Zionism without Judaism, and there never has been.... The difference between Israeli identity as defined by Yehoshua, and Jewish identity, is the difference between the fact of existence and the right to existence.... If, heaven forbid, we cut ourselves off from the line that links us to the Jewish people, if we cut ourselves off from thousands of years of Judaism and reject our being the realization of two thousand years of Jewish aspiration – for the next year in Jerusalem – then we lose the right to our existence. And in losing that right, we will be lost.[20]

The chorus of Yehoshua's angry critics has been joined by Avraham Burg, former speaker of the Israeli Knesset. Yehoshua, says Burg, has been a long-time adherent of Ben-Gurion's policy of negating the Diaspora. "It was vital for the old-school Zionists to find for themselves a distinctiveness that would define them, to separate themselves from what had been, to build a new world out of the dying shtetl." But what was long ago "a bitter ideological conflict between the innovative and rebellious Zionists and a withered, sclerotic Judaism, kept going on even after the establishment of the State of Israel, this time intended as an aid to help Israelis overcome the temptation of America." Today, to preach the position taken by Yehoshua at the AJC conference is to advocate fundamentalist isolationism that seeks to freeze the passage of time and to relegate Jewish life to an anachronism.[21]

Burg also rejects the long-term predictions – echoed in Yehoshua's remarks – about the "normal" and inevitable disappearance of Diaspora Jewry as a result of its assimilation. This was also the view of Yair Sheleg who, in defending Yehoshua, warned Diaspora Jewry that "their Jewish identity, if it doesn't disappear altogether is, at best, likely to become a charming piece of ethnic folklore."[22] In his response, Burg admits that "throughout Jewish history and in the early days of Zionism, we were practically the only nation that had a homeland but whose sons and daughters were scattered throughout the entire world." But this has long ceased to be the case.

> Today millions of Chinese, Japanese, Italians and Irishmen have robbed us of this unique status. China is not alienated from its émigré children, Korea looks for every possible way to strengthen the bond between its scattered emigrant communities and the motherland. And only among us is there an attempt by spiritual Zionist navigators to sever the link between all the Jewish molecules that make our matter so interesting and unique.[23]

Tony Karon goes a good deal further in championing the cause of the Diaspora. "Judaism's survival," he contends, "depends...on its ability to offer a sustaining moral and ethical anchor." And this can only happen, insists Karon, if indeed the Jews are scattered among the nations. "Judaism's universal ethical calling can't really be answered if we live only among ourselves." And this is the current situation, Karon continues, because the Zionist ingathering of the exiles is based on imperatives of nationalism that are rapidly becoming outdated. "Israel's own experience suggests it's hard to live only among ourselves without doing injustice to others.... All of the great Jewish intellectual, philosophical, moral and cultural contributions to humanity I can think of were products not of Jews living apart, but of our dispersal among the cultures of the world. Maimonides or Spinoza, Marx, Freud, Einstein or Derrida; Kafka, Proust or Primo Levi; Serge Gainsbourg or Daniel Barenboim; Lenny Bruce or Bob Dylan – I could go on ad nauseam – are all products of our interaction with diverse influences in the Diaspora."[24]

Karon's thesis parallels a central criticism of Yehoshua voiced by progressive Israelis. Jewish life could be "immeasurably fuller and broader and more meaningful" in Israel, argues Yair Caspi, not because Jews are the majority or responsible for making decisions there but rather because the structure of life in Israel stems from a basic Jewish vision about the proper way that a society and humankind should behave. In Caspi's view, this was the vision that the Zionist movement tried to resurrect through the "exemplary society" it set out to create in Eretz Israel.[25] In other words, what makes something fully Jewish – indeed, what guarantees Jewish survival – is not numbers but values. This is echoed by Burg noting that

> the Jewish people did not survive for two millenia in order to pioneer new weaponry, computer security programs or anti-missile missiles. We were supposed to be a light unto the nations. In this we have failed.
>
> It turns out that the two-thousand-year struggle for Jewish survival comes down to a state of settlements, run by an amoral clique of corrupt lawbreakers who are deaf both to their citizens and to their enemies. A state lacking justice cannot survive. More and more Israelis are coming to understand this as they ask their children where they expect to live in twenty-five years. Children who are honest admit, to their parents' shock, that they do not know.[26]

Similar notions were voiced by Yossi Sarid when he said provocatively that if Jewishness is based on the creation of an "exemplary society" then Diaspora Jewry had no reason for having feelings of inferiority.

> Just this last month [May 2006] Jews tried to awaken and stimulate American and international public opinion, which has been gradually ignoring the genocide in Darfur, whereas here, the land of the survivor and the remnants, not a peep has been heard. Here, before we deport them, we lock up 150 Sudanese refugees from the sword, who are fleeing from their slaughterers....
>
> Many good Jews showed up last week in support of the illegal workers in America – 11 million people who can be expected to be used and then thrown away. But what happens in Israel? The Jewish Immigration Authority traps foreign workers as though they were animals, making life a misery for entire families, and no one says a word....
>
> Across the sea they understand the meaning of "religious pluralism" and the equality of all the religious streams in Judaism,

whereas here we are still living under monopolistic Orthodoxy that meddles in the lives of citizens who seek the good of their country, and makes those lives a misery.... In many respects the Jewish community in the United States is more Jewish than the Jewish "community" in Israel.[27]

It was perhaps ironic that the context of Yehoshua's remarks happened to be the centennial celebrations of the American Jewish Committee (AJC). In 1950 the then president of the AJC, Jacob Blaustein, got Israel's prime minister David Ben-Gurion to agree to the following declaration. "(1) Jews of the United States, as a community and as individuals, have only one political attachment, namely to the United States of America; (2) the Government and people of Israel respect the integrity of Jewish life in the democratic countries and the right of the Jewish communities to pursue their own social, economic and cultural aspirations in accordance with their own needs and institutions; and (3) Israel fully accepts the fact that the Jews of the United States do not live "in exile" and that America is their homeland."[28] Ben-Gurion's signing of the agreement was an act of pragmatism in which he knowingly relinquished certain core Zionist principles so as not to alienate an essential ally, the American Jewish community. But this was not enough to bridge the enormous gulf between the Israeli and American Jewish visions of Jewish identity and between their respective forecasts of what lay ahead for the Jewish people.

The Yehoshua polemic highlights the fact that this gulf has become even deeper. One month after Yehoshua's bitter onslaught, Steven M. Cohen, professor of Jewish social policy at Hebrew Union College – Jewish Institute of Religion in New York, and Jack Wertheimer, professor of Jewish history at the Jewish Theological Seminary, published the following assessment of the state of Israeli-American Jewish relations:

In 1989, a national survey conducted for the American Jewish Committee found 73 percent of Jews agreeing that "caring about Israel is a very important part of my being a Jew"; in 2005, a mere decade-and-a-half later, the corresponding figure had fallen to 57 percent. Younger adults, moreover, exhibit weaker attachment to Israel than do their elders.

Nor is it just a matter of Israel. According to the 2000/2001 National Jewish Population Study, younger adults are significantly less likely than their elders to agree strongly that "Jews in the United States and Jews around the world share a common destiny" or that "when people are in distress, American Jews have a greater responsibility to rescue Jews than non-Jews." Responses to the simple statement, "I have a strong sense of belonging to the Jewish people," are especially telling. The proportions strongly agreeing drop steadily from a high of 75 percent among those aged sixty-five or over to a low of 47 percent for adults under thirty-five.[29]

It would seem, therefore, that the number of American Jews who support the "post-Zionist" or "Canaanite" vision – presented by Yehoshua as the vision separating the destinies of Israeli and American Jews – is greater than suggested by the angry reaction of his audience at the AJC conference. Most importantly, the above survey reconfirms the complex and elusive nature of Jewish identity in the modern world.

CHAPTER 20

JEWISH IDENTITY – THE CHALLENGE OF PEOPLEHOOD TODAY

In his book *Achizat Moledet* (Homeland's grip), A. B. Yehoshua suggests somewhat bitterly that no other nation is so persistently absorbed with the issue of identity as are the Jews. As a result, numerous books, essays, seminars and symposiums have been devoted to such questions as: Who is a Jew? What is the meaning of being a Jew? Which definitions of the term are legitimate? Do all Jews belong to one people or one religion? Are the Jews one people or one religion? Are assimilated Jews in the Diaspora as authentic as those living in Israel? There is something very odd, says Yehoshua, about a nation with thousands of years of history behind it, that still compulsively and endlessly struggles with the question of its identity. It would seem that this judgment is truer today than ever before.

The sweeping and cataclysmic changes of the twentieth century have created new and profound challenges for the Jewish identity. This process of change has not yet reached its end. As a result, the Jewish world is apparently heading for a further period of flux and an unpredictable future. The destruction of European Jewry, the establishment of the Jewish State of Israel, globalization and the emergence of new analytical concepts such as postmodernism have created new fissures in Jewish identity both in Israel and the Diaspora. Differences of view have also emerged between Jewish identity in the Diaspora and national Israeli-Jewish identity. Ultimately the question remains: Do these fundamental and tumultuous changes endanger the continuity of Jewish life in a globalized world?

It was reasonable to assume – as did the Zionist movement over a long period of time – that the "normalization" of the Jews in a sovereign Jewish state would lessen hostility toward the Jewish people as a whole. But this didn't happen. The enmity directed at Israel (where half of all Jews in the world now live) is far greater than the bitterness that even a prolonged and deep-rooted conflict really warrants. In the eyes of the nations of the world, the Israel of today has become "the Jew," so that the anti-Semitism felt toward the Jews of the Diaspora is effectively directed at the Jewish state.

Israel's ongoing existential struggles have left Israelis with a Jewish-Israeli identity, the dual nature of which becomes increasingly evident. Gone is the "new Jew," the anti-Diaspora persona so idolized by the early Zionist pioneers and the first generation of Israelis. From the 1960s and on, the Holocaust and anti-Semitism increasingly became the cornerstones of Israeli identity. As Israelis feel more and more vulnerable in their interminable conflict with the Arab world, so the Jewish dimension of their identity is reinforced. On the other hand, periods of relative quiet and stability push the bulk of Israelis in an opposite direction toward a distinct Israeli identity that is detached from Diaspora Jewry. Seemingly, Israelis fluctuate between emphasizing their Israeli and their Jewish identities, depending on their existential situation.

Since the Holocaust, the Jews of the United States and Europe are also preoccupied by existential fears. For them the Holocaust is no less important a component of their identity than it is for Israelis. Today, American and European Jews must cope with the persistence of anti-Semitism: Has the Holocaust led to Western society rising above itself and put an end to a centuries-old cultural norm that engenders hatred of Jews? Can a millennium of such hatred just dissipate within a mere few decades? And if someone thinks that the answer to these questions is yes, how does he or she explain the rise of extreme, Nazi-like anti-Semitism in the Muslim world? These questions have a significant impact on the way in which the Jews of today identify with the State of Israel, and especially on the quandary of whether or not there is still a need for Israel as a place of refuge for Jews from anti-Semitism.

At the very same time, in the United States Jewish citizens enjoy an unprecedented sense of security, free of the kind of existential struggles experienced by Israelis and untroubled by the suspicion of having a double loyalty. In today's pluralist, postmodern world, American Jews are free to hold double loyalties or hybrid loyalties without fear that they might be seen as detracting from their Americanism. At any rate, the question is whether American or European Jewry can sustain its existence in an environment of such freedom and with such an adulterated ethnic or religious identity, without – not to say outside of – the supportive confines of a Jewish state. Is a non-Orthodox Jewish identity viable in a world of increased integration? The simple answer is that we don't yet know.

We don't know if the many complex and continually changing Jewish identities in today's pluralistic and postmodern world can maintain their existence under the single roof of Judaism. In my view it is necessary that they should do so. But in order for this to happen Jews must not merely react to their traumatic past, painful as that may have been. They must also internalize the core ideas of multiculturalism – pluralism and diversity – so that they can create a Jewishness that is multifaceted, all inclusive, and positively reflects the freedoms of the world of today.

NOTES AND SOURCES

Translator's note: Books, essays and articles first published in Hebrew and then re-published in English are referred to by their English edition, but page numbers have been omitted.

INTRODUCTION

1 Jeremy Dauber, *Antonio's Devils: Writers of the Jewish Enlightenment and the Birth of Modern Hebrew and Yiddish Literature* (Palo Alto: Stanford University Press, 2004), 67–102; Benjamin Harshav, *Language in Time of Revolution* (Berkeley and Los Angeles: University of California Press, 1993); David E. Fishman, *The Rise of Modern Yiddish Culture* (Pittsburgh: University of Pittsburgh Press, 2005), 5–32; David Biale, "A Journey Between Worlds: East European Jewish Culture from the Partitions of Poland to the Holocaust," in *Cultures of the Jews: A New History*, ed. David Biale (New York: Schocken Books, 2002), 820–854.

CHAPTER 1: THE RISE OF NATIONALISM

1 Anita Shapira, "Zionism in the Age of Revolution," *Modern Judaism* 18, no. 3 (1998): 217.

2 Hannah Arendt, "A Heroine of Revolution," *New York Review of Books* 7, no. 5 (October 1966): 23.

3 Isaiah Berlin, *Against the Current: Essays in the History of Ideas* (London: Pimlico, 1979).

4   Hans Kohn, *Nationalism: Its Meaning and History* (New York: Krieger Publishing, 1982), 10.

5   Ernest Renan, "What is a Nation?," in *Becoming National: A Reader*, ed. Geoff Eley and Ronald Grigor Suny (New York and Oxford University Press, 1996), 41–55. See also Elie Kedourie, *Nationalism* (Oxford: Blackwell, 1993), 80–82.

6   Ernest Gellner, *Nations and Nationalism: New Perspectives on the Past* (Ithaca, NY: Cornell University Press, 1983), 57, 124.

7   Eric Hobsbawm, *Nations and Nationalism since 1780* (Cambridge: Cambridge University Press, 1990), 11–12.

8   Benedict Anderson, *Imagined Communities: Reflections on the Origin and Spread of Nationalism*, rev. ed. (London: Verso, 2006), 5–7.

9   Anthony D. Smith, *National Identity* (London: Penguin Books, 1993), 14–17, 19–20.

10 Ibid., 20.

11 Ibid.

12 Ibid., 47–49.

13 Ibid., 49.

14 Kohn, *Nationalism*, 11–12.

15 Arnold Toynbee, "Modern Nationalism," *Foreign Affairs XVII* (1939).

16 E. J. Hobsbawm, "Some Reflections on Nationalism," in *Imagination and Precision in the Social Sciences: Essays in Memory of Peter Netl*, ed. T. J. Nossiter (London: Faber, 1972), 388.

17 Anderson, *Imagined Communities*, 84.

18 Kedourie, *Nationalism*; Edward Hallett Carr, *Nationalism and After* (New York: Macmillan, 1967), 27–31

19 Carr, ibid., 15–16, 20.

20 Kohn, *Nationalism*, 27–29; Anthony D. Smith, *Theories of Nationalism* (New York: Holmes Meier, 1983), 27–29

21 Jacob L. Talmon, "The National Brotherhood and the International Confraternity," in *The Unique and Universal: Some Historical Reflections* (London: Secker & Warburg, 1965), 26.

22 Kohn, *Nationalism*, 31–32. Also see Rogers Brubacker, *Nationalism Reframed: Nationhood and the National Question in the New Europe* (Cambridge: Cambridge University Press, 1996), 55–76.

23 E. J. Hobsbawm, *Nations and Nationalism: Programme, Myth, Reality* (Cambridge: Cambridge University Press, 1990) 101–130.

24 J. Stalin, "Marxism and the National Question," *Prosveshcheniye* nos. 3–5 (March–May 1913): 1.

CHAPTER 2: THE EMERGENCE OF ZIONISM

1   Shlomo Avineri, "Zionism as a National Liberation Movement," *The Jerusalem Quarterly* 10 (Winter 1979): 133–136.

2   Ibid., 139–143.

3   Jonathan Frankel, *Prophecy and Politics: Socialism, Nationalism, and the Russian Jews, 1862–1917* (Cambridge University Press, 1981).

4   Eliezer Schweid, *HaYahadut v'hatarbut hachilonit* (Tel Aviv: Hakibbutz Hameuchad, 1981), 65.

5   David Vital, *The Origins of Zionism* (Oxford: Oxford University Press, 1975), 14–15.

6   Isaiah Berlin, *Against the Current: Essays in the History of Ideas* (London: Pimlico, 1979).

7   Ibid., 324; Shlomo Avineri, *The Making of Modern Zionism: Intellectual Origins of the Jewish State* (New York: Basic Books, 1981), 39–42.

8   David Vital, *A People Apart: The Jews of Europe, 1789–1939* (Oxford: Oxford University Press, 1999), 281–290.

9   Avineri, *Modern Zionism*. For Hovevei Zion in general, see David Vital, *Hamahapechah haTzionit* (Tel Aviv: Am Oved, 1978).

10 Tomasz Kamusella, *The Politics of Language and Nationalism in Modern Central Europe* (New York: Palgrave Macmillan, 2009), 1–6, 42–56, 905–919.

11 Hobsbawm, *Nations and Nationalism*, 110.

12 Avineri, "Zionism as a National Liberation Movement,"102 .

13 On Ben-Yehuda and the revival of the Hebrew language see: Robert St John, *Tongue of the Prophets: The Life Story of Eliezer Ben Yehuda* (Greenwood

Publishing Group, 1972,1962); Jack Fellman, *Revival of a Classical Tongue: Eliezer Ben Yehuda and the Modern Hebrew Language* (Berlin and New York: Walter de Gruyter, 1973); Benjamin Harshav, *Language in Time of Revolution* (Stanford University Press, 1993) 83–93.

14   Avineri, "Zionism as a National Liberation Movement," 109.

15   Walter Laqueur, *A History of Zionism: From the French Revolution to the Establishment of the State of Israel* (New York: MJF Books, 1997), 132–133.

16   Ibid., 121.

17   David Vital, "The Afflictions of the Jews and the Afflictions of Zionism: The Meaning and Consequences of the 'Uganda' Controversy," in *Essential Papers on Zionism*, ed. Jehuda Reinharz and Anita Shapira (New York: New York University Press, 1995), 119–132.

18   Shulamit Laskov, *Chayei Achad Ha'am: Pesifas mitoch ketavav u'chtavim acherim* (Jerusalem: The Zionist Library, 2006), 33.

19   Ahad Ha'am, "The Jewish State and the Jewish Problem" (1897).

20   Laqueur, *A History of Zionism*, 140–141.

21   Ibid., 187.

22   Leonard J. Stein, *The Balfour Declaration* (New York: Simon and Schuster, 1961).

23   Laqueur, *A History of Zionism*, 201–204.

24   At the time there were three separate political factions: (1) Achdut Ha'avodah established in 1919 following the merger between the Marxist Poalei Zion party (led by David Ben-Gurion and Yitzhak Ben Zvi) and a large group of non-affiliated workers (led by Berl Katzanelson); (2) The non-Marxist party Hapoel Hatzair (whose most prominent thinker was A. D. Gordon). In 1930 it merged with Achdut Ha'avodah under the banner of Poalei Eretz Israel (Mapai); (3) Hashomer Hatzair, a new Marxist party that originated in Galicia in the midst of World War I. In Eretz Israel, Hashomer Hatzair began to take root during the Third Aliyah (1919–1924), inspired to quite an extent by Martin Buber and German Romanticism.

25   On both, see Frankel, *Prophecy and Politics*, 329–409; Matityahu Mintz, "Ber Borokhov," in *Essential Papers on Jews and the Left*, ed. Ezra Mendelsohn (New York: New York University Press, 1997), 122–144.

26   Avineri, "Zionism as a National Liberation Movement," 246.

CHAPTER 3: REINVENTING JEWISH IDENTITY: DIASPORA NEGATION

1   Ahad Ha'am, *"Shelilat hagalut,"* in *Kol kitvei Achad Ha'am* (Dvir: Tel Aviv, 1949), 399–403.

2   Amnon Raz-Krakotzkin strongly supports this thesis and emphasizes that negation of the Diaspora and the stress on military valor are new features of Jewish identity that were unknown in the Diaspora and were inconsistent with Jewish identity there. Anita Shapira, on the other hand, argues that such an analysis – and the classification of Jewish characteristics in the Diaspora as opposed to those of Israeli Jews – has led to a conflict of interest between the Diaspora and Israel and polarizes the relations between the two sides. See Amnon Raz-Krakotzkin, *"Galut betoch ribonut: L'vikoret 'shelilat hagalut' betarbut haYisraelit,"* *Te'oriah u'vikoret* 4 (Autumn 1993): 23–55; Anita Shapira, *Yehudim chadashim, Yehudim yeshanim* (Tel Aviv: Am Oved, 1997), 20–21.

3   Anita Shapira, *"HaTanach v'hazehut haYisraelit,"* in *Yehudim, Tzionim u'ma she'benehem* (Tel Aviv: Am Oved,2007), 163–176.

4   Yedidya Itzhaki *"Shelilat hagolah,"* in *Tarbut haYehudit hachilonit: Hegut chadashah b'Yisrael*, ed. Ya'akov Malkin (Jerusalem: Keter, 2008), 250–251.

5   Shapira, *Yehudim, Tzionim u'ma she'benehem*, 101.

6   Itzhaki, *"Shelilat hagolah,"* 251.

7   Shapira, *Yehudim, Tzionim u'ma she'benehem*, 101.

8   Ibid., 108–109.

9   A. B. Yehoshua, *Achizat Moledet: Esrim maamarim v'rishum echad* (Tel Aviv: Hakibbutz Hameuchad, 2008)176 .

10 Tom Segev, *The Seventh Million: The Israelis and the Holocaust* (New York: Hill and Wang, 1993); Idith Zertal, *Israel's Holocaust and the Politics of Nationhood* (Cambridge: Cambridge University Press, 2005); Moshe Zuckerman, *Shoah b'cheder ha'atum* (Tel Aviv: Hakibbutz Hameuchad, 1993).

11 Segev, *Seventh Million*.

12 Shabtai Beit Zvi, *HaTzionut hapost-Ugandit b'mashber haShoah: Mechkar b'gormei mishgeh shel hatenuah haTzionit* (Tel Aviv: Bronfman, 1977), 181–182; Dina Porat, *Hanhagah b'malkod: HaYishuv nochach haShoah, 1942–1945* (Tel Aviv: Am Oved, 1986), 63.

13 Segev, *Seventh Million.*

14 Ibid.

15 Vital, *Afflictions*, 121.

16 Segev, *Seventh Million.*

17 Porat, *Hanhagah b'malkod*, 469–470.

18 Ibid., 80–82.

19 Shapira, *Yehudim chadashim*, 104–107.

20 Boaz Evron, *Hacheshbon haleumi*, 2nd ed. (Or Yehuda: Dvir 2002), 282–283.

21 Eliezer Don-Yehiya, "Memory and Political Culture: Israeli Society and Holocaust," *Studies in Contemporary Jewry* 9 (1993): 143–149.

22 Shapira, *Yehudim chadashim*, 153.

23 Theodor Herzl, *The Jewish State* (1896).

24 For Edmund Burke's speech see William Cobbett, *The Parliamentary History of England from the Earliest Period to the Year 1803* (London: TC Hansard, 1806), 223–224.

25 Yoram Hazony, "The Guardian of the Jews," in *New Essays on Zionism*, ed. David Hazony, Michael B. Oren and Yoram Hazony (Jerusalem: Shalem, 2006), 38–49.

CHAPTER 4: HARBINGERS OF POST-ZIONIST IDENTITY: BEFORE AND AFTER STATEHOOD

1 Israel Kolatt, "The Zionist Movement and the Arabs," in *Essential Papers on Zionism*, Reinharz and Shapira, 625–628; Susan Lee Hattis, *The Bi-National Idea During Mandatory Times* (Haifa: Shikmona, 1970), 48–80.

2 Kolatt, ibid., 628–639; Hattis, ibid.

3 Paul R. Mendes-Flohr, ed., *A Land of Two Peoples: Martin Buber on Jews and Arabs* (Oxford: Oxford University Press, 1983), 3–34.

4 Arthur A. Goren, *Dissenter in Zion: From the Writings of Judah L. Magnes* (Cambridge, MA: Harvard University Press, 1982), 27.

5 Benny Morris, *Righteous Victims: A History of the Zionist-Arab Conflict, 1881–2001* (New York: Alfred Knopf, 1991).

6   Shabtai Teveth, *Ben-Gurion and the Palestinian Arabs: From Peace to War* (New York: Oxford University Press, 1985).

7   Ibid.

8   Kolatt, "Zionist Movement," 631–632.

9   Ibid., 636–638.

10 Buber, *Land of Two Peoples*, 245.

11 Yoram Hazony, *The Jewish State: The Struggle for Israel's Soul* (New York: Basic Books, 2000). Hazony's study aroused scathing criticism by David Biale, who pointed out that Hazony was a member of the Likud and a former aide to Benjamin Netanyahu. In comparing Hazony's worldview to McCarthyism, Biale claimed that Hazony was trying to enforce a "party line," which he does not define precisely. On this matter, Biale got entangled in one of the main issues around which the struggle over the Jewish identities revolved: What is Zionism today? What are its current positions? How should Jewish identity adapt to new realities? See David Biale, *"Zion Uber Ales,"* *Tikkun* 15, no. 5 (September/October 2000): 77–79.

12 Hazony, ibid., 287–288.

13 Interview with Joshua Prawer, January 25, 1984, Oral History Archives (117), tape 26A, 10, cited in Hazony, *Jewish State*, 290.

14 Ibid., 290.

15 Ibid., 291.

16 These include Avigdor Cherikover, Ben-Zion Dinur (a Mapai member of the first Knesset and the minister of education from 1951 to 1955), Naftali Herz Tur Sinai, Moshe David Cassuto, Jacob Nahum Epstein, Gedaliah Alon and Benjamin Mazar. See Hillel Halkin, "The Zionist Idea," *Commentary* 110, no. 1 (July/August 2000): 63–69.

17 Hazony, *Jewish State*, 292.

18 Ibid., 293.

19 Ibid., 293–295.

20 Ibid., 292.

CHAPTER 5: HANNAH ARENDT: ON THE FAULT LINE OF CLASHING IDENTITIES

1   Amos Elon, *The Pity of It All: A Portrait of the German-Jewish Epoch, 1743–1933* (Metropolitan Books, 2002); Alexander Altmann, *Moses Mendelssohn: A Biographical Study* (Birmingham: University of Alabama Press, 1973).

2   Hannah Arendt, *Men in Dark Times* (New York: Harcourt, Brace and World, 1968), 16.

3   Elisabeth Young-Bruehl, *Hannah Arendt: For Love of the World* (Binghamton, NY: Vail-Ballou, 1982).

4   Richard J. Bernstein, "Hannah Arendt's Zionism?" in *Hannah Arendt in Jerusalem*, ed. Steven E. Aschheim (Berkeley: University of California Press, 2001), 195.

5   Young-Bruehl, *For Love of the World*.

6   Hannah Arendt, *The Origins of Totalitarianism*, rev. ed. (1951; repr., New York: Schocken, 2004, includes all the prefaces and additions from the 1958, 1968 and 1972 editions).

7   Young-Bruehl, *For Love of the World*.

8   Elhanan Yakira, "Hannah Arendt, the Holocaust, and Zionism: A Story of Failure," *Israel Studies* 11, no. 3 (Fall 2006): 40.

9   Hannah Arendt, "From the Dreyfus Affair to France Today," *Jewish Social Studies* 4, no. 3 (July 1942): 238–239; Hannah Arendt, "Herzl and Lazare," in *The Jew as Pariah: Jewish Identity and Politics in the Modern Age*, ed. Ron H. Feldman (New York: Grove, 1978), 125–130; Sharon Muller, "The Origins of Eichmann in Jerusalem: Hannah Arendt's Interpretation of Jewish History," *Jewish Social Studies* 34, nos. 3–4 (Summer–Autumn 1981): 248; Richard J. Bernstein, *Hannah Arendt and the Jewish Question* (Boston: MIT Press, 1996), 61.

10 Muller, "Origins of Eichmann," 249.

11 Hannah Arendt, "Zionism Reconsidered," *Menorah Journal* 32, no. 2 (October–December 1945), reprinted in *Hannah Arendt: The Jewish Writings* (New York: Schocken, 2007), 367, 370.

12 Yakira, "Hannah Arendt," 41.

13 Walter Laqueur, "The Arendt Cult: Hannah Arendt as Political Commentator," in Aschheim, *Hannah Arendt in Jerusalem*.

14 Anita Shapira, *The Eichmann Trial: Changing Perspectives* (Jerusalem: Yad Vashem, 2002).

15 Yakira, "Hannah Arendt," 42–43, 45; David Cesarani, *Becoming Eichmann: Rethinking the Life, Crimes and Trial of a "Desk Murderer"* (Cambridge, MA: Da Capo, 2006), 197, 347.

16 Yakira, "Hannah Arendt," 43; Shapira, *Eichmann Trial*.

17 Yakira, ibid., 58, note 15.

18 Laqueur, "Arendt Cult," 63.

19 Yakira, "Hannah Arendt," 43.

20 Shapira, *Eichmann Trial*.

21 Ibid.

22 Yakira, "Hannah Arendt," 48.

23 Hannah Arendt, *Eichmann in Jerusalem: A Report on the Banality of Evil* (Penguin, 1963).

24 Ibid.

25 Ibid.

26 Ibid.

27 Ibid.

28 Ibid. For a scholarly analysis of this, see Muller, "Origins of Eichmann," 126–238.

29 Arendt, *Eichmann in Jerusalem*.

30 Muller, "Origins of Eichmann," 242.

31 Hannah Arendt, "Privileged Jews," *Jewish Social Studies* 8 (January 1946): 28–29. Cited in Muller, "Origins of Eichmann," 246.

32 Hannah Arendt, "Portrait of a Period," *Menorah Journal* (October 1943), reprinted in Feldman, *Jew as Pariah*, 121, cited in Muller, "Origins of Eichmann," 245–246.

33 Muller, "Origins of Eichmann," 244; Arendt, *Origins of Totalitarianism*, 65–73.

34 Arendt, "Privileged Jews," 4, 9; Muller, "Origins of Eichmann," 244, 247.

35 Arendt, "Privileged Jews," 5–6.

36 Arendt, "Privileged Jews," 5–6.

37 Young-Bruehl, *For Love of the World*.

38 Hannah Arendt's letter to the American Jewish Congress, June 11, 1963, Library of Congress, cited in Young-Bruehl, ibid.

39 Hannah Arendt's letter to Herman Pomerantz, January 27, 1964, ibid., cited in Young-Bruehl, ibid.; Marie Syrkin, "Miss Arendt Surveys the Holocaust," *Jewish Frontier* 30 (May 1963): 7–14.

40 Arendt, *Eichmann in Jerusalem*, 10, 40, 58, 61, 76; Muller, "Origins of Eichmann," 238–239.

41 Young-Bruehl, *For Love of the World*.

42 Cynthia Ozick, "The Heretic: The Mythic Passions of Gershom Scholem," *New Yorker*, September 2002.

43 Gershom Scholem's letter to Hannah Arendt, which appeared in the Israeli daily *Davar*, January 31, 1964. It was reprinted in *Devarim b'go*, a collection of Scholem's essays (Tel Aviv: Am Oved, 1979), 91–95.

44 Feldman, *Jew as Pariah*, 245–251.

45 Hannah Arendt, *Responsibility and Judgment* (New York: Schocken, 2003), 81.

46 Cesarani, *Becoming Eichmann*, 346.

47 Yehuda Bauer, *Rethinking the Holocaust* (New Haven: Yale University Press, 2001), 78–79, 128.

48 Ibid., 79.

49 Yakira, "Hannah Arendt," 33, 54–57; Idith Zertal, *Israel's Holocaust and the Politics of Nationhood* (Cambridge: Cambridge University Press, 2005).

50 Moshe Zimmerman, "Hannah Arendt: Early 'Post-Zionist,'" in Aschheim, *Hannah Arendt in Jerusalem*.

51 Yakira, "Hannah Arendt," 55.

52 Letters to Jaspers, June 1 and October 10, 1967, cited in Gabriel Piterberg, "Zion's Rebel Daughter: Hannah Arendt on Palestine and Jewish Politics," *New Left Review* 48 (November/December 2007): 10.

53 Young-Bruehl, *For Love of the World*.

54 Ibid.

55 Ibid.

56 Yakira, "Hanna Arendt," 54–55.

CHAPTER 6: JEWS ASSIMILATED AND POST-ASSIMILATED

1   Todd Endelman, "Jewish Self-Identification and West European Categories of Belonging: From the Enlightenment to World War II," in *Religion or Ethnicity? Jewish Identities in Evolution* , ed. Zvi Gitelman (New Brunswick, NJ: Rutgers University Press, 2009), 104.

2   Zygmunt Bauman, *Modernity and Ambivalence* (Cambridge: Polity, 1993), 110–112.

3   Lloyd P. Gartner, *History of the Jews in Modern Times* (Oxford: Oxford University Press, 2001), 88–94; Sander L. Gilman, *Jewish Self-Hatred, Anti-Semitism and the Hidden Language of the Jews* (Baltimore: John Hopkins University Press, 1986), 98.

4   Gartner, *History of the Jews*, 98–99; Shmuel Feiner, *The Jewish Enlightenment* (Philadelphia: University of Pennsylvania Press, 2003), 121–122; Christian Wilhelm von Dohm, "Concerning the Amelioration of the Civil Status of the Jews," in *The Jew in the Modern World: A Documentary History*, ed. Paul Mendes-Flohr and Jehuda Reinharz, 2nd ed. (Oxford University Press, 1995), 28–36.

5   Aviva Cantor, *Jewish Women/Jewish Men: The Legacy of Patriarchy in Jewish Life* (San Francisco: Harper Collins, 1995), 157–158.

6   Bauman, *Modernity and Ambivalence*, 112.

7   George L. Mosse, "Jewish Emancipation: Between Bildung and Respectability," in *The Jewish Response to German Culture: From the Enlightenment to the Second World War*, ed. Jehuda Reinharz and Walter Schatzberg (Hanover and London: University Press of New England, 1985), 1–5.

8   Amos Elon, *The Pity of It All: A Portrait of the German-Jewish Epoch, 1743–1933* (Metropolitan Books, 2002).

9   Gilman, *Jewish Self-Hatred*, 39; Sander L. Gilman, *Creating Beauty to Cure the Soul: Race and Psychology in the Shaping of Aesthetic Surgery* (Durham, NC: Duke University Press, 1998), 90; Joshua Trachtenberg, *The Devil and the Jews: The Medieval Conception of the Jew and Its Relation to Modern Anti-Semitism* (New Haven: Yale University Press, 1943), 47–50; Sander L.

Gilman, "The Jewish Nose: Are Jews White? Or, the History of the Nose Job," in *The Other in Jewish Thought and History: Constructions of Jewish Culture and Identity*, ed. Laurence J. Silberstein and Robert L. Cohn (New York: New York University Press, 1994), 368–371.

10 Gilman, "The Jewish Nose," 387; Sander L. Gilman, *The Jew's Body* (London: Routledge, 1991), 96, 126–127; Sander L. Gilman, *Jewish Frontiers: Essays on Bodies, Histories and Identities* (London: Palgrave Macmillan, 2003), 116.

11 Gilman, "The Jewish Nose," 389.

12 Zygmunt Bauman, "Exit Visas and Entry Tickets: Paradoxes of Jewish Assimilation," *Telos* 77 (Fall 1988): 52–53.

13 Michael Stanislawski, *Zionism in the Fin de Siècle: Cosmopolitanism and Nationalism from Nordau to Jabotinsky* (Berkeley: University of California Press, 2001), 7.

14 Gershom Scholem, "Germans and Jews," in *On Jews and Judaism in Crisis: Selected Essays*, ed. Gershom Scholem, trans. Werner J. Dannhauser (New York: Schocken, 1976), 76–77; Scott Spector, "Beyond Assimilation: Introducing Subjectivity to German-Jewish History," in *Religion or Ethnicity*, Gitelman, 92.

15 Gilman, *Jewish Self-Hatred*, 2–3.

16 Cantor, *Jewish Women*, 157.

17 Bauman, "Exit Visas and Entry Tickets," 56.

18 Gilman, *Jewish Self-Hatred*, 3, 149.

19 Bauman, *Modernity and Ambivalence*, 113, citations of S. S. Prawer, *Heine's Jewish Comedy* (Oxford: Oxford University Press, 1983), 760–761.

20 Bauman, ibid., 114.

21 Bauman, ibid., 115.

22 Jacob Wassermann, *My Life as German and Jew*, trans. S. N. Brainin (New York: Coward-McCann, 1933), 226–227.

23 Scholem, 37; Michael R. Marrus, "European Jewry and the Politics of Assimilation: Assessment and Reassessment," in *Jewish Assimilation in Modern Times*, ed. Bela Vago (Boulder: Westview Press, 1981), 6–8.

24 Paul R. Mendes-Flohr, "The Throes of Assimilation: Self Hatred and the Jewish Revolutionary," *European Judaism* (Spring 1978): 34.

25 Kurt Lewin, *Resolving Social Conflicts* (New York: Harper, 1948), 193, cited in Raphael Patai, *The Jewish Mind* (New York: Charles Scribner's Sons, 1977), 46.

26 Bauman, "Exit Visas and Entry Tickets," 57–63.

27 Yigal Lucein, *Heine: The Double Life* (Tel Aviv: Schocken, 2000), 1–23.

28 Isaiah Berlin, "The Life and Opinions of Moses Hess," in *Essential Papers on Jews and the Left*, ed. Ezra Mendelsohn (New York: New York University Press, 1997), 21–57; David Vital, *Hamahapechah haTzionit* (Tel Aviv: Am Oved, 1978); Stanislawski, *Zionism and the Fin de Siècle*, 109–146, 237–269 passim.

29 Barry Rubin, *Assimilation and Its Discontents* (New York: Times, 1995), 32–61; Abraham Ascher, *Pavel Axelrod and the Development of Menshevism* (Cambridge, MA: Harvard University Press, 1972), 69–81, 339–340; Erich Haberer, *Jews and Revolution in Nineteenth-Century Russia* (Cambridge: Cambridge University Press, 1995), 174.

30 Bauman, "Exit Visas and Entry Tickets," 52–53.

31 Shulamit Volkov, "The Dynamics of Dissimilation: The Ostjuden and German Jews," in *Jewish Response*, Reinharz and Schatzberg, 196–200.

32 David Sorkin, "Emancipation and Assimilation: Two Concepts and Their Application to German-Jewish History," *Leo Baeck Institute Year Book* 35 (1990): 17–35.

33 Spector, "Beyond Assimilation," 95.

34 Scholem, "Germans and Jews," 76–77.

35 Endelman, "Jewish Self-Identification," 114–115.

36 Ibid.,11 .

37 Dolores L. Augustine, *Patricians and Parvenus: Wealth and High Society in Wilhelmine Germany* (Oxford: Berg, 1994), 240.

38 Marion Kaplan, "Friendship on the Margins: Jewish Social Relations in Imperial Germany," *Central European History* 34, no. 4 (2001): 274.

39 Endelman, "Jewish Self-Identification," 119.

40 Paul Mendes-Flohr, "Introduction," and "In the Shadow of the World War," in *German-Jewish History in Modern Times*, ed. Michael A. Meyer (New York: Columbia University Press, 1998), 4:2–21.

41 Zygmunt Bauman, "Assimilation into Exile: The Jew as a Polish Writer," *Politics Today* 17, no. 4 (Winter 1996): 570–578.

42 Zvi Gitelman, "Secularism in Post-Soviet Russia and Ukraine," in *Religion or Ethnicity*, Gitelman, 262.

43 In 1963, sociologists Nathan Glazer and Daniel Patrick Moynihan noted that most of the Jews in New York were not affiliated with a synagogue, and were linked, first and foremost, by a "sense of common destiny" – a destiny that is "ultimately defined by a connection to a single religion, to which each Jew is attached from birth and by virtue of tradition, if not by action and faith." In the seventies, Isaiah Charles Liebman and Steven Cohen claimed that "the ties to tradition and the minority experience are far more important than the common faith – a phenomenon which, in many ways, creates a collective that is more ethnic than religious." See Nathan Glazer and Daniel Patrick Moynihan, *Beyond the Melting Pot* (Cambridge, MA: MIT Press, 1963), 140–142; Wade Clark Roof and William McKinney, *American Mainline Religion: Its Changing Shape and Future* (New Brunswick, NJ: Rutgers University Press, 1987), 102, cited in Zvi Gitelman, "Conclusion," in *Religion or Ethnicity*, Gitelman, 303.

44 Charles Liebman and Steven Cohen, *Two Worlds of Judaism* (New Haven: Yale University Press, 1990), 17.

45 Gitelman, "Conclusion," 312.

46 Gitelman, "Secularism," 262; "Conclusion," 312–313.

47 Stephen Whitfield, *In Search of American Jewish Culture* (Hanover: Brandeis University Press, 1999), 224, cited in Gitelman, "Conclusion," 318–319.

48 Jonathan D. Sarna, *American Judaism: A History* (New Haven: Yale University Press, 2004), 357–358, 362–364.

49 Gitelman, "Conclusion," 312, 318–319.

CHAPTER 7: AMERICAN JEWISH IDENTITY IN THE NAZI ERA AND AT THE TIME OF ISRAELI STATEHOOD

1   Gulie Ne'eman Arad, *America, Its Jews and the Rise of Nazism* (Indiana University Press, 2000); J. D. Sarna, *American Judaism: A History* (New Haven: Yale University Press, 2004), 51–52, 60, 125–129.

2   Arad, ibid., 28–31. For the Damascus Affair, see Jonathan Frankel, *The Damascus Affair, Ritual Murder, Politics, and the Jews in 1840* (Cambridge:

Cambridge University Press, 1997).

3   Arad, ibid., 55.

4   Ibid., 72.

5   Ibid., 72–73. See also Leonard Dinnerstein, *Anti-Semitism in American History* (New York: Oxford University, 1995).

6   Arad, ibid,66 .

7   Ibid., 83–8.

8   Ibid., 129.

9   Ibid., 142.

10 Ibid.,127 , 146; David Wyman, *Paper Walls: America and the Refugee Crisis, 1938–1941* (New York: Pantheon, 1985), 14–23.

11 Arad, ibid., 131.

12 Joseph Ernest McAfee, "Jewish Solidarity in America," *Christian Century* 3 (June 1934).

13 Arad, ibid., 103.

14 Ibid., passim; Charles Silberman, *A Certain People: American Jews and Their Lives Today* (New York: Summit, 1985), 30.

15 Arad, ibid., passim.

16 Ibid., 173.

17 Ibid., 232.

18 Maurice Halbwachs, *On Collective Memory*, trans. and ed. Lewis A. Coser (Chicago: Chicago University Press, 1992), 38.

19 Ibid., 15–23.

20 Lewis A. Coser, "The Revival of the Sociology of Culture: The Case of Collective Memory," *Sociological Forum* 7, no. 2 (1992): 368.

21 Peter Novick, *The Holocaust in American Life* (New York: Mariner, 2000), 3, 5–6.

22 Ibid., 165–175.

23 Ibid., 30.

24 Laurel Leff, "How the New York Times Missed the Story of the Holocaust While It Was Happening," *History News Network* (4 April 2005); Laurel

Leff, *Buried by the Times: The Holocaust and America's Most Important Newspaper* (Cambridge: Cambridge University Press, 2005).

25 Novick, *Holocaust*, 40.

26 Ibid., 269.

27 Ibid., 7.

28 Zvi Ganin, *An Uneasy Relationship: American Jewish Leadership and Israel, 1948–1957* (Syracuse: Syracuse University Press, 2005), xvi, 3–4, 12; Zvi Ganin, *Truman, American Jewry, and Israel, 1945–1948* (Teaneck, NJ: Holmes and Meier, 1978).

29 Ibid., 3–6.

30 Ibid., 31–34.

31 Ibid., 19–20, 26–27, 36–37, 90–92.

CHAPTER 8: IDENTITY STRUGGLES WITHIN ISRAEL

1   Anita Shapira, *Yehudim chadashim, Yehudim yeshanim* (Tel Aviv: Am Oved, 1997),10.

2   Mordechai Bar-On, "New Historiography and National Identity: Reflections on Changes in the Self-Perception of Israelis and Recent Israeli Revisionist Historiography," in: Anita Shapira (ed.), *Israeli Identity in Transition*, (Westport, CT: Praeger, 2004), 5; E.H. Erikson, "Identity: Youth and Crisis," (New York: Norton, 1974), 15–17

3   Bar-On, "New Historiography," 5; G.W. Allport, "The Nature of Prejudice," (Reading, Mass: Addison-Welsey, 1954), 293–294; E.H. Erikson, "Dimensions of a New Identity," (New York: Norton, 1974), 95–96

4   Shapira, *Yehudim chadashim*, 10–15.

5   Jean-François Lyotard, *The Postmodern Condition* (Manchester: Manchester University Press, 1984), xxiv; Jean-François Lyotard and J. Thebaud, *Just Gaming* (Manchester: Manchester University Press, 1986), 96; David Harvey, *The Conditions of Postmodernity: An Inquiry into the Origins of Cultural Change* (Cambridge: Blackwell, 1989), 44–46.

6   Stuart Hall, "Cultural Identity and Diaspora," in *Identity, Community, and Cultural Difference*, ed. Jonathan Rutherford (London: Lawrence and Wishart, 1990), 223.

7   Laurence J. Silberstein, "Others Within and Others Without: Rethinking Jewish Identity and Culture," in *The Other in Jewish Thought and History: Constructions of Jewish Culture and Identity*, ed. Laurence J. Silberstein and Robert L. Cohn (New York: New York University Press, 1994), 2–5.

8   Jacques Derrida, "Deconstruction and the Other," an interview with Jacques Derrida, in *Dialogues with Contemporary Continental Thinkers*, ed. Richard Kearney (Manchester: University of Manchester Press, 1984), 116.

9   See, for example, Michel Foucault, *Madness and Civilization: A History of Insanity in the Age of Reason* (New York: Random House, 1965); Michel Foucault, *Discipline and Punish: The Birth of Prison* (New York: Random House, 1979); Michel Foucault, *The Order of Things: An Archeology of the Human Sciences* (New York: Random House, 1970).

10 Silberstein, "Others Within," 6.

11 Ibid., 11–12.

12 Virginia Dominguez, *People as Subject / People as Object: Selfhood and Peoplehood in Contemporary Israel* (Madison: University of.Wisconsin Press, 1989), 20, 157–169; cited in Silberstein, ibid., 12–14.

13 Bar-On, "New Historiography," 6–7.

14 Baruch Kimmerling, *Ketz shilton ha'achusolim (Ashkenazim, chilonim, vatikim, sotzialistim v'leumiim)* (Jerusalem: Keter, 2001), 30–31.

15 David Ohana, *The Origins of Israeli Mythology: Neither Canaanites nor Crusaders* (Cambridge: Cambridge University Press, 2012).

16 Bar-On, "New Historiography," 6.

17 Uri Ram, "Memory and Identity: The Sociology of the Historians' Debate in Israel," *Theory and Criticism* 8 (1996): 9–33.

18 Bar-On, "New Historiography," 5–6.

19 Aharon Megged, "The Israeli Urge for Suicide," *Haaretz*, June 10, 1994.

20 Benny Morris, *Righteous Victims: A History of the Zionist-Arab Conflict, 1881–2001* (New York: Alfred Knopf, 1991).

21 Walter Laqueur, *A History of Zionism: From the French Revolution to the Establishment of the State of Israel* (New York: MJF Books, 1997), 200.

22 Ibid., 210.

23 Ibid., 215–217.

24 Ibid., 219–221.

25 Ibid., 214.

26 Benny Morris, *The Birth of the Palestinian Refugee Problem Revisited* (Cambridge: Cambridge University Press, 2004), 10.

27 Ibid., 17.

28 Ibid., 20.

29 Benny Morris, *1948: A History of the First Arab-Israeli War* (New Haven: Yale University Press, 2008).

30 Morris, *Birth*.

31 Anita Shapira, *Yehudim, Tzionim u'ma she'benehem* (Tel Aviv: Am Oved, 2007), 13–40.

32 Morris, *Birth*.

33 The second edition was based on additional archival material and the minutes of Israeli cabinet meetings held during 1948–1949. But Morris admits that his research is not the last word on the Palestinian refugee problem because many documents are still not available. See ibid, 3.

34 Ibid.

35 For the traditional Israeli and Zionist argument regarding the exodus of Palestinian refugees from Israeli territory, see Mark Tessler, *A History of the Israeli-Palestinian Conflict* (Bloomington: Indiana University Press, 1994), 291–307.

36 For the traditional Arab version of a preconceived Israeli "transfer" plan, see Nur Masalha, *Expulsion of the Palestinians: The Concept of "Transfer" in Zionist Political Thought, 1882–1948* (Washington: Institute of Palestine Studies, 1992); Nur Masahla, "A Critique of Benny Morris," *Journal of Palestine Studies* 21, no. 1 (1991): 90–97. For Morris's arguments opposing this view, see Benny Morris, "Response to Finkelstein and Masalha," *Journal of Palestine Studies* 21, no. 1 (1991): 99–114.

37 Shabtai Teveth, "Charging Israel with Original Sin," *Commentary* 88 (September 1989), 24–33; Anita Shapira, "The Past Is Not a Foreign Country," *The New Republic* 221, no. 22 (29 November 1999): 26–38.

38 Baruch Kimmerling and Joel Samuel Migdal, *Palestinim: Am b'hivatzruto* (Jerusalem: Keter, 1999).

39 Benny Morris, "Revisiting the Palestinian Exodus of 1948," in *The War for Palestine: Rewriting the History of 1948*, ed. Eugene L. Rogan and Avi Shlaim (Cambridge: Cambridge University Press, 2001), 37.

40 Kimmerling and Migdal, *Palestinim*, 130–131.

41 Yoav Gelber, *Kommemiyut v'nakbah: Yisrael, haPalestinim, v'medinot Arav* (Or Yehuda: Dvir, 2004), 131–135.

42 Kimmerling and Migdal, *Palestinim*, 137–138.

43 Ibid., 139.

44 Gelber, *Kommemiyut v'nakbah*, 171; Morris, *Birth*, 166.

45 Gelber, ibid., 169–170; Morris, ibid., 166.

46 Morris, ibid., 153–171.

47 Yoav Gelber, *Palestine 1948: War, Escape and the Emergence of the Palestinian Refugee Problem* (London: Sussex Academic Press, 2006), 208, 223–228.

48 Shapira, *Not a Foreign Country*, 27.

49 Morris, *1948*, 439.

50 Morris, *Birth*, 310.

51 Ibid., 32.

52 Ibid., 555.

53 Bar-On, "New Historiography," 17.

54 Adi Ophir, *Avodat hahoveh: Masot al tarbut Yisraelit bazman hazeh* (Tel Aviv: Hakibbutz Hameuchad, 2002).

55 Motti Golani, *Milchamot lo korot me'atzman: Al zikaron, koach, u'vechirah* (Ben Shemen: Modan, 2002).

56 Yona Hadari, *Mashiach rachuv al tank: Hamachshavah hatziburit b'Yisrael ben Mivtza Sinai l'Milchemet Yom Hakippurim, 1956–1973* (Jerusalem: Shalom Hartman Institute, 2002).

57 Idith Zertal, *Israel's Holocaust and the Politics of Nationhood* (Cambridge: Cambridge University Press, 2005), 3.

58 Ibid., 167.

59 Bar-On, "New Historiography," 19.

CHAPTER 9: POST-ZIONISM

1   Laurence J. Silberstein, *The Post-Zionism Debates: Knowledge and Power in Israeli Culture* (New York and London: Routledge, 1999), 2; Ephraim Nimni, *The Challenge of Post-Zionism* (London: Zed Books, 2003), 3; Danny Ben-Moshe, "Post-Zionism in the Oslo Era and the Implications for the Diaspora," *Israel Affairs* 10, nos. 1–2 (Autumn/Winter 2004): 314.

2   Nimni, *Challenge of Post-Zionism*, 2–3; Charles Taylor, *Multiculturalism: Examining the Politics of Recognition* (Princeton: Princeton University Press, 1994).

3   Yosef Gorny, "Zionism Then and Now," *Tel Aviv University News* (Winter 1996/1997): 26; Ben-Moshe, "Post-Zionism in the Oslo Era," 314.

4   Uri Ram, "Four Perspectives on Civil Society and Post-Zionism in Israel," *Palestine-Israel Journal* 12, no. 1 (2005): 35; Mark Levine, "Is Post-Zionism Post-Modern?" *Currents* (Winter/Spring 1996): 14–27.

5   Silberstein, *Post-Zionism Debates*, 3.

6   Rogers Brubaker, *Citizenship and Nationhood in France and Germany* (Cambridge, MA: Harvard University Press, 1994), cited in Ram, "Four Perspectives," 35.

7   Ram, ibid.

8   Ram, ibid.; Amnon Raz-Krakotzkin, "*Galut betoch ribonut: L'vikoret 'shelilat hagalut' betarbut haYisraelit,*" *Te'oriah u'vikoret* 4 (Autumn 1993): 23–55, *Te'oriah u'vikoret* 5 (Autumn 1994): 113–132; Ilan Gur-Zeev, *Likrat chinuch l'galutiyut: Rav-tarbutiyut, Kolonialism, v'chinuch she'k'neged b'idan hapost-moderni* (Tel Aviv: Resling, 2004).

9   Ram, ibid.; Said, *Orientalism* (New York: Vintage, 1979), Yehouda Shenhav, *HaYehudim haAravim: Leumiyut, dat v'etniyut* (Tel Aviv: Am Oved, 2003); Ella Shohat, *Israeli Cinema: East/West and the Politics of Representation* (Texas: University of Texas Press, 1989); Ella Shohat, *Zichronot asurim* (Tel Aviv: Kedem and the author, 2001).

10 Ram, ibid.

11 Gershon Shafir, *Land, Labor and the Origins of the Israeli-Palestinian Conflict, 1882–1914* (Cambridge: Cambridge University Press, 1989), 8–21; Gershon Shafir, "Israeli Society: A Counterview," *Israel Studies* 1, no. 2 (Fall 1996): 189–213; Baruch Kimmerling, *Zionism and Territory: The Socio-Territorial Dimensions of Zionist Politics* (Berkeley: University of

California Press, 2000), 8, 29–30; Uri Ram, "The Colonization Perspective in Israeli Sociology," in *The Israel/Palestine Question*, ed. Ilan Pappé (New York: Routledge, 1999), 49–71; Uri Ram, *The Changing Agenda of Israeli Sociology: Theory, Ideology and Identity* (New York: SUNY Press, 1995); Ronen Shamir, *The Colonies of Law: Colonialism, Zionism, and the Law in Early Mandate Palestine* (Cambridge: Cambridge University Press, 1999); Ronen Shamir, "Jewish Bourgeoisie in Colonial Palestine: Guidelines for a Research Agenda," *Sotziologiya Yisraelit* 3, no. 1 (2000): 133–148; Amir Ben-Porat, "They Did Not Lie on the Fence: Opportunity, Longing and the Breakthrough to Palestine," *Studies in the Revival of Israel* 4 (1994): 298–278. For a critique of their analysis, see Avi Bareli, "Forgetting Europe: Perspectives on the Debate about Zionism and Colonialism," in *Israeli Historical Revisionism: From Left to Right*, ed. Anita Shapira and Derek J. Penslar (New York: Routledge, 2002), 99–116.

12 Ilan Pappé, "Zionism as Colonialism: A Comparative View of 'Diluted' Colonialism in Asia and Africa," in *Between Vision and Revision: A Century of Zionist Historiography*, ed. Yehi'am Weitz (Jerusalem: Shazar Center, 1998); Ilan Pappé, *The Modern Middle East* (New York: Routledge, 2005), 19–20.

13 Ilan Pappé, *A History of Modern Palestine* (Cambridge: Cambridge University Press, 2004), 11.

14 "History and Power in the Middle East: A Conversation with Ilan Pappé," *Logos* 3, no. 1 (Winter 2004).

15 Shlomo Avineri, "Post-Zionism Doesn't Exist," *Haaretz*, July 6, 2007.

16 David Hirsh, "Anti-Zionism and Anti-Semitism: Cosmopolitan Reflections," Working Paper Series (The Yale Initiative for the Interdisciplinary Study of Anti-Semitism, 2008), 23.

17 ibid, 27, 34; Uri Davis, *Apartheid Israel: Possibilities for the Struggle Within* (London: Zed Books, 2000).

18 Anthony Julius, "Jewish Anti-Zionism Unraveled: The Morality of Vanity," part 1, April 2008, www.z-word.com. For American Jewry, see Michael B. Oren, *Power, Faith and Fantasy: America in the Middle East, 1776 to the Present* (New York: W. W. Norton, 2007), 351–352. The reality described by Julius led Israeli historian Tom Segev to conclude that "contrary to the prevailing wisdom in Israel today, the Zionist movement's principal opponents were thus Jews. The movement did not succeed in convincing most of the Jewish people that it was viable." Clearly, that was indeed the case in

central and western Europe and the United States, but not in eastern Europe and the western part of the Russian Empire, where Jews were essentially presumed to be a separate nation: in the elections held in these areas after the First World War, the Zionists were the main electoral force. See Tom Segev, *Elvis in Jerusalem: Post-Zionism and the Americanization of Israel* (New York: Metropolitan Books/Henry Holt, 2002), 22; Ezra Mendelsohn, *The Jews of East Central Europe Between the World Wars* (Bloomington: Indiana University Press, 1987), 50–52.

19 Julius, "Jewish Anti-Zionism Unraveled," 2–3.

20 Isaac Deutscher, "Israel's Spiritual Climate," reprinted in *The Non-Jewish Jew and Other Essays* (London: Oxford University Press, 1968), 111–112.

21 Julius, "Jewish Anti-Zionism Unraveled," 3.

22 Ibid., 4.

23 Jacqueline Rose, response to Edward Said, in *Freud and the Non-European*, by Edward W. Said (London: Verso, 2003), 71, cited in Julius, "Jewish Anti-Zionism Unraveled," 4.

24 Ibid.

25 Marcel Liebman, *Born Jewish: A Childhood in Occupied Europe* (London: Verso, 2005), 176, cited in Julius, ibid., 4. See also Joel Kovel, interview, in Seth Farber, *Radicals, Rabbis, and Peacemakers* (Monroe, ME: Common Courage, 2005), 63.

26 Brian Klug, "Climate of the Debate over Israel," http://engageonline. wordpress.com/, 5 May 2007.

27 Julius, "Jewish Anti-Zionism Unraveled," 4.

28 Brian Klug, "Who Speaks for Jews in England?" *Guardian*, 5 February 2007, cited in Julius, ibid., 3–4.

29 Letter, *Guardian*, April 25, 2007; *Jewish Chronicle*, April 27, 2007, cited in Julius, ibid.

30 Reuven Kaminer, *The Politics of Protest: The Israeli Peace Movement and the Palestinian Intifada* (London: Sussex Academic Press, 1995), 12–13.

31 Shlomo Sand, *The Invention of the Jewish People* (New York: Verso, 2009), passim; Anita Shapira, "The Jewish People Deniers," *Journal of Israeli History* 28, no. 1 (March 2009).

32 Rochelle Furstenberg, *Post-Zionism: The Challenge to Israel* (New York:

American Jewish Committee and Bar Ilan University, 1997), vi.

33 Norman K. Finkelstein, *Beyond Chutzpah: On the Misuse of Anti-Semitism and the Abuse of History*, 2nd ed. (Berkeley and Los Angeles: University of California Press, 2008), 66–88; Michael Neumann, "What Is Anti-Semitism?" *Counterpunch* (4 June 2002); Brian Klug, "The Myth of the New Anti-Semitism," *The Nation* (2 February 2004); Tony Greenstein, "The Seamy Side of Solidarity," *Guardian*, 17 February 2007; Arthur Nelsen, "When an Anti-Semite Is not an Anti-Semite," *Guardian*, 5 April 2007; Paul Eisen, "Jewish Power," 19 August 2004, RighteousJews.org; Anthony Julius, "Jewish Anti-Zionism Unraveled," part 2, April 2008, www.z-word.com, 2.

34 Gilad Atzmon, "Aaronovitch's Tantrum and the Demolition of Jewish Power," Palestine Think Tank, 7 April 2009; Gilad Atzmon, "On Anti-Semitism," 20 December 2003, www.Gilad.co.uk.

35 Hirsh, "Anti-Zionism," 22.

36 Segev, *Elvis in Jerusalem*, 7.

37 Robert Wistrich, "Israel Past and Future," *Partisan Review* 3 (Summer 1996): 75, cited in Ben-Moshe, "Post-Zionism in the Oslo Era," 315.

38 Ram, "Four Perspectives," 33; A. B. Yehoshua, *Bi'zechut hanormaliyut: Chamesh masot b'she'elat haTzionut* (Jerusalem: Schocken, 1980). Ram notes that the philosopher Menachem Brinker also proposed this type of post-Zionism. See Menachem Brinker, *"Acharei haTzionut," Siman Keriah* 19: 21–29.

39 Ram, "Four Perspectives," 33–34; Daniel Bell, *The End of Ideology* (Glencoe, IL: Free Press, 1960); S. N. Eisenstadt, *Japanese Civilization: A Comparative Review* (Chicago: University of Chicago Press, 1996); Charles S. Liebman and Eliezer Don-Yehiya, *Civil Religion in Israel* (Berkeley: University of California Press, 1983); Baruch Kimmerling, *The Invention and Decline of Israeliness: State, Society and the Military* (Berkeley and Los Angeles: University of California Press, 2001).

40 Ram, "Four Perspectives," 34; Michael Billing, *Banal Nationalism* (New York: Sage, 1995).

41 Amos Elon, "Israel and the End of Zionism," *New York Review of Books* 43, no. 20 (19 December 1996): 27–28, cited in Ben-Moshe, "Post-Zionism in the Oslo Era," 323.

42 Silberstein, *Post-Zionism Debates*, 2.

43 Meyrav Wurmser, "Can Israel Survive Post-Zionism?" *Middle East Quarterly* VI, no. 1 (March 1999).

44 Interview with Benny Morris, June 10, 2009.

45 Edward Said, "New History, Old Ideas," *Al-Ahram Weekly* (May 1998): 21– 27, cited in Nimni, *Challenge of Post-Zionism*, 6, 8.

46 See, for example, the statements made by Michael Neumann, whose position created an uproar in anti-Zionist circles: "My principal reason for supporting a two-state solution is that, like many, I don't feel there's the slightest chance that Israelis would accept a [Palestinian] one-state solution…, or that anyone could dictate it to them" (Michael Neumann, "Two States, One State and Snake Oil," *Counterpunch* [15 May 2007]).

47 "South Africa, Israel-Palestine, and the Contours of the Contemporary Global Order," Noam Chomsky interviewed by Christopher J. Lee, *Safundi*, 9 March 2004. Also see "Justice for Palestine?" Noam Chomsky interviewed by Stephen R. Shalom and Justin Podur, *Z-net*, 30 March 2004; Interview with Noam Chomsky by Timo Stollenwerk, *Z Magazine*, 11 June 2004.

48 Ben-Moshe, "Post-Zionism in the Oslo Era," 320; Ben-Moshe's data is in Yair Auron, "Jewish-Israeli Identity among Israel's Future Teachers," *Jerusalem Letter/Viewpoints*, Jerusalem Center for Public Affairs no. 334 (1 May 1996): 3.

49 "Re-evaluating the Law of Return," *Policy Dispatch* no. 5, Institute of the World Jewish Congress, (January 1995): 4, cited in Ben-Moshe, "Post-Zionism in the Oslo Era," 322.

50 David Clayman, "The Law of Return Reconsidered," Jerusalem Center for Public Affairs, 16 July 1995 cited in Ben-Moshe, "Post-Zionism in the Oslo Era," 322.

51 Interview with A. B. Yehoshua, *Politics* (December 1986).

52 Elon, "Israel and the End of Zionism," 28.

53 *Al Hamishmar*, December 20, 1991, cited in Ben-Moshe, "Post-Zionism in the Oslo Era," 323.

54 Ibid.

55 Ibid, 32.

56 Ibid, 332.

57 A transcript of a conversation with Avraham Burg and Omer Bartov, New York Public Library, 1 December 2008, 24.

CHAPTER 10: ZIONISM: A PRODUCT OF COLONIALISM AND IMPERIALISM?

1 Joel Kovel, "Zionism's Bad Conscience," *Tikkun* 17, no. 5 (September/October 2002): 21.

2 "Le conflit israélo-arabe," *Les Temps Modernes* (June 1967). For a review of some articles that appeared in the same issue, including an article by Rodinson, see I. F. Stone, "Holy War," *New York Review of Books* 9, no. 2 (3 August 1967).

3 Maxime Rodinson, *Israel: A Colonial-Settler State?* (New York: Pathfinder, 1973).

4 Ibid., 91.

5 Ibid., 92.

6 Ibid., 36.

7 Ibid., 56.

8 Ibid., 88.

9 Ibid., 64–65.

10 Ibid., 86–87.

11 Ibid., 90.

12 These scholars, it should be noted, do not necessarily represent post-colonialism – i.e., the postmodern intellectual discourse that criticizes colonialism from an ideological point of view. One can have a post-colonial approach without necessarily thinking that Zionism is a colonial phenomenon. For post-colonialism, see Edward Said, *Orientalism* (New York: Vintage, 1979); Edward Said, *Culture and Imperialism* (New York: Vintage, 1994); Edward Said, *Power, Politics and Culture* (New York: Vintage, 2002); Homi Bhabha, *The Location of Culture* (London: Routledge, 1994); Bart J. Moore-Gilbert, *Postcolonial Theory: Contexts, Practices, Politics* (New York: Verso, 1997); Ran Aaronsohn, "Settlement in Eretz Israel – A Colonialist Enterprise? 'Critical' Scholarship and Historical Geography," *Israel Studies* 1, no. 2 (Fall 1996): 215; Laurence J. Silberstein, *The Post-Zionism Debates: Knowledge and Power in Israeli Culture* (New York and London: Routledge, 1999), 102–111.

13 Aaronsohn, ibid; Silberstein, *Post-Zionism Debates*, 102–111; Baruch Kimmerling, *Zionism and Territory: The Socio-Territorial Dimensions of Zionist Politics* (Berkeley: University of California Press, 2000), 8, 29–30.

14 Kimmerling, ibid.

15 Gershon Shafir, *Land, Labor and the Origins of the Israeli-Palestinian Conflict, 1882–1914* (Cambridge: Cambridge University Press, 1989), xi, 5.

16 Silberstein, *Post-Zionism Debates*, 103.

17 Gershon Shafir, *Land, Labor and the Origins of the Israeli-Palestinian Conflict, 1882–1914*, 2nd ed. (Cambridge: Cambridge University Press, 1996), 7.

18 Ibid., 5.

19 The author thanks Prof. Henry Cripps, chairman of arts and humanities at Claremont Graduate University, CA, for directing her attention to this important issue.

20 A. B. Yehoshua, *"Ben zechut l'zechut," Bi'zechut hanormaliyut*, 97–99.

21 Amos Oz, "From Jerusalem to Cairo: Escaping from the Shadow of the Past," *Encounter* (April 1982).

22 Amos Oz, "The Meaning of a Homeland," in *Who Is Left? Zionism Answers Back* (Jerusalem: Alpha, 1971), 158.

23 Uri Avnery, "An Apology," http://zope.gush-shalom.org/home/en/channels/avnery/1213478638/, 14 June 2008.

24 Aharonson, *"Hahityashvut b'Eretz Yisrael – mif'al kolonialisti?"* 349.

25 Samuel Katz, *Battleground: Fact and Fantasy in Eretz Israel* (Tel Aviv: Karni, 1972), 93.

26 Ibid.

27 James Parkes, *Whose Land? A History of the Peoples in Palestine* (London: Penguin, 1970), 266.

28 Katz, *Battleground*, 95–96; Jacob de Hass, *History of Palestine: The Last Two Thousand Years* (New York: Macmillan, 1934), 52.

29 Katz, ibid., 98–99.

30 Michael G. Kort, "Letters from the War," in "Israel: After the War and Before the Peace," ed. Bill Novak special issue, *Response* 7, no. 1 (Winter 1973/74): 11; Avi Bareli, "Forgetting Europe: Perspectives on the Debate about Zionism and Colonialism," in *Israeli Historical Revisionism: From Left to Right*, ed. Anita Shapira and Derek J. Penslar (New York: Routledge, 2002), 99–116.

31 Kort, ibid., 12; Jacob L. Talmon, *Myth of the Nation and Vision of Revolution:*

Ideological Polarization in the Twentieth Century (New Brunswick, NJ: Transaction, 1991); Shmuel Ettinger, "The Origins of Modern Anti-Semitism," *Dispersion and Unity* 9 (1969): 31–32; Stanislav Andreski, "An Economic Interpretation of Anti-Semitism in Eastern Europe," *Jewish Journal of Sociology* 5, no. 2 (December 1963): 206–209; Werner J. Cahnman, "Socio-Economic Causes of Anti-Semitism," *Social Problems* 5, no. 1 (July 1957): 25–26.

32 Kort, ibid., 12–13; A. H. Hourani, *Minorities in the Arab World* (Oxford: Oxford University Press, 1947); Norman A. Stillman, "Middle Eastern and North African Jewries Confront Modernity: Orientation, Disorientation, Reorientation," in *Sephardi and Middle Eastern Jewries: History and Culture in the Modern Era*, ed. Harvey E. Goldberg (Bloomington: Indiana University Press, 1996), 59–72.

33 Aharonson, *"Hahityashvut,"* 342–343.

34 Ibid., 343

35 Ibid., 343, 348.

36 Ibid., 348.

37 Ibid.

38 Boaz Evron, "The Israeli-Arab Impasse: Reflections on a Constructive Alternative," in *Who is Left? Zionism Answers Back*, 128–130.

39 Kovel, "Zionism's Bad Conscience," 22.

CHAPTER 11: JEWISH SOVEREIGNTY AND DEMOCRACY

1 Sammy Smooha, "Ethnic Democracy: Israel as an Archetype," *Israel Studies* 2, no. 2 (Fall 1997): 198–199.

2 Ibid., 199.

3 Ibid., 200.

4 Ibid.

5 Oren Yiftachel, "Israeli Society and Jewish-Palestinian Reconciliation: 'Ethnocracy' and Its Territorial Contradictions," *Middle East Journal* 51, no. 4 (1997): 505–519; Oren Yiftachel, in *Shel mi ha'aretz hazot?*, ed. Uzi Benziman (Jerusalem: Israel Democracy Institute, 2006), 147.

6 Sammy Smooha, in Benziman, *Shel mi ha'aretz*, 17, 23.

7 Shulamit Aloni, *Demokratiyah b'azikim* (Tel Aviv: Am Oved, 2008), 28.

8   Ibid., 33.

9   Ibid., 38, 302.

10 Kimmerling, *Invention*, 181–182, 186–187.

11 Ibid., 187–198.

12 Ibid., 186.

13 Ibid., 186–187.

14 Ibid., 205–228.

15 Ruth Gavison, "Jewish and Democratic? A Rejoinder to the 'Ethnic Democracy' Debate," *Israel Studies* 4, no. 1 (Spring 1999): 44, 47–48.

16 Ibid., 52–53.

17 Ibid., 50, 56, 61.

18 Ibid., 58, 65.

19 Segev, *Elvis in Jerusalem*, 73–78.

20 Alexander Yakobson, "Jewish Peoplehood and the Jewish State, How Unique? A Comparative Survey," *Israel Studies* 13, no. 2 (Summer 2008): 4–5.

21 Ibid., 5.

22 Ibid., 6–8.

CHAPTER 12: WHO IS A JEW?

1   The Law of Return, 1950, July 5, 1950, the website of the Ministry of Foreign Affairs, http://www.mfa.gov.il/MFA/MFAArchive/1950_1959/ Law of Return 205710-1950. See also Morris Kertzer, *What Is a Jew?* (New York: Touchstone, 1996), 7–8; Gary J. Jacobsohn, *Apple of Gold: Constitutionalism in Israel and the United States* (Princeton: Princeton University Press, 1994), 3–17, 251–254; Shulamit Aloni, *Demokratiyah b'azikim* (Tel Aviv: Am Oved, 2008), 46.

2   The Law of Return (amendment no. 2), 1970, the website of the Ministry of Foreign Affairs, http://www.mfa.gov.il.

3   Maya Leibowitz, David Ariel-Yoel and Moti Inbari, *Mihu Yehudi b'yamenu?: Rav-siach* Symposium on Jewish Identity, translated by Tamar Fox (Tel Aviv: Yedioth Ahronoth, Hemed, 2006 Hebrew), 7; Joseph Telushkin, *Jewish Literacy: The Most Important Things to Know about the Jewish Religion*

(New York: William Morrow, 1991), 359.

4   Oswald Rufeisen v. the Minister of the Interior, Israel High Court of Justice Case 72/62.

5   Haim Cohen, *B'tarbut haYahadut hachilonit: Hegut chadashah b'Yisrael* (Jerusalem: Keter, 2003), 225–227.

6   Benjamin Shalit v. Minister of the Interior, Verdict 23 (2), Israel High Court of Justice Case 68/58.

7   Punk Shlesinger, Israel High Court of Justice, 5070/95 and 2901/97.

8   Leibowitz, Ariel-Yoel and Inbari, *Mihu Yehudi*, 64–65.

9   Ibid., 21–23.

10   Ibid., 26–27.

11   Ibid., 24–25.

12   Ibid., 35, 40.

13   Ibid., 87.

14   Ibid., 90–91.

15   Aloni, *Demokratiyah b'azikim*, 162–163.

16   Leibowitz, Ariel-Yoel and Inbari, *Mihu Yehudi*, 58.

17   Ibid., 63.

CHAPTER 13: THE MIZRACHIM: THE JEWISH "OTHER" IN ISRAEL

1   Mizrachim comprised 51.6 percent of Israel's population in 1988 and 47.3 percent in 1996 – as a percentage of the total population their share declined because of the mass immigration from the former USSR in the early nineties. See Youssef Courbage, "Reshuffling the Demographic Cards in Israel/ Palestine," *Journal of Palestine Studies* 28, no. 4 (Summer 1999): 21–39.

2   Sami Shalom Chetrit, *Hama'avak haMizrachi b'Yisrael: Ben dichui l'shichrur, ben hizdahut l'alternativah, 1948–2003* (Tel Aviv: Am Oved, 2004), 7.

3   No fewer than 80 percent of the transit-camp residents were Mizrachim. The transit camps, which continued to exist until 1963, evolved over the years into towns or were annexed to neighboring communities. See Miriam Kachenski, *Hama'abarot*, Israeli Center for Israeli Technology, http://lib.cet.ac.il/pages/

item.asp?item=12939.

4   Meyrav Wurmser, "The Post-Zionist Critique: Post-Zionism and the Sephardi Question," *Middle East Quarterly* 12, no. 2 (Spring 2005): 22; Ella Shohat, "Sephardim in Israel: Zionism from the Standpoint of its Jewish Victims," *Social Text* 19 (Fall 1988): 24; Yael Zadok, "*Yaldei Teman: Hakonflikt she'merov pachad mechanim oto shed v'machnisim oto l'bakbuk,*" *Kedma*, December 2000.

5   Sammy Smooha, "The Implications of the Transition to Peace for Israeli Society," Annals *AAPSS* 555 (January 1998): 40.

6   Ibid, 39–40; Sammy Smooha, "Jewish Ethnicity in Israel: Symbolic or Real?" in *Jews in Israel: Contemporary Social and Cultural Patterns*, ed. Uzi Rebhun and Chaim I. Waxman (Boston: Brandeis Press, 2003), 68; Eliezer Ben-Rafael, *The Emergence of Ethnicity: Cultural Groups and Social Conflict in Israel* (Westport, CT: Greenwood, 1982); Eliezer Ben-Rafael and Stephen Sharot, *Ethnicity, Religion and Class in Israeli Society* (New York: Cambridge University Press, 1991); Wurmser, "Post-Zionist Critique," 26.

7   Smooha, "Implications," 40–41; see also Smooha, "Jewish Ethnicity in Israel," in: Keith Kyle and Joel Peters (eds.), "Whither Israel? The Domestic Challenges," (London: I. B. Tauris, 1993), 76–161; Shlomo Swirski, *Israel: The Oriental Majority* (London: Zed Books, 1989).

8   Chetrit, *Hama'avak haMizrachi*, 70.

9   Sami Shalom Chetrit, "Mizrahi Politics in Israel: Between Integration and Alternative," *Journal of Palestine Studies* 29, no. 4 (Summer 2000): 59–60, 62.

10   Wurmser, "Post-Zionist Critique," 22; Chetrit, *Hama'avak haMizrachi*, 70.

11   Shlomo Swirski, *Zeraim shel e-shivyon* (Tel Aviv: Breirot Publications 1995); Ella Shohat" ,Dislocated Identities :Reflections of an Arab-Jew ",*Movement Research: Performance Journal* 5 (Fall/Winter 1992); Ella Shohat, "Notes on the 'Post-Colonial,'" *Social Text* 31/32 (1992).

12   Shohat, "Sephardim," 3, 7, 9; Maxime Rodinson, "A Few Simple Thoughts on Anti-Semitism," in *Cult, Ghetto, and State* (London: Al Saqi Books, 1983).

13   Chetrit, *Hama'avak haMizrachi*, 52; For violent outbreaks of anti-Semitism in the Islamic world, see Bernard Lewis, *The Jews of Islam* (Princeton: Princeton University Press, 1987), 154–192; Mark R. Cohen, *Under Crescent and Cross: The Jews in the Middle Ages* (Princeton: Princeton University

Press, 1995), 162–200; Norman Stillman, *The Jews of Arab Lands: A History and Source Book* (Philadelphia: Jewish Publications Society, 1979), 64–95; Norman Stillman, *Jews in Arab Lands in Modern Times* (Philadelphia: Jewish Publications Society, 2003).

14 Norman A. Stillman, "Middle Eastern and North African Jewries Confront Modernity: Orientation, Disorientation, Reorientation," in *Sephardi and Middle Eastern Jewries: History and Culture in the Modern Era*, ed. Harvey E. Goldberg (Bloomington: Indiana University Press, 1996), 59.

15 Ibid., 60.

16 Ibid., 63.

17 Ibid., 64.

18 Ibid., 61.

19 Ibid., 63–65.

20 Ibid., 68.

21 Chetrit, *Hama'avak haMizrachi*, 15,49 .

22 Ibid., 80–82.

23 David Ben-Gurion, *Netzach Yisrael* (Tel Aviv: Ayanot, 1964), 34, cited in Shohat, "Sephardim," 4.

24 Sammy Smooha, *Israel: Pluralism and Conflict* (Berkeley: University of California Press, 1978), 88.

25 Chetrit, *Hama'avak haMizrachi*, 65.

26 Ibid., 91.

27 Ibid., 104, 147–155.

28 Amnon Raz-Krakotzkin, "*Galut betoch ribonut: L'vikoret 'shelilat hagalut' betarbut haYisraelit*," *Te'oriah u'vikoret* 4 (Fall 1993): 23–55, cited in Laurence J. Silberstein, *The Post-Zionism Debates: Knowledge and Power in Israeli Culture* (New York and London: Routledge, 1999), 179–180.

29 Kimmerling, *Invention*, 93–95, 131.

30 Ibid., 132–133.

31 Hanna Yablonka, "Oriental Jewry and the Holocaust: A Tri-Generational Perspective," *Israel Studies* 14, no. 1 (April 2009): 94–122.

CHAPTER 14: JEWISH IDENTITY IN TODAY'S DIASPORA

1   Deborah Dash Moore and S. Ilan Troen, introduction to *Divergent Jewish Cultures: Israel and America* (New Haven: Yale University Press, 2001), 5.

2   Caryn Aviv and David Shneer, *New Jews: The End of the Jewish Diaspora* (New York: New York University Press, 2005), 16, cited in Biale, *Cultures of the Jews*, passim.

3   Aviv and Shneer, ibid., 16; For Ivri-Nasawi, see Loolwa Khazoom, "United Jewish Feminist Front," in *Yentl's Revenge*, ed. Danya Ruttenberg (San Francisco: Seal, 2000), 168–180.

4   Aviv and Shneer, ibid., 17.

5   Howard Wettstein, introduction to *Diasporas and Exiles: Varieties of Jewish Identity* (Berkeley and Los Angeles: University of California, 2002), 1–2.

6   Homi Bhabha, *The Location of Culture* (London: Routledge, 1994).

7   Aviv and Shneer, *New Jews*, 17; Laurence J. Silberstein, ed., *Mapping Jewish Identities* (New York: New York University Press, 2000), 19.

8   Michael Galchinsky, "Scattered Seeds: A Dialogue of Diasporas," in *Insider/Outsider: American Jews and Multiculturalism*, ed. David Biale, Michael Galchinsky and Susannah Heschel (Berkeley: University of California Press, 1998), 186.

9   Paul Gilroy, *The Black Atlantic: Modernity and Double Consciousness* (Cambridge, MA: Harvard University Press, 1993), 1, 7, 111–146, 205–223; Stanley Aronowitz, "The Double Bind: America and the African Diaspora," *Transition* 6 (1), no. 69 (1996): 227–228.

10 Larry Tye, *Homelands: Portraits of the New Jewish Diaspora* (New York: Owl, 2000); Howard Sachar, *Diaspora: An Inquiry into the Contemporary Jewish World* (New York: HarperCollins, 1985); James Ross, *Fragile Branches: Travels through the Jewish Diaspora* (New York: Riverhead, 2001), cited in Aviv and Shneer, *New Jews*, 17.

11 Richard Marienstras, "On the Notion of Diaspora," in *Minority Peoples in the Age of Nation-States*, ed. G. Chaliand (London: South Asia Books, 1990), 119–125, cited in Aviv and Shneer, ibid., 18.

12 Leah Garrett, *Journeys Beyond the Pale: Yiddish Travel Writing in the Modern World* (Madison: University of Wisconsin Press, 2003), 170–171.

13 Daniel Boyarin and Jonathan Boyarin, "Diaspora: Generation and the Ground of Jewish Identity," *Critical Inquiry* 19, no. 4 (1993): 712–713.

14 Ibid., 711.

15 Aviv and Shneer, *New Jews*, 17; Boyarin and Boyarin, ibid., 714.

16 Todd M. Endelman, "The Legitimization of the Diaspora Experience in Recent Jewish Historiography," *Modern Judaism* 11, no. 2 (May 1991): 205.

17 Judit Bokser-Liwerant, "Globalization and Collective Identities," *Social Compass* 49, no. 2 (2002): 253–271; Bernardo Sorj, "Diaspora, Judaism, and Social Theory," www.bernardosorj.com, 1–2.

18 Endelman, "Legitimization," 205–206.

19 Sorj, "Diaspora," 9.

20 Galchinsky, "Scattered Seeds," 186–187.

21 Daniel Boyarin, Daniel Itzkovitz and Ann Pellegrini, "Strange Bedfellows: An Introduction," in *Queer Theory and the Jewish Question* (New York: Columbia University Press, 2003), 1.

22 John Boswell, *Christianity, Social Tolerance, and Homosexuality: Gay People in Western Europe from the Beginning of the Christian Era to the Fourteenth Century* (Chicago: University of Chicago Press, 1980), 15–16; In any case, Boswell qualifies the analogy by adding the following: "But there are significant differences.... Judaism, for example, is consciously passed from parents to children, and it has been able to transmit, along with its ethical precepts, political wisdom gleaned from centuries of oppression and harassment: advice about how to placate, reason with, or avoid hostile majorities; how and when to maintain a low profile; when to make public gestures; how to conduct business with potential enemies. Moreover, it has been able to offer its adherents at least the solace of solidarity in the face of oppression.... Gay people are for the most part not born into gay families. They suffer oppression individually and alone without benefit of advice or frequently even emotional support from relatives or friends."

23 Sander L. Gilman, *Freud, Race, and Gender* (Princeton: Princeton University Press, 1993); Jay Geller, "A Paleontological View of Freud's Study of Religion: Unearthing the *Leitfossil* Circumcision," *Modern Judaism* 13 (1993): 49–70.

24 George L. Mosse, *Nationalism and Sexuality: Middle-Class Morality and Sexual Norms in Modern Europe* (Madison: University of Wisconsin Press, 1985).

25 Jay Geller, "(G)nos(e)ology: The Cultural Construction of Other," in *People of the Body: Jews and Judaism from an Embodied Perspective*, ed. Howard Eilberg-Schwartz (Albany: SUNY Press, 1992), 82–243.

26 Boyarin, Itzkovitz and Pellegrini, "Strange Bedfellows," 2.

27 Ibid., 4.

28 Marjorie Garber, "Category Crises: The Way of the Cross and the Jewish Star," in *Queer Theory*, Boyarin, Itzkovitz and Pellegrini, 29–30; Sander L. Gilman, *Sexuality: An Illustrated History* (New York: Wiley, 1989), 266.

29 Gilman, ibid., 267, cited in Garber, "Category Crises," 32.

30 Nancy A. Harrowitz, "Weininger and Lombrose: A Question of Influence," in *Jews and Gender: Responses to Otto Weininger*, ed. Nancy A. Harrowitz and Barbara Hyams (Philadelphia: Temple University Press, 1995), 73–90; Garber, "Category Crises," 28; Chandak Seengoopta, *Otto Weininger: Sex, Science, and Self in Imperial Vienna* (Chicago: University of Chicago Press, 2000).

31 Aviva Cantor, *Jewish Women/Jewish Men: The Legacy of Patriarchy in Jewish Life* (San Francisco: Harper Collins, 1995), 79–82.

32 Ibid., 83–87.

33 Ibid., 87–88.

34 Ibid., 89–90.

35 Ibid., 92.

36 Ibid., 91–98.

37 Daniel Boyarin, *Unheroic Conduct: The Rise of Heterosexuality and the Invention of the Jewish Man* (Berkeley and Los Angeles: University of California Press, 1997), 3, 124–127.

38 Ibid., 23, 68.

39 Ibid., 4–5.

40 Ibid., 7–9, 143.

41 Ibid., 354; Boyarin, Itzkovitz and Pellegrini, "Strange Bedfellows," 1–2, 5.

42 Boyarin, Itzkovitz and Pellegrini, ibid., 3. For the emergence of the modern homosexual, see Arnold Davidson, "Sex and the Emergence of Sexuality," in *Forms of Desire: Sexual Orientation and the Social Constructionist*, ed. Edward Stein (New York: Routledge, 1992), 89–132; John D'Emilio, "Capitalism and Gay Identity," in *The Lesbian and Gay Studies Reader*, ed. Henry Abelove, Michele Aina Barale and David M. Halperin (New York: Routledge, 1993), 467–476; Lisa Duggan, *Sapphic Slashers: Sex, Violence,*

and American Modernity (Durham, NC: Duke University Press, 2000); Michel Foucault, *The History of Sexuality: An Introduction* (New York: Vintage, 1980).

43 Sander L. Gilman, "Sibling, Incest, Madness, and the 'Jews,'" *Jewish Social Studies* 4, no. 2 (January 1998): 158–159.

44 Ibid., 158, 163.

45 Sander L. Gilman, *Jewish Self-Hatred, Anti-Semitism and the Hidden Language of the Jews* (Baltimore: John Hopkins University Press, 1986).

46 Boyarin, Itzkovitz and Pellegrini, "Strange Bedfellows," 3.

47 Moshe Zimmerman, "Muscle Jews versus Nervous Jews," in *Emancipation Through Muscles: Jews and Sports in Europe*, ed. Michael Brener and Gideon Reuveni (Lincoln, NE: University of Nebraska Press, 2006), 13–14.

48 Erick Alvarez, *Muscle Boys: Gay Gym Culture* (New York: Harrington Park, 2008).

49 Andrew Sullivan, "The End of Gay Culture," *New Republic* 233, no. 17 (24 October 2005).

50 Peter Barry, "Lesbian/Gay Criticism," in *Beginning Theory: An Introduction to Literary and Cultural Theory* (Manchester: Manchester University Press, 2002), 139–155.

CHAPTER 15: FORCE AND JEWISH IDENTITY

1 Anita Shapira, *Land and Power: The Zionist Resort to Force, 1881–1948* (Palo Alto: Stanford University Press, 2000), 39.

2 David Biale, *Power and Powerlessness in Jewish History* (New York: Schocken, 1986), 139–140.

3 Shapira, *Land and Power*, 60.

4 Michael Brener, "Introduction: Why Jews and Sports," in *Emancipation Through Muscles: Jews and Sports in Europe*, ed. Michael Brener and Gideon Reuveni (Lincoln, NE: University of Nebraska Press, 2006), 1–12.

5 Biale, *Power and Powerlessness*, 137.

6 Shapira, *Land and Power*, 66.

7 Ibid., 69.

8   Ibid., 46.

9   Ibid., 82.

10 Ibid., 108.

11 Ibid., 132.

12 Ibid., 144; Ruth Wisse, *Jews and Power* (New York: Schocken, 2007), 121; Tom Segev, *One Palestine, Complete* (Metropolitan Books, 2000), 106–107.

13 Shapira, *Land and Power*, 182.

14 Wisse, *Jews and Power*, 220.

15 Shapira, *Land and Power*, 222.

16 Ibid., 224.

17 Avi Shlaim, *Kir habarzel: Yisrael v'haolam haAravi* (Tel Aviv: Yedioth Ahronoth, 2005).

18 Wisse, *Jews and Power*, 256.

19 Shapira, *Land and Power*, 272. Shapira notes that Jabotinsky was opposed to Ahimeir's vision of a violent revolution. But he wanted to speed up the steps toward independence, and this paved the way for acts of resistance and the use of force.

20 Ibid., 287.

21 Ibid., 350.

22 Ibid.

23 Ibid., 351.

24 Ibid., 364.

25 Ibid., 380.

26 Ibid., 382.

27 Biale, *Power and Powerlessness*, 4.

28 Ibid., 5.

29 Michael Selzer, introduction to *Zionism Reconsidered: The Rejection of Jewish Normalcy* (New York: Macmillan, 1979), 11.

30 Biale, *Power and Powerlessness*, 141–145.

31 David Ben-Gurion, *Paamei medinah* (Tel Aviv: Am Oved, 1993),338 .

32 Shapira, *Land and Power*, 494.

33 Tom Segev, *1967: Israel, the War and the Year that Transformed the Middle East* (Metropolitan Books, 2007).

34 Interview with Tom Segev, June 7, 2009.

35 Avraham Burg, *Lenatze'ach et Hitler* (Tel Aviv: Yedioth Ahronoth, 2007).

36 Interview with Tom Segev, June 15, 2009; interview with A. B. Yehoshua, June 15, 2009; interview with Benny Morris, June 10, 2009.

37 Interview with Tom Segev. The museum and educational center, which were established by Arab attorney Khaled Mahmid, were explicitly designed to increase awareness and understanding of the Holocaust among Arabs in Israel in order to advance the cause of peace and reconciliation between them and Israeli Jews.

38 Biale, *Power and Powerlessness*, 162.

39 Shlaim, *Kir habarzel*; Ian S. Lustick, "Abandoning the Iron Wall: Israel and 'The Middle Eastern Muck,'" *Middle East Policy* 15, no. 3 (Fall 2008).

40 Biale, *Power and Powerlessness*, 3.

41 Ibid., ix.

42 Wisse, *Jews and Power*, 173.

43 Ibid., 176.

44 Ibid., xiv; interview with Ruth Wisse, May 15, 2009.

CHAPTER 16: RELIGIOUS JEWISH IDENTITY

1 Mendes-Flohr and Reinharz, *The Jew in the Modern World: A Documentary History*, 2nd ed. (Oxford University Press, 1995), 156.

2 Nathaniel Katzburg, "Orthodoxy," Encyclopaedia Judaica, 2nd ed., vol. 15 (New York: Macmillan Reference USA, 2006), 493.

3 Emmanuel Rackman, "Orthodoxy," ibid., 497.

4 Samuel C. Heilman, "Haredim," Encyclopaedia Judaica, 2nd ed., vol. 8 (New York: Macmillan Reference USA, 2006), 348.

5 Rackman, "Orthodoxy," 499.

6 Heilman, "Haredim," 348–349.

7   Rackman, "Orthodoxy," 497.

8   Ibid., 498.

9   Heilman, "Haredim," 348; Jeffrey S. Gurock, *Orthodox Jews in America* (Bloomington: Indiana University Press, 2009), 18, 217.

10 Rackman, "Orthodoxy," 496, 498; Gurock, ibid., 256–257; Walter S. Wurzburger, "Orthodoxy," Encyclopaedia Judaica, 2nd ed., vol. 15 (New York: Macmillan Reference USA, 2006), 493.

11 Heilman, "Haredim," 350–351.

12 Gurock, *Orthodox Jews*, 19.

13 Ibid., 84–110, 148–183.

14 Ibid., 256–272.

15 Wurzburger, "Orthodoxy," 495.

16 Fred Skonlik, "Haredim," Encyclopaedia Judaica, 2nd ed., vol. 8 (New York: Macmillan Reference USA, 2006), 351; Evan R. Goldstein, "Israel's Ultra-Orthodox Welfare Kings," *Wall Street Journal*, November 12, 2010.

17 Mendes-Flohr and Reinharz, *Jew in the Modern World*, 156.

18 Dana Evan Kaplan, "Reform Judaism," Encyclopaedia Judaica, 2nd ed., vol. 17 (New York: Macmillan Reference USA, 2006), 166.

19 Robert M. Seltzer, *Jewish People, Jewish Thought: The Jewish Experience in History* (New York: Macmillan, 1980), 580–582.

20 Ibid., 582.

21 Ibid.; Kaplan, "Reform Judaism," 166; Mendes-Flohr and Reinharz, *Jew in the Modern World*, 157.

22 Kaplan, ibid., 166, 173.

23 The Protocol of the Brunswick Conference in 1844. Quoted in Mendes-Flohr and Reinharz, *Jew in the Modern World*, 158. See also David Philipson ,*The Reform Movement in Judaism*, rev. ed., ed. S. B. Freehof (New York: Ktav Publishing House, 1967), 145.

24 *Solomon Maimon: An Autobiography*, translated from the German, with additions and notes by J. Clark Murray (Cupples and Hurd: Boston, 1888).

25 Kaplan, "Reform Judaism," 168–169.

26 Ibid., 166.

27 Ibid., 169.

28 Marc Lee Raphael, *Profiles in American Judaism: The Reform, Conservative, Orthodox, and Reconstructionist Traditions in Historical Perspective* (San Francisco: Harper and Row, 1985), 28–31.

29 Yaakov Ariel, "Miss Daisy's Planet: The Strange World of Reform Judaism in the United States, 1870–1930," in *Platforms and Prayer Books: Theological and Liturgical Perspectives on Reform Judaism*, ed. Dana Evan Kaplan (Oxford: Roman and Littlefield, 2002), 50.

30 Raphael, *Profiles*, 39–40.

31 Ibid., 41–47; Kaplan, "Reform Judaism," 169.

32 Kaplan, ibid., 173–174.

33 Ibid., 175–180; Dana Evan Kaplan, *Contemporary American Judaism: Transformation and Renewal* (New York: Columbia University Press, 2009), 229–234, 254–255.

34 Kaplan, "Reform Judaism," 181–182.

35 Shmuel Ettinger, *A History of the Jewish People* (Cambridge, MA: Harvard University Press, 1985), 836.

36 Raphael, *Profiles*, 86.

37 Ibid., 89.

38 Kaplan, *Contemporary American Judaism*, 23.

39 Ibid., 95–96; Mordecai M. Kaplan, "Unity in Diversity in the Conservative Movement," in *Tradition and Change: The Development of Conservative Judaism*, ed. Mordecai Waxman (New York: Burning Bush, 1970), 212.

40 Raphael, *Profiles*, 96.

41 Kaplan, *Contemporary American Judaism*, 23–24.

42 Raphael, *Profiles*, 96–97, 105–106.

43 Ibid., 98.

44 Ibid., 99.

45 Ibid., 103–105.

46 David Golinkin and Michael Panitz, "Conservative Judaism," Encyclopaedia Judaica, 2nd ed., vol. 5 (New York: Macmillan Reference USA, 2006), 173–175; Dana Evan Kaplan, "Trends in American Judaism from 1945 to the

Present," in *The Cambridge Companion to American Judaism* (Cambridge: Cambridge University Press, 2005), 65–66; Kaplan, *Contemporary American Judaism*, 29, 236–238.

47 J. D. Sarna, *American Judaism: A History* (New Haven: Yale University Press, 2004), 243; Kaplan, *Contemporary American Judaism*, 133.

48 Sarna, ibid., 244–245.

49 Ibid.,245 ; Richard Hirsch, "Reconstructionism," Encyclopaedia Judaica, 2nd ed., vol. 17 (New York: Macmillan Reference USA, 2006), 147–148.

50 Hirsch, "Reconstructionism," 147; Raphael, *Profiles*, 183.

51 Raphael, ibid., 184–185.

52 Kaplan, *Contemporary American Judaism*, 133, 136.

53 Hirsch, "Reconstructionism," 147–148.

54 Ibid., 148.

55 Ibid.; Sarna, *American Judaism*, 246.

56 Sarna, ibid., 247–248.

57 Kaplan, *Contemporary American Judaism*, 137.

CHAPTER 17: MODERN JEWISH FUNDAMENTALISM

1 Gershon Gorenberg, *The Accidental Empire: Israel and the Birth of the Settlements, 1967–1977* (New York: Henry Holt, 2006), 3–5.

2 Seth Schwartz, *Imperialism and Jewish Society, 200 BCE to 640 CE* (Princeton: Princeton University Press, 2001), 78–87.

3 Jacob Neusner, *First Century Judaism in Crisis: Yohanan ben Zakkai and the Renaissance of Torah* (Nashville: Abingdon, 1975); Benjamin Isaac and Aharon Oppenheimer, "The Revolt of Bar Kokhba: Ideology and Modern Scholarship," *Journal of Jewish Social Studies* 36, no. 1 (Spring 1985): 33–60.

4 Gershom Scholem, *Sabbatai Sevi: The Mystical Messiah, 1626–1676*, trans. R. J. Zwi Werblowsky (Princeton University Press, 1975).

5 Ibid.

6 David Vital, *Hamahapechah haTzionit* (Tel Aviv: Am Oved, 1978), 161–168.

7   Ehud Sprinzak, *Not Bound by the Law: Legal Disobedience in Israeli Society* (Tel Aviv: Sifriyat Hapoalim, 1986).

8   Ian S. Lustick, "Israel's Dangerous Fundamentalists," *Foreign Policy* 68 (Fall 1987): 121–122.

9   Eliezer Don-Yehiya, "Jewish Messianism, Religious Zionism and Israeli Politics: The Impact and Origins of Gush Emunim," *Middle Eastern Studies* 23, no. 2 (April 1987): 225–228; Gershon Shafir, "Changing Nationalism and Israel's 'Open Frontier' on the West Bank," *Theory and Society* 13, no. 6 (November 1984): 818–819.

10 Amnon Rubinstein, *The Zionist Dream Revisited: From Herzl to Gush Emunim and Back* (Jerusalem: Schocken, 1980).

11 Ian S. Lustick, *For the Land and the Lord: Jewish Fundamentalism in Israel* (New York: Council on Foreign Relations Press, 1988), 44–46.

12 Ibid., 46–48.

13 Ibid., 55–56; Zvi Raanan, *Gush Emunim* (New York: Sifriyat Hapoalim, 1980), 46–47.

14 Ian S. Lustick, "Israel and the West Bank after Elon Moreh: The Mechanics of *de facto* Annexation," *Middle East Journal* 35, no. 4 (Autumn 1980): 557–577.

15 Jan Demarest Abu Shakra, *Israeli Settler Violence in the Occupied Territories: 1980–1984* (Chicago: Palestine Human Rights Campaign, 1985).

16 Lustick, *For the Land*, 66–71.

17 Ibid., 122–131.

CHAPTER 18: ANTI-SEMITISM AND JEWISH IDENTITY

1   Robert S. Wistrich, *A Lethal Obsession: Anti-Semitism from Antiquity to the Global Jihad* (New York: Random House, 2010), 79.

2   Gavin I. Langmuir, *History, Religion, and Antisemitism* (Berkeley and Los Angeles: University of California Press, 1990), 275–305.

3   Wistrich, *Lethal Obsession*, 79; Gavin I. Langmuir, *Toward a Definition of Antisemitism* (Berkeley and Los Angeles: University of California Press, 1990), 195–298.

4   Lloyd P. Gartner, *History of the Jews in Modern Times* (Oxford: Oxford University Press, 2001), 215.

5   Shmuel Ettinger, "Jew Hatred in Its Historical Context," in *Anti-Semitism Through the Ages*, ed. Shmuel Almog (New York and Jerusalem: Pergamon Press and the Vidal Sassoon International Center for the Study of Anti-Semitism of the Hebrew University of Jerusalem, 1988), 9–10; Yehuda Bauer, "In Search of a Definition of Anti-Semitism," in *Approaches to Anti-Semitism: Context and Curriculum*, ed. Michael Brown (New York: American Jewish Committee, 1994), 15–16.

6   Eugen Weber, "Jews, Anti-Semitism, and the Origins of the Holocaust," *Historical Reflections* 5, no. 1 (Summer 1978): 5.

7   Shmuel Ettinger, "The Modern Period," in *A History of the Jewish People* (Cambridge, MA: Harvard University Press, 1985), 871.

8   Esther Benbassa, *Suffering as Identity: The Jewish Paradigm*, trans. G. M. Goshgarian (London: Verso, 2010), 3–4.

9   Ibid., 30.

10   Mark R. Cohen, *Under Crescent and Cross: The Jews in the Middle Ages* (Princeton: Princeton University Press, 1995), 178–179.

11   Benbassa, *Suffering*, 92.

12   Ibid., 49–51.

13   Ibid., 52–57.

14   Ibid., 42–45; Salo W. Baron, *A Social and Religious History of the Jews*, 2nd ed., vol. 11 (New York and Philadelphia, 1983), 4–13,18–22. See also Yosef Hayim Yerushalmi, "Response to Rosemary Ruether," in *Auschwitz: Beginning of a New Era? Reflections on the Holocaust*, ed. Eva Fleischner (New York: Ktav, 1977), 98–100. For a more moderate interpretation of Baron's criticism of the "crybaby" approach, see Cohen, *Under Crescent*, 45–46.

15   Martin Gilbert, preface to *Jewish History Atlas*, 2nd ed. (London: Weidenfeld and Nicolson, 1976).

16   Benbassa, *Suffering*, 77–78.

17   Ibid., 2.

18   Ibid., 9; A. B. Yehoshua, *"Nisayon l'zihui v'havanah shel tashtit ha'antishemiyut,"* *Alpayim* 28 (2005): 14–15.

19 Harold Fisch, *The Zionist Revolution: A New Perspective* (London: Weidenfeld and Nicolson, 1978), 86–87; Avi Sagi, "The Holocaust and the Foundation of Jewish Identity," *Azure* 39, no. 42 (Autumn 2010): 41–42.

20 Robert S. Wistrich, "Israel and the Holocaust Trauma," *Jewish History* 11, no. 2 (Fall 1997): 15.

21 Ibid., 16.

22 Yehoshua, *"Nisayon l'zihui,"* 69–70.

23 David Horowitz, "The Passion of the Jews," *Ramparts* 13, no. 3 (October 1974): 21–22, reprinted in David Horowitz, *Left Illusions: An Intellectual Odyssey* (Dallas, TX: Spence, 2003), 46–47.

24 Jacob (Yaakov) Talmon, *"Hamoledet b'sakanah,"* *Haaretz*, March 13, 1980.

25 Tom Segev, *The Seventh Million: The Israelis and the Holocaust* (New York: Hill and Wang, 1993), 514.

26 Alan Dowty, "Israeli Foreign Policy and the Jewish Question," *Middle East Review of International Affairs* 3, no. 1 (March 1999), http://meria.idc.ac.il/journal/1999/issue1/.

27 Segev, *Seventh Million*, 154; Wistrich, "Israel and the Holocaust Trauma," 16–17.

28 Amos Elon, *The Israelis: Founders and Sons* (New York: Holt, Rinehart and Winston, 1971), 200–201.

29 Segev, *Seventh Million*, 514.

30 Ibid., 369.

31 Amos Oz, *In the Land of Israel* (San Diego: Harcourt Brace Jovanovich, 1983), 99.

32 Segev, *Seventh Million*, 366–367; Dowty, "Israeli Foreign Policy," 4.

33 Cited in Segev, ibid., 365.

34 Uri Ramon, *"Hamaskanot shel haShoah b'Milchemet Sheshet Hayamim,"* *Dapim l'cheker haShoah v'hamered*, file A (1969): 59 and thereafter; quoted in Segev, *Seventh Million*, 392.

35 Segev, ibid., 393.

36 Benbassa, *Suffering*, 131.

37 Segev, 394–395; an addendum to the original Hebrew text.

38 Dowty, "Israeli Foreign Policy," 5.

39 Benbassa, *Suffering*, 131–132.

40 Dowty, "Israeli Foreign Policy," 6.

41 Ibid., 4; Segev, *Seventh Million*, 471–472; Benbassa, *Suffering*, 133; Eliezer Don-Yehiya, "Memory and Political Culture: Israeli Society and Holocaust," *Studies in Contemporary Jewry* 9 (1993): 139–162.

42 Natan Sharansky, *I am Jewish: Personal Reflections Inspired by the Last Words of Daniel Pearl* (Woodstock, VT: Jewish Lights, 2004), 32–33.

43 Patrick Weil, "The History and Memory of Discrimination in the Domain of French Nationality: The Case of Jews and Algerian Muslims," *HAGAR: International Social Science Review* 6, no. 1 (2005): 63; Annette Wieviorka, *L'ère du témoin* (Paris: Pluriel, 2002), 137.

44 André Harris and Alain de Sédouy, *Juif et Français* (Paris: Grasset, 1979), 176.

45 Mark Kurlansky, *The Chosen Few: The Resurrection of European Jewry* (New York: Ballantine, 2002), 177.

46 Jonathan Judaken, "French-Jewish Intellectuals After 1968," *Encyclopedia of Modern Jewish Culture*, vol. 1.

47 Natan Sharansky, "3D Test of Anti-Semitism: Demonization, Double Standards, Delegitimization," *Jewish Political Studies Review* 16, nos. 3–4 (Fall 2004), 5–8.

48 Ibid.; examples of demonization included a comparison of Arab or Palestinian towns with the Warsaw Ghetto; showing pictures of Anne Frank wearing a keffiyeh; or juxtaposing a picture of the Palestinian child Muhammad al-Durrah (whose killing in an exchange of gunfire at the beginning of the Second Intifada in autumn 2000 was not indisputably attributed to either Israeli soldiers or Palestinian fighters) with the iconic picture of the Jewish child standing with raised hands in the Warsaw Ghetto. See Manfred Gerstenfeld, "Holocaust Inversion: The Portraying of Israel and Jews as Nazis," *Post-Holocaust and Anti-Semitism* 55 (April 2007).

49 Pierre-André Taguieff, *Rising from the Muck: The New Anti-Semitism in Europe* (Chicago: Ivan R. Dee, 2004), 62.

50 Walter Laqueur, *The Changing Face of Anti-Semitism: From Ancient Times to the Present Day* (Oxford: Oxford University Press, 2006), 8; Jonathan

Judaken, "So What's New? Rethinking the 'New Anti-Semitism' in a Global Age," *Patterns of Prejudice* 42, nos. 4–5 (2008): 554.

51   Wistrich, *Lethal Obsession*, 35, 403–408.

52   "Israel Outraged as EU Poll Names It as a Threat to Peace," *Guardian*, November 2, 2003, http://www.guardian.co.uk/world/2003/nov/02/israel.eu.

53   Wistrich, *Lethal Obsession*, 4, 44–45.

54   Danny Ben-Moshe, "The New Anti-Semitism, Jewish Identity, and the Question of Zionism," in *Israel, The Diaspora, and Jewish Identity*, ed. Danny Ben-Moshe and Zohar Segev (London: Sussex Academic Press, 2007), 11, 16; Ian Katz, *International Jerusalem Post*, October 20, 2004.

55   Ben-Moshe, ibid, 11, 18–19.

56   Michael Neumann, "What Is Anti-Semitism?" *Counterpunch* (4 June 2002): 7.

57   Ibid., 12.

58   Segev, 516 (an addendum to the original Hebrew text).

59   Benbassa, *Suffering*, 134–135.

60   Zygmunt Bauman, "The Holocaust's Life as a Ghost: Lingering Psychological Effects," in *Tikkun Reader: Twentieth Anniversary*, ed. Michael Lerner (Lanham: Rowman and Littlefield, 2007), 174, 178–179.

61   Oz, *In the Land of Israel*, 76.

62   Bauman, "The Holocaust's Life as a Ghost," 181.

63   Yehuda Elkana, *"Bizechut hashichechah,"* *Haaretz*, March 2, 1988.

64   Segev, 517 (an addendum to the original Hebrew text).

65   Sagi, "Holocaust," 54–55.

66   Benbassa, *Suffering*, 177.

CHAPTER 19: THE A. B. YEHOSHUA POLEMIC

1   A. B. Yehoshua, *"Shiur moledet,"* *Haaretz* supplement, May 13, 2006.

2   A. B. Yehoshua, "A Brief Epilogue," August 2006; reprinted in *The A. B. Yehoshua Controversy: An Israel-Diaspora Dialogue on Jewishness, Israeliness, and Identity* (New York: American Jewish Committee, 2006), 13.

3   Yehoshua, "*Shiur moledet.*"

4   See, for example, Zeev Bielski, "*Ta'uto shel A. B. Yehoshua,*" *Haaretz*, May 2006.

5   The transcript of A. B. Yehoshua's remarks at an event marking a hundred years since the founding of the American Jewish Committee, May 1, 2006. Reprinted in *Yehoshua Controversy*, 62–66.

6   Yehoshua, "*Shiur moledet.*"

7   David Grossman, *Sleeping on a Wire: Conversations with Palestinians in Israel* (Picador, 2003).

8   *Yehoshua Controversy*, 63–64.

9   Gilbert N. Kahn, "Distant Relations: Why Israelis Don't 'Get' Diaspora Jewry," *New Jersey Jewish News*, May 6, 2006; Gary Rosenblatt, "Still One People," *New York Jewish Week*, June 30, 2006.

10   *Yehoshua Controversy*, 63.

11   Cited in Allan C. Brownfield, "American Jews Belong in Israel, Declare Israeli Authors Yehoshua and Halkin," *Washington Report on Middle East Affairs* 25, no. 6 (August 2006): 54.

12   *Jerusalem Post*, March 13, 2003.

13   A. B. Yeshoshua, "An Apology to Those Who Attended the.Symposium," August 2006, reprinted in *Yehoshua Controversy*, 12.

14   Samuel Freedman, "In the Diaspora: You're Taking us for Granted – Don't," *Jerusalem Post*, June 27, 2006.

15   Hillel Halkin, "More Right than Wrong," *Jerusalem Post*, May 11, 2006.

16   Tzvia Greenfeld "*Mashma'aut Yisraelit,*" *Haaretz*, May 11, 2006.

17   Leonard Fein, "Israeliness or Judaism — Must We Choose One?" PeaceNowConversation.org, 8 May 2006, reprinted in *Yehoshua Controversy*, 32–33.

18   Tony Karon, "How Jewish Is Israel?" *Haaretz*, May 21, 2006, English edition.

19   Fein, "Israeliness or Judaism," *Yehoshua Controversy*, 33.

20   Natan Sharansky, "*Pegiah b'etzem kiyumenu,*" *Haaretz*, May 12, 2006.

21   Avraham Burg, "*V'todah l'A. B. Yehoshua,*" *Haaretz*, May 22, 2006.

22   Yair Sheleg, "*Bameh tzadak Yehoshua,*" *Haaretz*, May 10, 2006.

23 Burg, *"V'todah l'A. B. Yehoshua."*

24 Tony Karon, "How Jewish Is Israel?"

25 Yair Caspi, "Israeli Judaism: The Judaism of Survival No Longer Works," *Haaretz*, May 18, 2006, English edition.

26 Avraham Burg, "A Failed Israeli Society is Collapsing," *International Herald Tribune*, September 6, 2003.

27 Yossi Sarid, *"Mi yilmad mimi?" Haaretz*, May 12, 2006.

28 Brownfield, "American Jews," 55.

29 Steven M. Cohen and Jack Wertheimer, "Whatever Happened to the Jewish People?" *Commentary* 121, no. 6 (June 2006): 33–37.

INDEX OF SUBJECTS AND PLACES

Hebron, 117, 118, 126, 207, 238
Herut Party, 108
Hibbat Zion, Hovevei Zion, 17, 18, 19, 20, 22, 24, 28, 29, 115, 164
Katowice Conference (1844), 28
Holocaust,
Echoes of in the United States, 101–105
fears of, 249–251
lessons of, 259, 261
memory of, 50, 103, 249
Holocaust Day, 50
Holocaust survivors, 70, 108, 111, 125, 127, 249, 257, 258
homosexuality, homosexuals, 193–194, 195, 198, 199–200
human rights, 137, 163, 259

Iceland, 169
identity,
collective identity, 92, 109–111, 114, 129, 183, 244
collective Sabra identity, 111
cultural identities, 112–113, 191
dual identity, 93, 95, 252
feminine identity, 193
homosexual and lesbian identity, 193
hybrid identity, 86, 93, 95, 133, 190, 191
Israeli national identity, 120
national identity, 4, 5, 12, 41, 42, 44, 97, 131, 136
Jewish national identity, xi, 52, 141, 211, 222
Jewish secular identity, 90, 92, 93, 95, 137, 189
Judaism's ethnic/national identity, 222, 225, 233
new Hebrew identity, 44

singular national identity, 217
imperialism,
Zionism as an offshoot of, 133–134, 144–158
Western imperialism, 157
Independent Jewish Voices, 137
Internationalism, 38, 136
socialist internationalism, 16
intifada,
the first *intifada*, 119
the second *intifada*, 143, 257
Ireland, 60, 160, 169
Irgun Bet (Organization B), 207, 209, *see also* Etzel
Islam, 7, 20, 31, 44, 62, 118, 128, 155, 183, 184, 236, 240, 255, 257
Islamic cultures, 113, 243
Islamic racism, 241
Israel Defense Forces (IDF), 125, 128, 213
attack on the Iraqi nuclear reactor (1981), 214
attack on the Syrian nuclear reactor (2007), 214
Israeli Communist Party (Maki), 108, 137
Israeli militarism, 56, 253
Israeli sovereignty over the whole of Eretz Israel, 237, 239
Israeli Supreme Court, 167, 221
"Brother Daniel" case, 172–173
Elon Moreh case, 239
Qa'adan case, 168
Shalit case, 174, 175, 177
Istanbul, 24, 33
Italy, 48, 209
Jews, 83
Ivri–Nasawi, 189

Jenin, 118

INDEX OF NAMES